FOXCATCHER

MARK SCHULTZ lives in Medford, Oregon.

Praise for *Foxcatcher*

"My recommendation: If you want to know all about what happened at Foxcatcher, preorder the book by Mark Schultz. It is a must-read, whether or not you know a lot about wrestling."
—Eddie Goldman, host of *No Holds Barred*

"While the film touches more on the tragedy of his brother, David, the book takes you through the triumphs of his athletic career, the personal struggles that led him to join up with du Pont, and a true inside perspective of what really went on at Foxcatcher Farms."
—MMAmania.com

"Raw, authentic, and powerful. It is a fantastic autobiography from start to finish, and it can be read in one or two sittings, since it will be difficult to put down."
—DigitalJournal.com

"This is a fascinating story that will draw the reader into the life and struggles of the gold medalist, Mark Schultz."
—*Grand Forks Herald*

"This is a book that will affect the reader from the moment he begins reading it. Mark Schultz's tale is a bold tale that is not afraid of the truth and it is well written and totally engaging."
—Amos Lassen

FOXCATCHER

THE TRUE STORY OF MY BROTHER'S MURDER,

JOHN DU PONT'S MADNESS,

AND THE QUEST FOR OLYMPIC GOLD

MARK SCHULTZ

WITH DAVID THOMAS

IP

A Plume Book

PLUME
An imprint of Penguin Random House LLC
375 Hudson Street
New York, New York 10014

First published in the United States of America by Dutton, an imprint of Penguin Random
House LLC, 2014
First Plume printing 2015
Plume ISBN 978-0-14-751648-0

P REGISTERED TRADEMARK—MARCA REGISTRADA

THE LIBRARY OF CONGRESS HAS CATALOGED THE DUTTON HARDCOVER EDITION AS FOLLOWS:
Schultz, Mark, 1960–
    Foxcatcher: the true story of my brother's murder, John du Pont's madness, and the quest for
Olympic gold / Mark Schultz, with David Thomas.
        pages cm
    ISBN 978-0-525-95503-0 (hardback)
    1. Schultz, Mark, 1960– 2. Schultz, David L. –1996. 3. Du Pont, John E. (John Eleuthère)
4. Wrestlers—United States—Biography. 5. Olympic athletes—United States—Biography.
6. Murder—United States—Case studies. 7. Wrestling—United States. I. Title.
GV1196.S39A3 2014
796.812092—dc23
[B]
                                                                          2014026863

Printed in the United States of America
10 9 8 7 6 5 4 3 2 1

Hardcover book design by Alissa Rose Theodor

Written for my kids and dedicated to my brother, Dave

Contents

Prologue

January 26, 1996

H i, Coach!"

Dave smiled and waved as he stepped toward John du Pont's silver Lincoln Town Car coming to a stop in his driveway, "P.U. Kids" jotted in the palm of Dave's right hand. It was my brother's day to pick up his two kids from school, and he had just finished repairing his car radio with a few minutes to spare.

Du Pont, rolling down his window, didn't return the greeting.

"You got a problem with me?" du Pont asked.

He didn't give Dave a chance to answer.

The first hollow-point bullet from du Pont's .44 Magnum revolver struck Dave's elbow—perhaps he had raised his arms to cover himself—and continued its spiraling path through his heart and into his lungs.

Dave cried out in pain and lunged forward, apparently hoping he could wrestle the gun away.

Right arm still extended, du Pont squeezed the trigger again. The second bullet entered Dave's stomach and did not stop until it had exited through his back, pierced through the back window of Dave's car, and shattered the front windshield.

Dave crumpled face-first onto the snow-covered driveway. His wife, who had been inside the house, started toward the front door after the first shot.

"John, stop!" Nancy shouted.

John, stepping out of his car, turned his gun toward her. She ducked back inside. John aimed the gun back at Dave as he crawled toward his car, a trail of red marking his path in the snow. The bastard shot my dying brother in the back.

My office phone rang. It was just another afternoon in the middle of wrestling season, spent opening mail and answering phone calls until my team's practice would begin shortly.

Until my dad called.

"Du Pont shot Dave and killed him."

I didn't hang up the phone; I threw it and screamed, grabbed the papers in front of me, and slung them against the wall. Notebooks and pens and anything else within reach followed. So did a clock and awards sitting on the file cabinet near my desk. I cursed loud enough for the highest heavens to hear.

Alone, I sat in the corner and sobbed for an hour until my assistant coach opened the door. I told him about my dad's call, and he sat down and wept with me.

By that point, John du Pont—heir to the du Pont family fortune and supposed best friend of amateur wrestling in the United States— had taken refuge in his sprawling mansion. Police swarmed to the Foxcatcher Farm estate they knew so well. Some had trained at du Pont's shooting range, which he had opened up to them. Some wore bulletproof vests and communicated on radios he had purchased for them.

Du Pont, ever taking advantage of his reputation as a philanthropist, had been hailed as a generous giver for all of his adult life.

But I knew better. I knew that he gave in order to take. John du Pont gave me the means to wrestle and then took my wrestling career from me. Now he had taken my brother from me.

The police, settling in for what would be a forty-eight-hour standoff, sent word warning me, even though I was more than two thousand miles from the scene, to stay away.

They were right to call me. I would have made one more trip to the farm if I had believed I had a chance of getting to John. And I would have killed him.

PART ONE

Making a Champion

CHAPTER 1

A Fighter's Chance

My brother was the one constant in my life until John du Pont murdered him.

Dave protected me, he set an example for me, and he suffered alongside me. Although born seventeen months apart—Dave was older—we were almost like twins.

The media liked to point out our differences. We looked different. Dave sported a thick, black beard most of his adult life and I was clean-shaven, making my dominant cheek and chin features more pronounced. My medium-brown hair was thick and wavy; Dave kept his hair shorter. Then later, Father Time made his hair even shorter. I was noticeably more muscular, Dave more chemistry professor–ish.

We wrestled differently, too, the media said. Dave was a brilliant technician on the mat. Perhaps our sport's greatest technician ever. I relied more on sheer strength, brute force even.

Sports Illustrated once portrayed Dave as "a Yoda-like master of the mats," capable of outsmarting opponents. I was the "sledgehammer," "a massively muscled head-on attacker" brawling my way to victory.

The contrasts made for great stories. Perhaps that's why we played along for fun during interviews. But the true story, despite the obvious physical differences, was how much alike we were.

And the better story would have been how much that was by design, because I tried to emulate my older brother in every way I could.

Ours had all the makings of a rags-to-riches tale. From poor beginnings, we fought our way through life and the world of wrestling to win a combined four National Collegiate Athletic Association championships, two Olympic gold medals, and three World Championship titles. But riches never came. We won plenty of gold, but we never found the brass ring that would allow us to compete without having to rely on the likes of John du Pont, a credibility-craving, controlling misfit of a multimillionaire I never would have associated with if USA Wrestling had provided better financial support for its most successful wrestlers.

Our parents divorced when I was three. Our dad and our mom didn't have one of those nasty divorces, so we didn't have to deal with parents trashing each other. We also were really close to our grandparents on our mom's side, and as far as kids of divorces go, we didn't have it too bad in our early years.

I wasn't quite yet five when I started school in Menlo Park, California, and as an October baby, I was the youngest in my class. Dave was a grade ahead and, unlike me, one of the bigger kids in his class. But Dave, who would eat just about anything and everything, was soft and uncoordinated. His physique would later result in his being nicknamed "Pudge."

Dave's lack of coordination came from his dyslexia. Instead of having one side of the brain that is dominant, which is what influences how people think and operate, individuals diagnosed with dyslexia have a brain with mixed dominance, and that negatively affects the brain's organization.

Not surprisingly, Dave had great difficulty reading. The letters *b*, *d*, *p*, and *q* flipped back and forth, up and down when he read. Dave's teachers placed him in remedial classes. Dave hated those classes because, like many dyslexics, he actually was very intelligent.

One day when Dave was a third-grader, a kid from his grade started making fun of him for being in remedial reading. Dave got mad, took the kid to the ground, and slammed his head against the concrete. That knocked the kid out, and an ambulance had to come to the school to take the kid to the hospital. Dave had cracked the kid's skull.

After that, Dave became known as the toughest kid in the school and, not surprisingly, didn't have to face teasing again for being in remedial reading. We did get picked on a lot, though, and I still don't know why. I remember one time when a group of girls kept calling me "conceited." They might have said that at least a dozen times, maybe a couple of dozen, in about an hour.

I didn't think I was conceited. I was a good athlete and I wasn't real talkative, but I wouldn't say I was conceited. I was small, though, and that made me an easy target.

One bully in particular kept picking on me, and that's when my protector stepped in on my behalf. Dave took the bully down and pounded on him until the bully started crying and got up and ran home.

Dave got cross with another kid at school named John. I can't remember what started their rift, but I think John had disrespected Dave. They agreed to settle it on the playground after school. Word got around that John and Dave were going to fight, and there was a lot of interest in the outcome because Dave was the school's tough guy and John was one of the best athletes, really coordinated and extremely fast.

After school, the kids formed a circle around John and Dave, and John quickly was revealed as no match for Dave. They wound up on the ground, and Dave got on top of him and started pounding on him. Dave's fists were flying, John's arms were trying to cover his head, and both kids were crying—John, on the bottom, because he was getting beat up, and Dave, on top, I guess because it was one of those deals where you're a kid in a fight and you have so much adrenaline flowing and you have no idea what's going to happen after the fight. A teacher heard the commotion and separated the two.

I don't know how Dave wound up on top of a kid as athletic as John so quickly, but he must have detected a spot where John left himself vulnerable and pounced on it. He was an excellent technician long before he discovered wrestling.

Even though because of my size I was more on the edge of the action than in the middle of it, fighting became a defense for both of us. We didn't have many advantages, but we did have toughness and the bullheadedness to never give in going for us.

My parents had told me after I turned four that I had six-pack abs and well-defined muscles, but my first recognition of my athletic talent came in second grade, when another student boasted that he could outrun me across a field. He took off before I could get started, but despite the boy's big head start, I caught up to him and beat him to the finish line.

That race provided me needed confidence, because even though I was the youngest member of the class, I learned I could do something athletically better than others. I was way too young to know about the science of fast-twitch muscle fibers that I would learn about in college, but discovering how quick I was compared with the others in my class led me to realize the advantage I had in terms of explosive power. After that boost of confidence, I became the goalkeeper in our recess soccer games and usually went back to class covered in dirt from diving to make saves. For the first time, I experienced the joy of being the best at something in sports.

O̲ur mother had remarried and attended graduate school at Stanford. Before my fourth-grade year, she accepted a job offer to be the costume designer for the Oregon Shakespeare Festival in Ashland, Oregon, the first city across the California border on Interstate 5. The move took us more than a six-hour drive from our home in Palo Alto, away from our dad and grandparents.

We had a good relationship with Dad. He and Mom gave me Dad's middle name—Philip—when I was born. My first name came from an uncle, Mark Bernstein, and I didn't like my name growing up because "Mark" sounded like a hare-lipped dog barking. Then I learned the name came from Mars, the Roman god of war, and I thought it was cool that I carried the name of a warrior.

Dad, a Stanford grad, was a comedian and drama professor, and he kept us laughing when we were around him. In our early years in Palo Alto, I developed a love for comedy, memorizing all of Steve Martin's *A Wild and Crazy Guy* album. Our maternal grandparents Willis and Dorothy Rich were smart and accomplished people; Grandpa was a professor at Stanford, and Grandma was a doctor. While our mom worked in the summers, we stayed

with them in nearby Menlo Park, and they loved on us every time
we were with them. My grandmother and I grew especially close.
But then we moved.

I hated Oregon. Not because of Oregon itself, but because
moving there took me away from the positive influences of my dad
and grandparents. I recently told my mom, Jeannie St. Germain,
that I still have negative feelings toward Oregon and wished that
we had never moved there, because that is where life began to turn
difficult for me.

Mom and our stepdad had two more kids, Seana and Michael,
whom I've always considered full-blooded siblings. Then Mom got
divorced again and her parents passed away. She had a brother who
stayed distant and wasn't around to help her (or us) at all. Her job
with the Shakespeare Festival was one of the best theater jobs in the
country, but it didn't leave her much time for us because she had to
work a lot of hours to support us financially. Mom definitely made
personal sacrifices to raise us the best she could.

Our house in Ashland was pretty small, probably about twelve
hundred square feet. There was my mom's room, a room Seana and
Michael shared, and a room that Dave and I could have made ours.
But that room had glass walls—a sunroom type of room—and
was cold most of the time because it wasn't insulated. So we took
up residence in a little building out back that we called "the bunkhouse."

The bunkhouse was uncomfortable and cold. There were no
beds; we slept on cots and wrapped ourselves in sleeping bags. The
walls were insulated, but the handle had fallen off the door and
cold air whisked right through the opening. The bunkhouse had a
small electric heater we would huddle over in the morning, with

sleeping bags draped over our backs, to warm up before we dressed
for school.

We lived a dirty existence there. The road to our house was all
dirt and filled with potholes. Some of our neighbors were sheep
farmers. We didn't have a lot of clothes, and the items we did have
were dirty, and we didn't wash them often. In sixth grade, I had
worn the same pair of socks for so long that the bottoms had become black and hard.

"That's sick, Schultzy," one of my teachers told me when she
saw my socks.

It was painfully embarrassing. Those were awful times, but
going through them made Dave and me tough and independent.
We had to grow up faster than most other kids around us.

The transition from Palo Alto to Ashland was difficult. I hated
our elementary school in Ashland. I was almost four hundred
miles away from my dad and grandparents, and the winters were
cold in that freezing bunkhouse. I couldn't wait for the weather to
warm up so I could build up calluses on the bottoms of my feet
that would enable me to hike barefoot on Mount Ashland behind
Lithia Park.

To me, school was boring, so I tapped into the comedian gene
passed along from my dad to create fun. I would listen to Bill Cos-
by's vinyl records over and over at home, memorizing his stories so
I could repeat them for my classmates and make them laugh.

I was a good, natural athlete; Dave wasn't. We both had stiff
shoulders and couldn't throw balls as far as some of the other boys.
Neither of us was good at distance running, either.

Sixth grade was a big year for me in sports, because I broke twenty of the school's twenty-five athletic records for my grade. Classmates voted me "most likely to win the Olympic long jump." Winning that honor was cool because I remembered Dave and me watching the 1968 Olympics in Mexico City when American Bob Beamon pulled off one of the greatest feats in all of sports, breaking the world record in the long jump by an amazing 21¾ inches.

In those days I didn't watch the Olympics and dream of some day competing in the Games. At that point I was still trying to figure out which sport I would make mine. I was good at many sports, so when I thought about specializing in a sport I thought it should be one at which I could make a lot of money because we were so poor.

During sixth grade, I read the book *American Miler: The Life and Times of Glenn Cunningham*, about one of the best Americans in the mile run during the 1930s. Cunningham competed in two Olympics and won the silver medal in the fifteen hundred meters at the 1936 Games in Berlin.

Cunningham's legs had been badly burned during a schoolhouse explosion, and doctors told him he would never walk again. The book described how Cunningham did learn to walk again and developed a running style in which he ran on the balls of his feet and placed one foot directly in front of the other, as though he were running on a straight line. I copied his form, and that gave me a bit of a distinct walk. I had the pleasure and honor of meeting Cunningham in 1988 and was able to tell him how he had affected the way I walked and ran. A week after we met, Cunningham died.

Dave took up wrestling in seventh grade. He made our junior high's junior varsity, and he had a 3-3-1 record in his first season. Dave absolutely fell in love with wrestling from the start. By that time, the other boys in his grade had caught up with him in size, so Dave used wrestling to maintain his status as the toughest kid in school. I loved Dave being the toughest kid, especially because I was the youngest in my grade and not very big compared with the others. Dave didn't miss a chance to step in and take up for me when I got bullied.

I think finding wrestling was a eureka moment for Dave. His reading troubles didn't matter in wrestling, but brutality did, and he had plenty of that. Plus, because he was so smart, he could take moves others did and improve them, and then create his own moves. Even when he first started wrestling, Dave could trick opponents into putting themselves in a position they thought would give them an advantage only to quickly learn they had instead stepped into Dave's trap. By then, it was too late.

Becoming a better wrestler was about the only thing Dave cared about. He carried his wrestling shoes with him at all times and wore a singlet underneath his clothes just in case he met up with someone who wanted to wrestle.

As Dave got into wrestling, we discovered that because his brain wasn't dominated by one side due to his dyslexia, he appeared to have the advantage of being ambidextrous. He wrote and threw with his left hand, kicked with his right foot, and shot guns right-eye dominant. Because he was neither left- nor right-handed, Dave was able to perform moves equally well from both sides. Opponents had trouble figuring out Dave's style and also were left vulnerable due to Dave's being able to attack a wrestler's weaker side—whichever side it was—with equal strength.

Because Dave basically lived wrestling, he rapidly improved. He made the junior high's varsity his eighth-grade year and placed fourth in the state. As a ninth-grader—our high school started with the tenth grade—he wrestled at the World Schoolboy Championships in Lima, Peru, and finished second behind a wrestler from Great Britain.

I was blown away that Dave had risen so fast in such a difficult sport. He, however, didn't make a big deal out of his accomplishments. He had a steady demeanor about him that would have kept you from guessing whether he was doing well in wrestling or stinking.

His dyslexia seemed to have another benefit, too. Dave had become accustomed to having to overcompensate for his dyslexia just to make him equal to his classmates. Then when he did reach a point where he matched up to them, Dave never stopped overcompensating. That really showed on the mat, as he caught and then surpassed others his age, and even older wrestlers, accomplishing feats in high school that have yet to be equaled in US high school wrestling history.

My introduction to wrestling wasn't quite as convincing for me as Dave's was to him.

Wrestling was mandatory in seventh-grade physical education class. We spent all of one period going over different moves and started a tournament the next day in which all seventh-grade boys were required to participate.

With matches held only during class time, it also was a long, drawn-out tournament. My first match came late in the first round, and I hated that. The longer I had to wait to wrestle, the more time I had to consider the potential ramifications to my status as best all-around athlete if I lost. It wasn't the first time I had felt butter-flies in my stomach before a sports contest, but it was the worst case of butterflies I had experienced to that point. (And the butter-flies appeared every time I wrestled during my career. I never fig-ured out how to eliminate them, but I did learn to control them and even use them to create adrenaline before a match.) Losing would have been humiliating, and I thought about it every day when I watched other classmates wrestle.

Finally, when my match rolled around, I was able to throw a headlock on my opponent and pin him. But there was no enjoying the victory, because I immediately began to feel the pressure of what would happen if I lost my second-round match.

As you can imagine, there wasn't much competition in the seventh grade, because none of us were experienced wrestlers. We had all undergone a whopping one period of training. Even though wrestling isn't an intuitive sport that anyone can be naturally good at, I was able to get by on my athletic abilities to win all four matches, with all four ending in a headlock followed by a pin.

Each time I won in our school tournament, I only dreaded the next match. Then when I won the final match, I was more relieved than anything else.

Later that school year, I decided to try out for the seventh-grade wrestling team. But just a few days later, Dave and I moved back to Palo Alto to live with our dad. I loved Mom, but Palo Alto always felt like home to me. Dad had a nicer house, too, and I didn't have to stay in the freezing bunkhouse anymore. Plus, Dad's work allowed him to be home and take care of the basic tasks, like laundry. It sounds simple, but just having clean clothes allowed me to train harder and sweat my clothes down completely, usually several times a day. Moving back to Palo Alto, though, meant I wouldn't get a chance to wrestle in seventh grade.

I made the eighth-grade team in Palo Alto. Our coach was also the swimming coach, and swimming was his primary sport. Our wrestling practices were unorganized, and we learned almost no techniques. The season lasted only six weeks, with three tournaments: District, Northern County, and County championships. Four guys were entered in each weight class in each of the tournaments. I finished second to the same guy in all three, and with a 3-3 record. The season didn't amount to much of anything, and I don't point to that year as when I "started wrestling."

When the season ended, I didn't feel I had learned much about how to wrestle. I didn't like the sport, because it was too exhausting.

Wrestling didn't come close to captivating me as it did my brother.

One day during my ninth-grade year, I went to watch Dave's high school team practice at Palo Alto High School and met Dave's coach, Ed Hart. Hart was also the school's gymnastics coach and taught me how to do a backflip. My immediate thought, in addition to its being cool and an ego boost that I could do something the others in my school couldn't, was that gymnastics would benefit me as an overall athlete by improving my flexibility, balance, and muscle strength.

Gymnastics became for me what wrestling had become for Dave. I embraced becoming a gymnast as though I would be one for the rest of my life, which I believe is the best way for someone to approach anything that he or she wants to be good at. I started training twice a day and met Stanford coach Sadao Hamada, who was one of the most respected gymnastics coaches in the world, and he started training me. I quickly learned a long list of gymnastics moves, and I could tell I was benefiting in the three areas in which I thought gymnastics would help me. In wrestling, a flurry of moves can leave a wrestler dizzy. Gymnasts don't become dizzy, because they have kinesthetic body awareness, which is a fancy way of saying they know where they are at all times. Gymnastics made me so flexible that I could do the splits. It made me so strong that at one point I could do fifty-five pull-ups with a little kip, which is a more-intense pull-up because it involves more of the body than a regular pull-up. Gymnastics also helped me face and defeat my fears.

To help defeat one fear, I picked a risky place to practice one move, the forward roll. There was an old bridge for trains that spanned San Francisquito Creek in Palo Alto. It was probably a fifty-foot drop to the creek below. I would shimmy up to the steel beam atop the bridge and wait for a train to come onto the bridge. Then I would do front rolls on the two-foot-wide beam above the train to prove to myself that I could overcome fear.

I spent most of my free time my ninth-grade year with Coach Hart, who was glad to keep working with me and let me compete with the high school team. With his help, I won the South Peninsula Athletic League's all-around championship for the gymnast with the most total points in all of the meet's events. But because I was still a grade shy of being in high school, the tournament director would not give me any of the medals I had earned. In turn, my Palo Alto teammates refused to accept any of their medals as a show of support for me.

Coach Hamada trained me at two places. One was a gym close to my house and the other was at Stanford's Encina Gym, where the university's gymnastics and wrestling teams worked out. At Encina Gym, I would work out on one side of the room while Dave practiced wrestling on the other. The gymnasts tended to go home after workouts, while the wrestlers liked to hang around after practice. When I was finished with gymnastics, I stayed at the gym to take part in games and competitions on the trampolines with some of the wrestlers.

Later that year, I won the fifteen- to sixteen-year-old Northern California all-around championship. That time, I received my medals.

Coach Hamada was a great coach and friend to me, and he taught me how to develop the best set of athletic skills I could have asked for. Based on the balance, flexibility, and strength I gained in gymnastics, I think gymnastics laid the best foundation I could have developed for any sport.

The mental advantages I picked up in gymnastics were also significant. Everything is mental. We all live in our minds, so whatever we think is reality to us. However, there is no separation between the body and the mind. We are one organism, and confidence must be based on fact. The fact that I learned to do things that other wrestlers could not would help me immensely.

I attribute a large amount of my success as a wrestler to two

factors: my foundation of gymnastics and the sibling rivalry I enjoyed with Dave combined with the brotherly love we shared for
each other. Knowing we would always be brothers no matter what,
we could get extremely brutal and merciless with each other.

Gymnastics and Dave prepared me both physically and mentally for just about anything that could occur during a match.

CHAPTER 2

From off the Mat to Champion

Gymnastics didn't have the ability to provide one thing I lacked: confidence.

As Dave's wrestling career progressed, his self-confidence grew in equal measure. But I went in the other direction. I just wasn't happy in life. My gymnastics medals seemed hollow. Lost, and confused about who I was and wondering what I would become, I kept getting into arguments with my dad and wound up quitting gymnastics.

Down deep inside, I knew what my problem was: my ego. While I was succeeding in gymnastics, my brother was doing even better in wrestling. He was receiving more attention, too, and college recruiters were slobbering all over the thought of getting Dave onto their campus. I complained about that once to my dad, and he slapped me.

Dad had thought after I won the Northern California state championship that gymnastics would be my ticket to college. I had, too. But I walked away from the sport, unsure of what I would do next.

At fifteen, I moved back to Ashland to live with my mom, Seana, and Michael, because I was starting to get high on marijuana, my dad found out about it, and he began clamping down on my activities to the point where I felt my freedom was being taken away.

Being back at my mom's meant that I was living with my mom, her boyfriend, my half brother, and my half sister. We were so poor that I would go to the school's lost and found to take a jacket I could wear in cold weather. I started hanging out with bad influences, especially one neighbor kid whom I would smoke marijuana with and who sadly ended up dying from a drug overdose.

One of the guys I hung out with got arrested for stealing a check out of a car, forging the person's signature, and trying to cash it. I was with him when he tried to cash the check. He hadn't offered to give me any of the money, and I didn't do anything wrong, but I got arrested as an accomplice or an associate. I was put on probation and warned to stay out of trouble, and I learned a lesson about being with the wrong people. I should have told him not to attempt to cash the check, although I knew it wouldn't have made a difference. He would have tried whether I was with him or not.

Getting arrested caused me to do a little soul-searching, and I realized two things. First, I didn't like myself. Second, the only way I could be happy was to be able to beat up everyone in the world. The latter can't be dismissed as just the thought process of a fifteen-year-old. That same desire drove me all the way through my last competition as an athlete, in ultimate fighting, in 1996.

That further affirmed my decision to quit gymnastics. I was good at gymnastics, but thinking back to watching Dave defend himself and me on the playground, I knew I was going to have to find a different avenue to the toughness I wanted to be known for.

Bruce Lee was big then, and watching him kick the crap out

of twenty guys in movies like *Fist of Fury* convinced me that striking martial arts was the way to go. But there wasn't a Bruce Lee studio near Ashland, so I opted for Chuck Norris's Tang Soo Do at a place up the road in Medford. My gymnastics gave me a leg up, literally, because I could hold one leg almost straight over my head.

We trained in a dojo that looked like a dance studio, with wooden floors and big mirrors on the walls. I worked as hard as I could at Tang Soo Do for the first four months. Spending my time training there separated me from my bad influences, and I sensed I was becoming a more disciplined person. I felt I had found my calling, until Dave came to visit for my birthday that fall and we got into a fight over something I don't recall. Typically when Dave and I spent time together, he would say something to push one of my buttons, and then it was go time for us.

I thought I was ready to whip Dave and teach big brother a lesson with my four months' experience in the fine art of Tang Soo Do.

We went out to Mom's front yard and I got in my stance and started egging Dave on. I took a big swing, and he ducked underneath and shot in for a quick takedown. Dave got on top of me and started pounding me in the head and face as I'd watched him do to others. (Believe me, the view was much worse from below.) The pounding Dave administered on me made me realize that most fights end up on the ground, and that's where becoming proficient at wrestling would come in handy.

I wanted to become a great fighter because I lacked confidence and got bullied and made fun of. I wasn't good at talking to girls. The only solution to my problems was to become the toughest guy in the world.

I quit Tang Soo Do and two weeks later tried out for the wrestling team at Ashland High.

When I walked into the Ashland gym on the first day of practice, I was singing this dumb little made-up song, "Wrestling is for wrestlers." I kept repeating that phrase over and over. I guess that was my way of saying to myself, *I'm going to be a wrestler. It's become a wrestler or die trying.*

Every day, I aimed to push myself to my physical limits. I hated running, but I would work on conditioning until I felt like throwing up. I studied the rules and learned every technique I could. I made sure that no one on the team worked out longer than I did.

I learned that wrestling is a simple sport, really. It's not easy, but it's simple, and it definitely isn't a sport for the weak, physically or mentally. There isn't much that's complicated about the concept of wrestling: Pin your opponent and you win.

A pin, also known as a fall, occurs when you take down your opponent, turn him over, and pin his shoulder blades to the mat. In freestyle and Greco-Roman, a pin was called a "touch fall" because all a wrestler had to do was touch both of his opponent's shoulder blades to the mat for a pin. In collegiate style, the shoulder blades had to be on the mat for one second for a pin.

If a match ended without a pin, the wrestler with the most points scored in the match was declared the winner. The moves for which points were awarded varied between the styles. But speaking in general terms, the ways to score points included: taking an opponent down to the mat (called a takedown); escaping from the control of your opponent (an escape); reversing your opponent when he has you in a down position and then getting on top of him (a reversal); almost pinning your opponent (a near fall); and a variety of penalties that can be called against your opponent, such as unsportsmanlike conduct, illegal holds, and stalling, to name a few.

Again, that's in general terms. There were no points for an escape in freestyle. Also, while I was competing, freestyle stopped penalizing points for stalling. When points were awarded for an opponent's stalling, freestyle and collegiate even had different methods of doing so. Stalling calls were judgment calls that gave a lot of power to referees. Sometimes too much power.

The near fall was another good example of how widely the rules varied. In collegiate wrestling, a near fall was scored when a wrestler turned his opponent onto his back and the opponent's shoulder blades broke a forty-five-degree angle to the mat for at least two seconds. If you held your opponent in that position for two seconds, you received two near-fall points; if you held him there for five seconds, you received three points. In freestyle, we called that a "turn." You could score two points for turning your opponent's shoulder blades beyond a ninety-degree angle. You could even just roll him over completely until he was back on his stomach, and if his shoulder blades met the ninety-degree angle standard, you could receive two points for the turn.

The number of points awarded for the different scoring moves also changed from style to style, but typically ranged from one to three points.

Matches consisted of periods. In collegiate wrestling before 1982, the first period lasted two minutes and the second and third lasted three minutes. That changed to a 3-2-2 format. Freestyle matches had three periods of three minutes each until 1981, when matches were shortened to two periods of three minutes each.

Wrestlers were divided into weight classes, with the wrestlers not allowed to weigh more than their designated weight class. When I competed, the Olympics had ten weight classes in both freestyle and Greco-Roman. Currently, there are seven in each. In college wrestling, there were ten classes, as is still the case.

One type of competition was a dual meet between two teams, with both putting one wrestler in each weight class. Each match won could count up to six points for a team, with points awarded depending on the type of victory. The team with the most points at the end of the meet won the dual.

Another format was a tournament featuring multiple teams, as at college national championship meets and high school meets such as a conference or state championship. Tournaments were double elimination, and a wrestler could lose as early in the tournament as his first match and still finish as high as third place.

Freestyle tournaments followed a round-robin format. In international meets, including the Olympics, wrestlers were divided into two pools, or groups. All the wrestlers in each pool would wrestle against each other, with the wrestler in each pool accumulating the most points (based on type of victories) advancing to the championship match.

When I decided to switch to wrestling, I was all in. I committed to train as hard as I could, even if it killed me. That's no exaggeration. I was unhappy with myself because I had been getting high too much and hanging around losers I didn't respect. To be successful in an area, you have to respect the people who are successful in that area, or you are disrespecting the very thing that you want to become. I was so unhappy that there no longer existed a difference between life and death to me. I sincerely didn't care anymore. I wanted to start associating with people I respected. Fortunately wrestling provided that.

My coach was Tim Brown, a heavyweight wrestler and football coach. He was a good coach and a good guy. Ashland's wrestling program was small, though, with only about ten guys at tryouts. Coach Brown understood the importance of stamina and wrestling, and he ran us like crazy to get us in tip-top shape.

Best I remember, we had twelve weight classes in high school wrestling when I competed. If necessary, coaches would choose weight classes for their wrestlers if there were weights unfilled, because forfeiting a weight class would give the opposing team six points in a dual match. Only one wrestler from a school could participate at each weight in a meet, so coaches would come up with ways to choose who would compete at weights.

I started wrestling in the 130-pound weight class. It was then that I experienced one of the worst parts of wrestling: cutting weight.

Cutting weight is the process of dropping weight, usually rapidly, to meet the weight maximum of a particular class. Cutting involves heavy workouts to make you sweat as much as you can; cutting back on food, or even cutting out food altogether; and, when a wrestler is really having to work hard to make weight, sticking a finger in your throat so you vomit. Done the wrong way—as in those extreme cases—cutting weight is dangerous. But it has been a part of the sport for as far back as I've heard it explained.

When I was competing in wrestling, the predominant philosophy was that cutting lots of weight gave a wrestler an advantage
in that he would be bigger than a wrestler who didn't cut to the
same weight. Basically, a wrestler who cut would lose body fat to
get down in weight and would have more muscle mass than the
other wrestler.

I thought it was a stupid philosophy, especially for someone
with a lean body type, which I had from gymnastics. I weighed
136. Six pounds may not sound like too much of a difference, but
because I was lean, I was cutting water weight and my body was
eating my muscles. When calories aren't coming in from outside
the body, energy must be found from what is stored in the body.
Carbs are burned during aerobic (with oxygen) actions, and pro-
teins are burned with anaerobic (without oxygen) actions. Because
I didn't have much body fat, the only way for me to lose weight was
to burn energy from muscle protein and by dehydrating water
weight through sweating. As a result, my ability to perform was
significantly hampered.

Wade Yates, one of my best friends, was a district runner-up
the previous season for Ashland in my weight. Coach Brown created a rule that if two wrestlers were in the same weight, they
would wrestle challenge matches each week for that weight's spot
on the varsity. Wade and I wrestled eleven times in ten weeks, and
I won ten times. I had to lift my level of intensity so high when I
wrestled Wade each week that I suffered a drop-off for the ensuing
competitions.

I think I got pinned in my first four matches and didn't have
a clue why I was getting destroyed.

Dave's reputation was that he became so good because of his vast knowledge of techniques. I was new to wrestling and didn't know any moves, so I set out to learn as many as I could. Dave and I had a friend named Jim Goguen who wrestled at Southern Oregon College (now Southern Oregon University) in Ashland.

I went over to the campus, and Jim introduced me to the concept of gaining hand control from the bottom to escape an opponent riding you on top. I call it the "hand-control standup."

Here's how it works: You're down on the mat, and your opponent has his arms around you. You grab his fingers so that he can't grab his own hand to get a locked grip around you or grab your hands so that he has what's known as hand control. Then you put your feet out in front of you, arch your back so that you can get your hips away from his hips, and then cut free from your opponent with a quick turn. That's an effective way of escaping your opponent.

The hand-control standup worked well because of one indisputable fact: The back of your head is harder than your opponent's face. If the other guy's face was behind my head, Jim told me, I should smash his face with my head. No opponent would want to hang on if he was being smashed in the face.

After Jim taught me that move, almost no one could hold me down. I employed that move all throughout high school and college and into national and international competitions. At the college level, scoring includes one point for riding time. Riding time comes when a wrestler is in control of an opponent on the mat, and the wrestler being controlled is unable to escape or score a reversal. At the end of the match, if a wrestler has one minute more of riding time than his opponent, one riding time point is added to his score. After my second year in college, no opponent scored a riding time point against me.

The hand-control concept was just as effective from on top. If I could control an opponent's hands, I could ride him pretty well. The funny thing is that the hand-control concept was so simple. I couldn't understand why more wrestlers—shoot, all wrestlers— weren't doing it. I never shared the secret of the hand-control standup with anyone.

Thanks to what Jim taught me, I improved at escapes. I was training as hard as I could, too. But still, the wins weren't coming. I made the mistake of believing that if I learned techniques like Dave, I'd be winning like him, too. The big difference didn't come, though, until I realized that I would need to add explosive power to the techniques to make them work.

After losing those first four matches, my record climbed to 4-6 by about halfway through the season. That's when Coach Brown decided to replace me with Wade to make our team better, even though I was still winning our weekly challenge matches.

I didn't like the fact that Coach had created the challenge system and then didn't follow it. He had established the rules we were playing by, but then he threw out the rules so he could have Wade wrestle in tournaments instead of me.

On top of that, we were forfeiting matches in the upper weights we couldn't fill because of our lack of heavier wrestlers. Our team was lousy, so I didn't understand the "make the team better" reason. And I didn't care about the team anyway. Sure, they added up points for team totals at tournaments, but as far as

I was concerned, wrestling was an individual sport. It was me against my opponent. That's all I cared about.

Instead of talking to Coach Brown, I went straight to the principal, who instructed Coach to put me back on varsity. Because of that, the situation was partly my fault, too. I should have talked to Coach Brown first. I could have talked to him about it, because he was a good coach. He made a judgment call I didn't agree with, and there was nothing more to it than that.

At least on the surface.

But when I look back, I think the reason I went to the principal first is that, mentally, I had already checked out of Ashland. I never was happy in Oregon, I wanted out of there, and I was willing to stir up trouble if that's what it took to make it happen.

I started skipping classes. I got into a fight in PE and broke my hand when I punched the kid in the back of the head. The only lesson I learned from that incident was to never again punch someone in the back of the head; it's too hard back there. With my hand in a cast, I flunked typing class. Then I cut off the cast because I got tired of wearing it. The hand didn't heal correctly.

I couldn't wait to flee Oregon, but I couldn't go back to Palo Alto until my probation period expired. Waiting out the remainder of my probation seemed to slow time significantly. I felt as if I had been ripped off in being arrested and put on probation anyway. Then there were the problems on the wrestling team, my broken hand, and wanting to get out of the same house as my mom's boyfriend.

Dave came for another visit after wrestling season, this one tied to recruiting. It seemed as if every college with a wrestling program was recruiting Dave, and that made me jealous of him. I had always been a better natural athlete than him and had won the gymnastics championship in California. I would look at Dave and think about how uncoordinated he had been and wonder how he had become so good at wrestling in such a short time. Dave's success confused me, but it also opened my eyes to the potential I could have as a wrestler. If nothing else, I knew that if I gave my full attention to wrestling, I would have a top-notch workout partner in my brother.

During the week Dave spent with us, Ron Finley, the coach at the University of Oregon, and Bob Rheim from Southern Oregon came to talk with him. While Mark and I were talking to the coaches, he called me a pothead. I couldn't beiieve he said that right in front of them.

D ave's senior season at Palo Alto High is the best any US high school wrestler has ever produced.

In November, he missed a few matches of his high school team to compete in Lincoln, Nebraska, at the prestigious Great Plains freestyle tournament. Despite being a high school wrestler, Dave advanced to the finals against Chuck Yagla. Dave was just a high school senior and he was going up against Yagla, who had completed his collegiate wrestling career at the University of Iowa a year earlier. Yagla had won the 1975 and '76 NCAA Championships and was named the meet's Outstanding Wrestler his senior year.

Dave was down a few points to Yagla when the two were chest to chest, arms around each other. Dave caught the two-time NCAA champ in a step-around body lock, taking a long step with his left leg and wrapping it around Chuck's right leg to trap it. Dave then drove Chuck straight to his back, keeping Chuck's right leg trapped with his left leg, and pinned him for the victory.

Winning at Great Plains qualified Dave for the Tbilisi tournament in Soviet Georgia, considered the best in the world because all the Soviet wrestlers took part and they formed the most dominant team in world and Olympic competitions. Dave placed second there, higher than any other American.

Dave had finished fourth at state his sophomore and junior years, but competing in Tbilisi kept him out of the high school tournaments that would have qualified him for the California state championship meet. Coach Hart petitioned the state coaches association to allow Dave to compete anyway, but in one class higher at 170 pounds. The coaches agreed, knowing Dave would win state. And he did, easily, with his closest score 12–1 in the finals.

After state, Dave took part in the Greco-Roman National Championships. In Greco-Roman, wrestlers are not allowed to use their legs to attack and cannot attack an opponent's legs. Dave won that tournament and the Gorriaran Award given to the wrestler who totals the most falls in the least amount of time.

College recruiters were lining up to make their best sales pitches to Dave.

Dave revolutionized wrestling because of his emphasis on technique. Before, most coaches had emphasized pure conditioning. At that time, freestyle matches were nine minutes long and college matches lasted eight minutes. In a nine-minute match, conditioning tended to be the only thing that mattered, because wrestlers with great technique but lousy conditioning could get wiped out by superconditioned wrestlers.

Dave changed that because he was well conditioned *and* possessed super technique. That's why as a high school senior he was able to beat some of the world's best wrestlers with a body that looked as if it belonged to, as one friend of ours liked to say, a chemistry professor. Dave's body was deceiving, though; he actually had incredible core strength.

My probation ended in the middle of my junior year, and I moved back to Palo Alto, although too late to try out for the wrestling team. I reached out to another one of Dave's wrestling friends, Chris Horpel, who had recently graduated from Stanford after earning All-American honors. Chris was seven years older than I was. At first, we had almost an older brother–younger brother relationship. I tried to make Chris like me by getting him to laugh at my Steve Martin imitations. After a while, he got pretty good at imitating Steve, too. Steve Martin was the best, and Chris and I cracked each other up with his comedy.

Chris coached me and wrestled against me the remainder of my junior year and during the summer. He also arranged for me to train with some of Stanford's wrestlers, and that would give me a huge advantage over other competitors my age. Unable to compete on the school team, I wrestled in amateur freestyle tournaments almost every weekend. Most of the time, I lost my first two matches and was eliminated. But I hit a growth spurt during that period and at the end of the summer won a pretty big tournament at West Valley College while wrestling at 145 pounds. Winning the tournament was great, but still my only motivation in wrestling was to become the greatest fighter in the world.

Coach Hart, Dave's coach, knew I would be wrestling for him the next school year at Palo Alto High, and he kept close tabs on my progress. He also worked out with me, and I took him down ten times.

Dave dutifully kept a wrestling notebook full of notes and observations. I copied Dave my junior year because I thought— and still think—that the way to become good at just about any- thing is to find someone who is good at it and copy what he does. So, like Dave, I decided to turn wrestling into an academic pursuit.

I organized my notebook into categories of tie-ups, or posi- tions I would find myself in before or after shots. Grabbing an opponent's wrist, for instance, is a tie-up. But grabbing a wrist and using it to execute an arm drag to a single leg would make the single leg the tie-up. I've noticed that most wrestlers tend to divide attacks into three steps: set-up, penetration, and finish.

Set-up, usually executed with the hands and arms, is setting up the opponent for an attack by getting him off-balance and cre- ating an opening to attack. Penetration, often referred to as "the shot," is the attack itself. The finish is the final move of the se- quence designed to score points or, ideally, lead to a pin.

On a basic move like the arm drag, for example, my set-up would be allowing my opponent to grab my right wrist with his left hand. Then I would lower my wrist to move his arm into the posi- tion I wanted. Next, I would grab the back of his triceps with my left hand and throw his arm directly sideways, which would break his grip. I would throw so hard that his arm would almost be hor- izontal to the ground, twisting his upper body away from me.

There wasn't much to the penetration. After I got my oppo- nent's arm horizontal, I would drop my hips and shoot. That was my penetration step. For the finish, after throwing his arm horizontal, I would keep both arms out wide, like a net, to catch anything I could (usually both legs, but sometimes just one). As I took the penetration step, I would wrap my stepping leg all the way around the back of my opponent's left leg/foot, trapping it and tripping him as I drove my left shoulder into his stomach/groin area. Trapping his leg would result in either my tackling him or my forcing him to fall backward to the mat.

In my notebook, I eliminated the penetration, because that was a given, and turned the three-step process into two steps.

If a technique didn't have a name, I created one for it.

Each page was dedicated to one tie-up. Examples of tie-ups are single leg, double leg, high-crotch, over-under, double overhook, double underhook, front headlock, and, for one with a funny name, the whizzer. I wrote the name of the tie-up at the top of a page and listed underneath all the different ways to finish from that tie-up. Upper-body finishes included throws, kick-ups, and trips. I discovered the seven basic categories of finishing all leg attacks: lift, trip, spin behind, switch to another move, crack the opponent down to his hip, run the pipe, and go out the back door. On the back of the page, I listed counters to each tie-up. Then I had separate pages for reversals, pinning combinations, and escapes. Inside the front cover, I listed hints to relieve pressure, stay focused, and perceive reality. All of that was designed, in my sixteen-year-old mind, to improve as quickly as possible.

I studied my wrestling notebook far more than any of my school textbooks, and I reread my notebook until I memorized every note on every page. I took mental snapshots of the pages, and when I got into a tie-up during a match, that particular page would flash into my mind and I could "see" a menu of moves to choose from. I would decide how to finish before I shot so there would be no hesitation.

My notebook was pretty full by the time I went to Joe Seay's Bakersfield Express camp the summer before my senior year. I roomed with Jeff Newman, who would also be a senior at Paly, as our school was commonly called. When Jeff saw me making notes in my book and I explained what I was doing, we got into a fun debate about the effectiveness of making such a book. Jeff was a good wrestler, and we would become training partners and good friends, but I knew the book worked for my big brother and that was the only point I needed to consider.

At the camp I developed the idea of "chain" wrestling, or transitioning from one move to another and then another and then another in an infinite chain of moves. I jotted down a lot of chains in my notebook until I concluded there was no limit to the chains and I stopped writing down moves. From that point, I focused on which moves and chains were the most effective and, ultimately, they became my most-guarded secrets. In fact, my most effective attack was so secretive that I didn't even realize how much I employed it until watching myself on video.

A couple of more traditional books greatly influenced me. One was a book on takedowns that was written by Bobby Douglas, an African American who broke racial barriers in wrestling, finished with a career record of 303-17, and was inducted into the National Wrestling Hall of Fame.

The second was *You Are the World* by Indian teacher J. Krishnamurti. I had read inspiring stories of Zen masters accomplishing incredible physical and mental feats, including one who had spent a day in meditation, sipping tea and relaxing, then got up and shot an arrow into a dark corridor and nailed the center of the target. As I checked out *You Are the World*, it looked as if it contained Zen philosophy. I flipped to a chapter about overcoming fear and began reading. I was so intrigued by the chapter that I read that book and then others by Krishnamurti.

At first, it was difficult to understand Krishnamurti. He didn't write books that offered, for instance, six easy steps to overcoming fear. He would ask questions but not provide answers. His books didn't tell me what I should or shouldn't think. Instead, he wrote in a way that seemed as if he were walking alongside me, teaching me how to live without him and not to depend on him.

Before reading Krishnamurti, I had never heard phrases like "dying to the past every moment"; "observing what is, not what should be, including my thoughts without judgment, and seeing what happens"; and "living totally in the present."

From Krishnamurti's writings, I learned to observe my thoughts and the world without judging. I learned to see my mind with complete attention and see what happens. I learned that the divisions and conflicts that existed in my mind between what is and what should be were the same sources of conflict and division that existed in the world. And I learned that the only thing that mattered to me was what was happening at that moment. I learned to live totally in the present and die to the past.

Realizing that in love there was no separation between the observer and the observed, I began to love everything, including my opponents. I no longer held grudges. That freed me from encumbrances that had previously been obstacles to my success. With the pains of my past no longer in my present, I had the energy I needed to move on and continue improving in every way I could.

Learning to live totally in the present and die to the past helped me get through training, because when I caught myself thinking that my body could take no more pain than it was already experiencing, I would tell myself that all the pain I had experienced up to that moment was in my past, and my past was dead and gone.

Life began anew every second, and that philosophy combined with wrestling brought me out of my darkness and made me happy again.

Before my senior year, I needed workout gear and asked Dad to buy me a sweatshirt. By coincidence, as far as I knew, he bought me a green sweatshirt. Our school colors were green and white. I wore that sweatshirt every day, and pulling it down over my head was like flipping a switch that transformed me into the person I was trying to become: confident and at ease with myself.

I pushed myself in my workouts to my absolute limits, training harder than anyone else and working myself into better shape than anyone else. I worked out twice a day. Some days, I worked out three or four times. Every day, more and more, I could see myself becoming the fighter I wanted to be.

I gained thirty pounds in one year and weighed a lean, mean 157 pounds when my senior year started. In California, one pound was added every month of the season until the state championships. My class started at 154 pounds and ended at 159. I figured that if I worked out hard and then dropped to the next lowest weight, that should be my ideal weight. I'd usually have to cut only a pound or two to wrestle at 154.

For a short period, Stanford had a club wrestling team that worked out at Gunn High School, Paly's crosstown rival. Through my connection with Chris Horpel, I was able to work out with the Stanford club after my practice at Paly. Bob McNeil, one of the Stanford wrestlers, was a master of the side roll, and that move I learned from him would become my go-to move.

Jeff Newman and I trained together every day, and he wrestled a weight higher than me, at 165. Jeff won every tournament and was undefeated, including a victory against Joe Guillory, the defending Central Coast Section champion at my weight.

Meanwhile, I didn't win any of our three regular-season tournaments. I lost to the eventual tournament champion in my first match at the first tournament. Coach Hart held me out of the second tournament because of a broken toe. At the third meet, I placed third.

I was faring well against Jeff in practice, so I knew I could beat Joe Guillory and the others he was beating. But mentally, I was struggling. The pressure of competing seemed to get to me. It didn't help that I was *the* Dave Schultz's little brother and that I had gone 4-6 the previous year at 130 pounds.

I don't know what changed, but something sure did. Dramatically. I won the nine-team South Peninsula Athletic League, pinning my opponent in the final, to qualify for Regionals. There, with wrestlers from about twenty schools competing, I won again and qualified for the Central Coast Section, which consisted of about ninety schools. At CCS, I defeated one opponent who had beaten me during the regular season, and advanced to the finals to face Joe Guillory.

Guillory took me down and rode me the entire first period. In the second period, I reversed him to his back for five points with the Bob McNeil side roll. I won the match by one point, was named the meet's Outstanding Wrestler, and qualified for the state championship at San Diego State University.

Most states broke down their state tournaments into different divisions or classifications based on the sizes of schools, so they wound up with multiple state champions in each weight class. California, despite having more than eight hundred schools that competed in wrestling, didn't do that. Schools of all sizes competed together, with one state champion crowned at each weight. A wrestler who won a state championship in California truly was *the* state champion.

Joe Guillory lost in the first round. There I was in my senior year, most likely my last season to wrestle, getting ready for my first match in my first state tournament, and a wrestler I knew firsthand was one of the best in the state had lost right off the bat.

You've got to be kidding me! I thought. *These guys are tough. I might be in over my head here.*

I relied on Krishnamurti's teachings and told myself to live totally in the present. I focused solely on my first match, not even taking a look beyond that match on the bracket sheet. For as long as I kept advancing through the tournament, I would continue to look only to my next opponent. That's a trick I used throughout my career to help keep me completely in the present.

My first match was against a wrestler who had finished fifth in the Southern Section. I was never in danger of losing during that match and gave up a takedown at the end to win by one point.

My next opponent was Tim Johnson of Vallejo's Hogan High. Johnson was undefeated and a favorite to win the championship. He led me 3–2 with ten seconds remaining when I escaped to tie the match and send us into overtime. We had a one-minute break before the start of overtime, and I had used up so much energy to rally for the tie that I lay down as soon as I reached my corner. I was so exhausted that I almost threw up.

About forty-five seconds into the break, Coach Hart looked at me, then over to my opponent, who was sitting up on a knee and talking to his coach. Johnson didn't appear tired at all, and here I was sucking wind. Coach Hart slapped me really hard and pulled me to my feet. I'd never seen him do anything like that, and his slap startled me. I felt a rush of needed adrenaline. Coach knew what he was doing!

Overtime consisted of three one-minute periods. We finished the first period scoreless, but I scored three points in each of the next two periods for a 6–0 win in overtime. Johnson, by the way, worked back through the consolation side of the bracket and placed third.

My semifinals match was against Kerry Hiatt of Poway High. Hiatt was undefeated, and Poway had won four state team titles. Plus, Poway was near San Diego State and had a large number of fans at the meet. Hiatt took me down in the first period and rode me the entire round. In the second round, I chose to start on the bottom and hit him with the side roll that I had used in every critical match that season. I put Hiatt on his back for five points and rode him for all of the third period to win 5–2.

When the ref raised my hand to signify my victory, I looked over to Coach Hart and gave him a thumbs-up. He knew what I was asking. The old gymnast in me had been doing backflips on the mat to signify big victories, and winning in the semifinals was a big victory to me. But Coach Hart waved me down and yelled, "No!" When I walked over to him, Coach told me, "Save it. It's not time."

Another undefeated wrestler awaited me in the final, Chris Bodine of Pleasant Hill. Bodine was a junior, but we both were seventeen.

The score was 4–4 starting the third period, and he chose bottom. Basically all he had to do to win state was escape. I rode him for about a minute, then he stood up, broke my grip, and turned to face me. Right before he completed the escape, I let go of his body, snatched his left leg, and held on with all I had. I didn't know what to do from there. But I did know that if I let him go, he would win. We both were exhausted, and I thought this might be the last time I would ever wrestle.

But with both arms clutching Bodine's leg, I died to the past. *You're not dead yet,* I told myself, then exploded one last time and did something I'd never done before: I lifted my opponent off the ground with a single leg and arched into a back suplay. We both began falling, and I turned into Bodine and landed on top of him when he hit the mat. He was lying right on his back, and I slapped him in a half nelson with one arm, grabbed his leg with my other arm, and locked my hands into a cradle. I held him on his back in the cradle for three points. He got off his back with a few seconds left on the clock, and I rode him out to win the state championship, 7–4. I punctuated my victory with a backflip.

That 1978 California State Wrestling Championships was the most miraculous tournament of my life, even of all my future t˙˙˙

naments on the national and international levels. Winning the
state championship made me start thinking that perhaps there was
a god after all.

Two years earlier, I had been a gymnast, not a wrestler. Then
in only sixteen months, I had progressed from a 4-6 record and
losing my spot on the team to walking toward the winners' podium as *the* California state champion. As I made the walk, I was
wearing the green sweatshirt my dad had bought me and that I
had poured dozens of gallons of sweat through.

After the medals ceremony, I went into the bathroom and
looked into the mirror, staring into my own eyes for probably five
minutes. I wondered why it was that this brain had enabled me to
be better than anyone else in the state.

Why me?

Whatever sins I had committed must have been forgiven for
me to receive this incredible blessing. For that, I could only give
thanks and pledge to do my best to preserve this feeling and parlay
it into even greater heights.

Again, I wondered, *Why me?*

Other wrestlers knew as much as I did, worked as hard as I
did, and wanted to win (probably) as much as I did. But yet somehow, there was something different I had that they didn't.

I didn't know what it was, but as I continued to look into that
mirror, I saw someone who had been granted a gift, an undefinable
edge. More important, I saw someone I loved. I was happy with
myself.

When I returned to Palo Alto, Dad threw me a party with a
cake, balloons, and a banner that read CONGRATULATIONS! That
was the first time in my life I felt that I had accomplished some-

thing Dad had never imagined I could do. My dad the comedian had made me laugh all throughout my growing-up years. But on this day, I was making him smile and laugh!

That state championship–winning move, in all its unplanned glory, was the luckiest thing that ever happened to me in my life. If it hadn't worked, I would have lost and become a US Marine and a former wrestler.

CHAPTER 3

John du Pont

On another coast and years before, John Eleuthère du Pont had a very different childhood. He grew up in a forty-plus-room mansion on an eight-hundred-acre estate in Newtown Square, Pennsylvania, just west of Philadelphia. The mansion was an exact replica of President James and Dolley Madison's Montpelier home in Virginia, which had been designed by Thomas Jefferson, a du Pont family friend.

The du Pont business acumen—most associated with the DuPont chemical and explosives company and, later, General Motors—elevated the family from French immigrants to American royalty, listed alongside the likes of the Rockefellers, the Astors, and the Vanderbilts.

As one of hundreds of heirs to the du Pont fortune, John was born with a silver spoon in his mouth. His life journey, though, evolved into an unfulfilled quest to taste Olympic gold—even after it had become painfully obvious that he would never be able to earn that chance through his own talents and abilities.

John du Pont became rich simply by being born. His great-great-grandfather, French-born Eleuthère Irénée du Pont, built a gunpowder mill in Wilmington, Delaware, in 1802 that would grow into the E. I. du Pont de Nemours and Company, which came to be called DuPont for short.

E.I.'s expertise at making gunpowder led to the company's establishing itself as a leading supplier of gunpowder to the US military. The company expanded into the production of smokeless gunpowder and dynamite.

In 1902, while DuPont celebrated its one hundredth anniversary, company president Eugene du Pont's death resulted in a transaction that would mark a new era in DuPont's history and position the company for remarkable growth.

Du Pont cousins T. Coleman, Pierre S., and Alfred I. purchased the company and transitioned DuPont into a scientific-research-driven chemical company. DuPont's profits allowed Pierre to later acquire controlling interest in the struggling General Motors company in which he was a shareholder. The DuPont company then invested in the automaker, perhaps saving GM from collapse. Pierre made his and DuPont's investments pay off richly when he became GM's president and steered the company into its spot as the world's largest automobile maker.

With its emphasis on science, DuPont entered the field of synthetic textile fibers and rose further in prominence. The company struck it big in the 1930s by introducing women's hosiery into the marketplace. During World War II, DuPont became a large supplier of the material used in parachutes and B-29 bomber tires. DuPont also played a key role in the Manhattan Project, which produced the first atomic bombs.

The family's business acumen led to the du Ponts' becoming one of America's wealthiest and most influential families.

The line from Eleuthère Irénée to John E. du Pont passed from E.I.'s son Henry to grandson William to great-grandson William Jr.

John was born in 1938 in Philadelphia, the youngest of the

four children of William Jr. and Jean Liseter Austin, who also hailed from a well-to-do family.

Jean's father had given the newlyweds more than six hundred acres of land called Liseter Hall in Newtown Square. William Jr.'s father then built the couple the mansion that John grew up in.

The Montpelier replica estate became part of a family legal squabble in the 1980s in which John was involved. Family members spent millions of dollars on legal fees alone before the matter was worked out.

The du Ponts resolved family problems by hiring lawyers; Dave and I settled our disputes with our fists.

John's father, president of the Delaware Trust Company, owned Thoroughbreds that raced under the colors of his Foxcatcher Farm stable, and he was also a major player in the construction of racetracks and steeplechase courses, gaining international acclaim for the more than twenty he designed. His love of foxhunting led to the establishment of his well-known Foxcatcher Hounds kennel. John's mother bred Welsh ponies and championship beagles for competition. She was highly regarded in equestrian circles for her, as she called them, Liseter Welsh ponies, and she won more than thirty-two thousand awards over seven decades of showing horses.

John had two sisters and a brother, the youngest of whom was already eleven when John was born. Their parents separated when John was only two, and his mother kept Liseter Hall in the divorce settlement. John's sisters and brother went off to boarding schools and then started their own families, but John attended a local private school and remained on the estate with his mother.

John's father married tennis star Margaret Osborne six years after the divorce. They had a son together, William III, and divorced while John was in his midtwenties.

William Jr. had little to do with John as his son grew up. John once told a reporter that he "spent a lifetime looking for a father." His mother, a strong-minded woman, did not remarry and lived in the mansion, overseeing the farm's operations, until she died at age ninety-one. Without his father's presence, and with his older siblings often away from home, John basically grew up alone with his mother. Perhaps that caused, or at least contributed to, his lifelong inability to have normal relationships.

Shy and a stutterer into adulthood, John faced teasing at the prestigious boys-only Haverford School. Classmates voted him, curiously, both the laziest student and the most likely to succeed. John participated in swimming and wrestling at Haverford. He once proudly showed me a picture of him on the wrestling team during his freshman year. He was on the bottom row at the very end of the line, wearing a Haverford singlet. That was the only photo I saw of him in a wrestling uniform from his school years.

John struggled to develop meaningful friendships at school, but he reveled in a graduation party he threw at his estate despite the fact that he had fallen behind in his classwork and would not graduate on time. John told the boys that none of them was allowed to bring a date. During the party, a few of the boys tried to drive a car into the estate's swimming pool.

That prank was one John would replicate later in life, but with a much more sinister purpose.

Du Pont graduated from high school in 1957 and enrolled at the University of Pennsylvania, but he did not finish out his freshman year before leaving. John did earn a college degree, in marine biology, from the University of Miami, where he competed on the swim team.

Du Pont dreamed of swimming in the Olympics, and he had the financial resources to train in California with the best swim club in the nation, the Santa Clara Swim Club.

John bought a home in Atherton, California, to live in during his training. Some twenty years before I would hear du Pont's name for the first time, John lived less than five miles from Dave and me.

The Santa Clara Swim Club trained Olympic champion swimmers. At that time, the club's list of Olympic gold medalists included—and certainly was not limited to—Mark Spitz, Lynn Burke, Donna de Varona, Chris von Saltza, and Steve Clark.

Du Pont was, at best, a good swimmer. He clearly could not compete at the level necessary to make an Olympic team.

In 1963, du Pont decided to take up the sport of modern pentathlon, which consisted of five events: cross-country running, fencing, freestyle swimming, pistol shooting, and show jumping.

I've heard two stories of how John reached that decision.

One said that the Santa Clara swim coach convinced John that he was not cut out for the Olympics in swimming and recommended that if John really wanted to achieve his goal of competing in an Olympic Game, pentathlon could be his best chance.

According to the second account, which was John's story, he visited the home of Lynn Burke, the 1960 Olympic backstroke champion, and her father told du Pont that, considering he already knew how to swim, fire pistols, and ride horses, he should try pentathlon and then introduced him to a fencing coach.

Both stories could be true.

Pentathlon made sense for John's Olympic dream because it wasn't a widely contested sport at the time. It required money to pay coaches to train an athlete in the different disciplines, which limited the number of hopefuls. John could pay for that training, and he also had the financial means to construct training facilities on his mother's property.

Du Pont built a pistol range, cleared out a cross-country course, and had an indoor Olympic-size swimming pool installed. Along the wall beside the pool, du Pont paid to have mounted a mosaic of himself performing each of the five disciplines. The tiny pieces of tile for the mosaic were shipped in from Florence, Italy.

Du Pont could also afford to cover the costs of traveling to other countries to compete. He won a tournament that was reported back home to be the Australian national championship in 1965, when there was very little interest in the sport there.

But in the United States, as with swimming, he just wasn't Olympic material. In 1967, he hosted the national championship in his backyard and, despite his home-field advantage, placed in the middle of the pack. The following year, in the competition to determine the US team members for the 1968 Games in Mexico City, du Pont finished next to last.

John's money had paid for the best coaching he could find in the United States. His money had allowed him to build practice facilities that allowed him to train without leaving home. But his abilities couldn't earn him a spot on the team.

For the 1976 Olympics, as a reward for his financial contributions to modern pentathlon, du Pont was given a manager's spot on the US team, allowing him to wear the team's warm-up suit and pose in the team photo.

But du Pont never possessed what it took to make it to the Olympics without buying his way in as a noncompetitor. The determination was there, along with more than enough resources, but the skills were not.

John was approaching thirty when he failed to make the Olympic team in modern pentathlon. With four years until the next Olympics, du Pont faced an insurmountable combination: At his age, he had run out of time to reach an elite level in the sports he had been best at, and he had run out of sports for which he could try to purchase another attempt at an Olympic bid.

John du Pont would never be an Olympian. The best he could do was associate with those who were.

With a nod to the name of his father's stable of Thoroughbreds, John concentrated on bringing in the best athletes for his Team Foxcatcher, recruiting and encouraging swimmers, triathletes, and pentathletes to train at what was known as "the farm."

He had already learned the benefits of association through his contributions to law enforcement. While training in California, he donated to the Atherton Police Activities League and showed off the badge he had been given by the Newtown Township Police Department back home as appreciation for donations he had made there.

His association with the Newtown Township police deepened beginning in 1970. He allowed the police to train at his indoor and outdoor shooting ranges. (He named the indoor range for FBI director J. Edgar Hoover.) As an expert marksman from pentathlon, he volunteered his time to train Newtown Township officers in shooting. He bought bulletproof vests and radios for the department and allowed the police to use his helicopter.

That association benefited him in a couple of ways. First, he was able to potentially gain a deeper level of protection, both legal and physical, that would buy him more power if he ever got in legal trouble. Second, and more immediate, he was able to wear a police uniform and perform volunteer, reserve-type duties. In look and in thought, he could be a cop. His badge and standing with the police department also provided him the ability to purchase high-powered guns.

John liked the feel of powerful weapons in his hands. There is one strange story from the late seventies, about a day when the fish weren't biting at the farm's pond. He became so enraged that he pulled out a gun and fired at geese on the water, almost shooting the son of a swim coach.

Du Pont and guns were a dangerous combination long before the months leading up to when he murdered Dave.

CHAPTER 4

One and Done at UCLA

Until I won the state championship, I was headed to the military after high school graduation. College coaches weren't pursuing me to wrestle for them, as they had with Dave, and I hadn't given much thought to attending college without a scholarship. I had already visited with a recruiter for the US Marine Corps because I didn't know what else I could do after high school.

But my state championship provided me an unexpected option. There are no guarantees in college recruiting, but because of California's reputation for producing elite high school wrestlers, winning a state championship just about guarantees an opportunity to wrestle in college. My problem was one of timing. I hadn't been on any college's radar, and my state title came at the point in the recruiting calendar when most of the wrestling scholarships had already been committed.

Two schools offered me scholarships: Oklahoma State and the University of California, Los Angeles.

Oklahoma State was a perennial national powerhouse, and UCLA, well, wasn't. At the time, Oklahoma State had won twenty-seven team national championships and had placed third my senior year. To show how dominant the Cowboys were (and are, with thirty-four championships currently), all these years

later, no other college team has as many championships even now
as Oklahoma State did back then.

Oklahoma State also happened to be Dave's team, as coach
Tommy Chesbro had been the fortunate soul to sign Dave out of
high school.

Honestly, I believe Coach Chesbro's offering me a scholarship
had more to do with Dave than with me. I think he feared that if
I went anywhere other than Oklahoma State, Dave would leave to
join me.

Dave had a 30-4-1 record as a freshman and placed third in
the NCAAs at 150 pounds, losing to the eventual champion, Mark
Churella, 13–10, in the semifinals. Dave was miserable at Oklahoma State, though. Coach Chesbro wanted to keep Dave at 150
so Ricky Stewart could wrestle at 158. College athletes have five
academic years in which to complete their four years of athletic
eligibility. Athletes can "redshirt" one year, which allows them to
attend classes and practice with their team but not participate in
competitions. The redshirt year doesn't count against their four
years of eligibility. It is most common for a redshirt to be used
during athletes' first year in college to allow them to adapt to college life and ease their transition into competing at the collegiate
level. Ricky had redshirted the 1978 season, his freshman year,
after an 88-0-1 high school career in Oklahoma that included
three state championships.

Dave was having to cut hard to make 150, but Ricky was
bigger than Dave and wouldn't be able to cut to 150.

My brother was good enough to wrestle at any weight, but
cutting weight is no fun, and it is especially difficult when you are
having to work as hard as Dave was to make weight. He also had

academic struggles. Dave went to college to wrestle, and classes were a necessary evil that allowed him to be in college to wrestle. Having dyslexia certainly didn't help with his attempt to remain eligible.

I had my own concerns about Oklahoma State. Going into OSU's wrestling room with two years of experience seemed like a recipe for possible disaster. Oklahoma State signed the most-talented wrestlers in the country each year, and going up against them in practice could have shattered my confidence.

Dave flat out told me not to go to Oklahoma State.

I chose UCLA, which had been looking like a better option for me anyway, because I had a much greater chance of making the starting lineup there. Oklahoma State had finished third at the 1978 NCAA championships with five All-Americans. UCLA had been a middle-of-the-pack team in the Pac-8 Conference but seemed to be putting together one of the nation's strongest recruiting classes to add to Fred Bohna, the best heavyweight in the country.

I had friends going to UCLA, including my high school teammate Jeff Newman and Pat O'Donnell, whom I had wrestled a couple of times (and lost to) in the summer before my senior year. Pat would become my roommate and later became an NCAA All-American at Cal Poly–San Luis Obispo.

I liked UCLA's coaches, too.

Dave Auble was head coach and a living legend in my eyes. He had won two NCAA championships, been selected Outstanding Wrestler once, and also placed fourth in the 1964 Summer

Games in Tokyo. I knew Coach Auble to be hard-nosed, hard-working, hard-playing, stubborn, aggressive, and fearless. Coach Auble was tough, and that's what I wanted to be known as more than anything. I wanted his toughness to rub off on me.

Brady Hall, one of the assistants, had accomplished something I could only dream of at that point by winning a national Amateur Athletic Union freestyle championship. Brady had roomed with Dave at the 1976 US training camp the summer after Dave's junior year, when Dave was the only high school wrestler at the camp. Brady had also become a successful businessman through what we now refer to as flipping real estate. I looked at Brady as someone I could learn from not only about wrestling but also about every area of life.

That year, Chris Horpel was hired as an assistant at UCLA. Coach Auble had been an assistant at Stanford when Chris wrestled there. I was already sold on UCLA, but adding Chris as an assistant made going to school there that much better.

Oh, and there was this one other recruit who wound up coming to UCLA whom I had heard of: this Dave guy from Oklahoma State. My brother decided to join me at UCLA and transferred in even though he would have to sit out one season because of NCAA transfer rules.

Dave and I had spent the entire summer working out together. I was thinking I was pretty good after winning state, but Dave turned summer into a nightmarish three months for me. He wanted to work out all the time, and I—reigning California state champion—wanted to enjoy my summer.

"You want to go work out?" Dave would ask.

"Not today," I'd say. "I don't feel like it."

"Pussy," Dave would say in an effeminate voice.

Dave really knew how to piss me off.

"Okay, that's it!" I'd say, all mad. "You're going to die today!"

Then we'd go work out and he'd destroy me.

That routine went on almost every day that summer.

"Want to go work out?"

"No."

"Pussy."

"Okay, let's go."

Dave would take me down what seemed like fifty times a day, and I'd never take him down. I dreaded wrestling against him each day.

Finally, after telling myself "This sucks" enough times to want to do something about it, I determined I had to develop a better strategy: If I couldn't score against Dave, then the least I could do was to keep him from scoring.

I started spending all my time on the mat with him backing up, stalling, breaking his hold, even running backward sometimes. I didn't care if I could score, but I'd do anything I could think of to prevent him from scoring. Pretty soon, I got good enough at stalling that I no longer had to back away from him. I could hold my ground and even push back a little and still stall. Every time I was on the mat with Dave, I'd go into a defensive shell. When I got proficient at that, I started making brief attempts at attacks. If my attack didn't work—and against Dave, it often didn't—I'd go right back into defensive mode.

My strategy worked. Instead of getting destroyed, I started losing by scores like 4–0 and 5–0. That pissed Dave off, and I didn't care. Actually, I enjoyed getting under his skin a little.

That summer turned out to be a game changer for me as a wrestler because of the emphasis I learned to place on defense. Eventually, my offense became as good as my defense, but my style developed with defense first.

The decision to attend UCLA appeared great in the beginning. With our recruiting class, I thought Coach Auble was building a West Coast dynasty. I was on a full-ride scholarship. Movie stars were seemingly everywhere in the area. (I sat in front of Lorenzo Lamas in a movie theater for the premiere of the wrestling movie *Take Down*.) Our wrestling room was huge, and it was always sunny in Southern California.

Every day, the choice to attend UCLA looked better and better.

My first year of college consisted of eating, sleeping, going to class, wrestling, and sneaking in extra workouts. As a freshman, I was required to take general studies courses as prerequisites. Philosophy was one of my classes. From studying Krishnamurti, I did well in that class and considered choosing philosophy as my major.

We were required to take a course about cancer in which the professor showed us pictures of people with horrible cases of cancer, mostly from using tobacco. Some of the pictures showed how people had parts of their faces cut off because of cancer, leaving them terribly deformed but at least still alive. I think the purpose of the course was to scare the crap out of us. It worked.

I also took a jazz appreciation class—although I didn't learn to appreciate jazz until after college—and a Western civilization course. What I remember most from the latter course was the professor telling us that in the history of Western civilization, whenever leaders had a choice between doing what was best for society or best for themselves, the leaders chose what was best for them, and that usually resulted in chaos, war, and the deaths of thousands of people.

I turned eighteen during my first quarter, and late that quarter, a couple of girls invited me to a party. The party was in a third-floor apartment, and everyone was loud and drinking. I didn't know anyone else there and quickly got bored. The girls asked if I wanted to leave, and I said I did.

We went downstairs and one girl went to go get her car and pull around to pick us up. The one waiting with me asked if I would show her how to wrestle. We went out onto the grass and I showed her a gentle version of the foot sweep, where you place your foot behind your opponent's calf and make a sweeping motion to take that foot off the floor and then take him to the mat.

The police had been called about the party, and a police car pulled up right as I was showing this girl the foot sweep. The policemen got out of the car and walked directly to me.

"Can I help you, officer?" I asked the first one.

"You can't even help yourself," he replied.

Then they started walking toward the elevator to bust up the party.

I followed them and decided I would take the stairs and warn everyone at the party that the cops were coming.

The cops stopped and turned toward me.

"What are you doing?" they asked me.

"I'm going upstairs," I answered.

"You can't go upstairs," they said.

"It's a free country," I said, then opened the door to the staircase.

One of the cops grabbed me from behind and tried to get me in what I call a "police academy headlock."

I immediately lifted him up and slammed him to the ground. That was easier than any match I'd been in. As soon as that cop hit the ground, the other tried to get me in the same headlock. I picked him up and put him on the ground, too. The first cop got off the ground and tried the exact same move again. I gave him the exact same treatment.

Then his partner got up and shoved me into a fire extinguisher case, but his hand was between me and the case. When I hit the case, the glass cover broke and blood started spurting from the officer's hand. They pulled out their handcuffs, but I kept moving my hands around and they couldn't cuff me. That's when the one with the cut hand took a swing at me. I ducked and grabbed both his legs and pulled them. He landed directly on his cut hand and started screaming in pain.

"That does it," the other said. "You're going to jail, dead or alive," and reached for his gun.

I immediately jumped over a fence and took off running.

By this point, the ruckus had gotten the attention of some at the party. One guy was all excited and ran after me. I was tired from the skirmish, and the guy caught up with me.

"Here, take my shirt," he said.

Mine had been torn off during the fight and the guy knew that the policemen would be looking for someone without a shirt. Seconds after I pulled his shirt on, a cop car drove past.

But then that guy flagged down the driver of a car at a stop sign, told him what had happened, and asked the driver to give us a ride to the dorms. The driver peeled out. I knew that guy wasn't going to be any help, so I gave him back his shirt and told him to leave me alone.

I jumped a fence and hid in bushes, but the owner of the place had seen me and called the police. A police helicopter was already in the air looking for me, and it wasn't long until officers had semi-circled the bushes.

Over a loudspeaker, they told me to give up. I wasn't convinced I should. I thought I could still get away and was preparing to make a run for it.

The clicking of their gun hammers changed my plans. I came out of the bushes with my hands up, and they cuffed me, threw me into the back of a police car, and hauled me off to jail.

My phone call went to Coach Auble. I told him what had happened. Half serious, half joking, he said, "Good job. I knew you had it in you." Then he told me he'd call my dad.

I had been placed in a holding cell at first, then they moved me alone into a cell with no pillow or mattress. A cop came up and asked me to take a Breathalyzer test. I said okay, and he looked a little too happy about my willingness to cooperate, so I changed my mind and told him to forget it.

The next day, I was charged with assault and battery on two LAPD officers and my dad put up five thousand dollars bail. Coach Auble helped connect me with a lawyer. One of the girls who had taken me to the party told the district attorney that I had not punched or kicked the officers, that I had only broken their holds and used their own force against them.

The charges were dropped, although my dad had to pay about a thousand dollars to the lawyer. Dad didn't make me pay him back for the lawyer, but years later I paid him back sevenfold.

———

Coach Auble was one tough man. He was about forty years old, and I wished I could have watched him wrestle in his prime. He could be a little unpredictable and had an aggressive nature, but that's what I assumed had made him so tough on the mat. Coach carried a mouthpiece wherever he went just in case he got into a fight. I admired him, and we got along great.

Coach had me fly with him once to a tournament in San Francisco while the rest of the team drove. I was injured and unable to wrestle, but he still wanted me to go with him. Coach and I went out for dinner, and he spotted an open parking spot right in front of our restaurant. We were in the far left lane and there was another car that was in front of the open spot and was about to back in and park there. Coach floored it and shoved the nose of the rental car into the spot, grabbed his mouthpiece, and told me to finish parking the car.

Coach got out and the other guy also got out of his car. I doubt the poor guy expected what came next. I don't know what was said between the two, but Coach put in his mouth guard and got right in the guy's face, started rubbing his ribs, and stuck his chest into the guy. Coach had broken two ribs years earlier, and for some reason, whenever he was acting tough, he'd rub those two ribs while sticking his chest out. The rest of us knew what that meant, but the guy from the other car didn't.

I finished parking the car, the other guy got in his car and drove off, and Coach came back to join me.

"Go wait in that alley by the restaurant," he told me, "and if that guy comes back to fight me, we're doing it in the alley. And maybe take his wallet." The last line was a joke. The part about fighting in the alley wasn't.

Coach cracked me up a lot.

At that San Francisco tournament, the guy who took my place was losing a match and Coach was in his corner screaming at him. Apparently, the two had had some issues the year before. Finally, Coach had seen enough. In the middle of the match, he pulled twenty bucks out of his pocket, grabbed the wrestler, handed him the money, and told him he was off the team. That left me as the only wrestler at my weight.

Coach had placed me at 150 to start the season. I had cut a lot of weight to get there.

Although I'd had to cut weight to make my weight class during high school, I had never had to cut to drop down into a lower class. I had witnessed Dave and others go through that, so I knew it was the worst part of our sport. But not until I actually had to experience it myself did I know just how bad cutting was.

Cutting isn't just tough on you physically; it also grates on you mentally. It's like a cloud hanging over your head that won't go away because you know that with the next meet, you'll be having to cut. Cutting is one of the biggest reasons that nothing in sports is more physically painful and psychologically demanding than wrestling, especially at college's top level. I believe there are only three groups of people who have it worse than college wrestlers: the terminally ill, soldiers on the front line, and prisoners on death row.

The smallest wrestlers tended to cut the most. Not percentagewise, but in total pounds. The smaller the wrestler, the more cutting weight became a bigger part of his life. I've known wrestlers through the years who wrestled at 118 pounds but walked around in the off-season at 150. It was unreal.

If you're a wrestler who has to cut a lot, it can almost ruin the sport for you. Dave hated the way he had to cut at Oklahoma State so much that he left.

There are differing philosophies on cutting weight. Mine before college had been to train as hard as I could and my body would assume its optimal weight. Then I would cut to whatever weight was just below that.

Coach Auble, though, believed in cutting lots of weight and thought that if I wrestled at 150, I would be better. But I was so lean that cutting to 150 meant almost total dehydration, which lowers the body's ability to consume oxygen and also decreases strength.

After a miserable road trip at 150, we realized it was a mistake and I shot up to 158 the next day. That was the only time I gave control over my weight to a coach. Good wrestlers must eliminate mistakes, and that was one mistake I would never make again. Wrestlers stand alone on the mat, so they have to be their own coach.

Don't get me wrong about Coach Auble. He was an excellent coach and a role model for me. But my cutting all the way down to 150 didn't work. I lost eight matches that year, and half of them were at 150.

I ended my freshman season with an 18-8 record. I placed third in the conference tournament to qualify for the NCAA tournament, but I lost my first-round match there and didn't place.

UCLA didn't turn out to be a dream place, as it had seemed at the start.

Something happened between Coach Auble and Chris Hor-pel that caused a noticeable tension between the two, and the team split into two groups when the wrestlers started taking sides. Dave and I felt stuck in the middle because we both liked Coach Auble and were also good friends with Chris.

Coach Auble represented the type of wrestler I wanted to become, and I pretty much wanted to be just like him when I grew up. I have a saying that I've followed through the years: It's not what you know, it's who you are. I believe a wrestler's personality, more than anything else, is what makes him win. Whatever it was about Coach Auble that made him win, I wanted those characteristics to rub off on me.

On the other hand, Chris had begun helping me back when I was in high school and was part of the reason I had become successful in wrestling. He continued supporting me at UCLA.

With Dave unable to wrestle in tournaments, all he could do that season was the daily workouts. The first time he and I worked out together came during the middle of the season. Dave was superaggressive with me. I thought he was trying to destroy my confidence.

Confidence is either built up or torn down every day. I was feeling a lot of pressure competing as a freshman, and cutting weight had been an extra burden for me. I thought Dave was trying to take advantage of where I was mentally to build his confidence on my back.

When I got pissed at how Dave was wrestling me and started stalling my ass off, Dave got annoyed and yelled at Chris to tell me to quit stalling.

"That's too bad, Dave," Chris shot back. "Deal with it."

In my mind, I was like, *Yesssss!!!* because Chris was supporting me and not making me do what Dave wanted.

So I, and Dave, never really took a side in the coaches' dispute.

The turmoil destabilized the team. We finished third in conference and Fred Bohna won the school's first wrestling national championship. But that West Coast dynasty never developed. Coach Auble left UCLA after that season and didn't return to coaching for several years. Chris Horpel left to become head coach at Stanford, his alma mater. Dave and I decided to get out, too, leaving after one year, with Dave never getting to take the mat as a Bruin.

UCLA wound up dropping wrestling as an intercollegiate sport a year later, citing a lack of practice space and the cost to remedy the problem. I think the decision had its roots in all the problems during our year there.

CHAPTER 5

Creating an Aura

The summer after our season at UCLA, Dave and I tried out for the Junior World Team, which trained at the US Olympic Training Center in Colorado Springs, Colorado. Neither of us had a car, and the only way we could get there was to hitchhike. Over the first hundred miles, we picked up about ten different rides. Then a woman pulled over to the side of the road and when we told her where we were headed, she said she could take us the rest of the way.

After training camp in Colorado Springs, we traveled to Brockport, New York, for the Junior World Team Trials. Dave and I weighed in for the trials at 165 pounds—the first time I had weighed as much as he did.

The team's head coach, Bill Weick, was a high school coaching legend in Chicago who been head coach of various US international teams and had been on the coaching staff of the 1972 Olympic team. Coach Weick later coached three Olympic teams in the 1980s, including teams for which Dave and I competed. He became one of my favorite coaches and corner men.

Coach knew that Dave could win Junior Worlds at 163, so he told me to try out at the next weight class up, 180.5. I agreed before learning that would mean I'd have to beat Ed Banach to make the team. Ed was a sensational wrestler who had redshirted his freshman year at the powerhouse that was the University of Iowa. In fact,

Ed's older brother, Steve, and his twin brother, Lou, also signed with Iowa. Their coach was Dan Gable, probably still the most-recognized name in all of wrestling. As a wrestler in high school and college, Dan had a 181-1 record, and he won gold at the 1972 Olympics. By the time he had retired from coaching at Iowa in 1997, Dan's teams had won fifteen national championships and he had coached 152 All-Americans. If Dan signed you to wrestle at Iowa, you were very good.

Finding out I would have to beat Ed drained me psychologically. My body started feeling tired. I think when a person knows he will have to go through an intense experience, his body starts conserving energy by getting tired. I knew I would have to conserve as much energy as I could. For the week or week and a half leading up to the trials, the only time I got out of bed was to eat and practice.

Ed and I wrestled best two-out-of-three matches to make the team. I got up on him 7–0 in the first match and he came back to beat me 12–11. Then he beat me pretty bad in the second match.

Dave easily won at 163, but Coach Weick wanted to see what Dave could do at the next weight up and switched Dave and me. Dave beat Banach handily, and I won at 163, so both of us made the Junior Worlds team. But it bugged me that my brother had beaten Ed and I hadn't. I looked at the two of us, and there was no comparison in our builds. Physically, I should have been the one beating Ed, but Dave beat him and I couldn't figure out why.

The night before the team was to leave for Mongolia for the Junior Worlds, a group of us went to a bar. I met the most beautiful girl in the world there. Or at least as beautiful as Dave's girlfriend,

Veronica, who had sought Dave out after Dave had defeated her boyfriend, a former World Cup champion, in a local tournament. But the girl in the bar had an ugly friend with her who wouldn't leave us alone. Dave stepped in and took her off away from us. That's what I call taking one for the team!

The girl I was with took me to her apartment so we could make out. I couldn't believe my luck in meeting this girl, but we left for Mongolia and I never saw her again. However, the fact that I had been able to make out with a girl that was as beautiful as Dave's girlfriend was a real confidence builder for me. Dave had a disarming confidence around girls, especially after the success of his high school wrestling career. It hadn't been easy for me to talk to girls growing up, but that began to change during my first year of doing the college scene.

The day before we left for the Junior World Team Trials in Brockport, I had learned how much I had progressed. Pat and I went to the swimming pool at the top of the hill above the dorms. With my gymnastics background, I was able to show off some tricks from the three-meter diving board. Then I joined Pat to sunbathe for a little while. After I had gotten comfortable and started soaking in the rays, all the talking around the pool ceased.

I looked up to see that an incredibly gorgeous girl had entered the pool area. She had superthick, straight brown hair all the way down to her lower back, a beautiful face, gigantic breasts, and a perfectly round, rock-hard rear. Everybody stopped to watch her make her way around the pool. She walked toward Pat and me and laid her towel down just a few yards from us. After she stretched out on her towel, the poolside conversations and activities resumed.

"I dare you to go over and talk to her," Pat said to me.

Why don't you? I thought to myself.

"Okay," I said, to Pat and myself.

I walked over to where she was sunbathing and either I tuned out everything around me or all the conversations halted again.

"Excuse me," I said, getting her attention. "My friend dared me to come over here and talk to you. Could you just go along with me, let me sit here for a minute, and act like you like me?"

"Sure," she said, and visibly invited me to sit next to her so my friend could see.

She gave me more than a minute—we talked for a few hours. She gave me her phone number and asked me to call her. Dave and I left the next day and I never saw her again.

I had already felt like I was beginning to turn a corner in my ability to talk with girls. I'd had some cute girlfriends my freshman year, but nothing like Veronica or the girls I met at the pool and in Brockport.

The first thing I noticed upon our arrival in Mongolia was the huge military presence. Everywhere we turned, there was some combination of military trucks, soldiers, portraits of Vladimir Lenin, and the communist hammer and sickle symbol.

Wrestling was huge in Mongolia. Genghis Khan's army used wrestling, horseback riding, and archery to conquer territories in creating the largest empire in the late twelfth and early thirteenth centuries. Through all the centuries since, those three skills had remained valued in Mongolia.

Our team visited an outdoor arena to watch an ancient traditional Mongolian wrestling exhibition at the Naadam festival. The entire field was covered with wrestlers, and they performed a strange dance around a "referee" holding a pole. As the wrestlers circled the pole, they slowly flapped their arms like birds.

Before each match, the two wrestlers would face each other, then slap the insides and outsides of their thighs.

There were no weight classes or time limits for matches. A match ended when one wrestler took down his opponent or forced him to touch his knees, hands, or other body part to the ground. The winners remained in the tournament until the final two wrestlers squared off for the championship.

It was interesting to see what wrestling might have been like centuries earlier. I'm not sure I liked the idea of not having weight classes, though. It had been tough enough going up one class to wrestle Banach at the trials!

The heavyweight on our team angered me. Back then, there was no weight limit on heavyweights. Our big boy didn't train as much as the rest of us, and when he did practice, he didn't try as hard as I thought he should. He was big and fat and using his weight to win instead of any skill. He didn't seem very mature, but then again all of us were under twenty.

But what really pissed me off about this guy was that he would eat and drink in front of the rest of us as we cut weight. The drinking part really annoyed me. When you're cutting and can't afford to drink even an ounce of water, it's cruel for another wrestler to walk near you with a cup in his hand.

He and Dave were the only ones on the team not starving themselves to make weight, and he had packed a suitcase full of food and counted every item every day to make sure one of us hadn't taken anything.

Near the end of our training camp back in the States, we had taken a psychological test, and the results showed that I was ready, motivated, and in top mental shape. I wasn't that way in Mongolia, though. I think Coach Weick overtrained us. He ran us like crazy. I felt like I was training for a marathon instead of a wrestling tournament. We ran around a soccer field on steaming hot days more times than I care to remember. I couldn't have gained weight if I had force-fed myself.

By the time the tournament in Mongolia started, I was so physically and mentally drained that I would have preferred to hop back on the plane and go home instead of wrestle.

Still, I won my first match 17–0 against a Korean opponent. It was such a mismatch that it didn't matter whether I wanted to be there or not. I barely won my next match, then lost the next two and didn't place.

I was typically starving after tournaments and would go on a hunt for chocolate. The Mongolian chocolate was pretty good, at least when I was able to avoid the occasional worm.

When Dave wrestled a Bulgarian after I was done, I didn't want to go back to the arena, so I stayed at the hotel and watched the match on television. TV must have been fairly new to the country, because there were only a few black-and-white TVs in the hotel, and the only thing showing on them was wrestling. For Dave's match, they weren't showing the score on the screen, so I scored the match in my head. At the end, I had Dave winning 11–3. But the ref raised the Bulgarian's hand instead. The Bulgarian won 12–11. I couldn't believe it! Dave also wrestled against the eventual tournament champion, a Russian. It was a close match, but the refs cheated badly and Dave lost.

After the last match, I sat against a wall with Dave, and he was so distraught over losing that he started punching himself in the face. Dave had always been extremely hard on himself when he lost.

That's another thing I learned from Dave—take your losses hard.

I had observed something similar from Korean wrestlers at the end of my freshman year at UCLA when Dave and I had been asked to compete against a Korean cultural exchange team at a high school in Los Angeles.

I wrestled first and got pinned by the same headlock that had caused me problems since I first started the sport. I asked the Korean coach for a rematch and defeated the same opponent 20–1. Our team went on to win the dual.

I walked through the door of the locker room and heard screaming and banging. The Koreans' captain was beating the crap out of his teammates with a kendo sword and ordering them to bash their heads against the lockers. Some were bleeding, and I think all of them were crying and yelling as though they had dishonored themselves by losing.

Standing there watching and feeling their wrestlers' deep sense of honor and pride, I immediately gained respect for the Koreans.

That's what they should be doing, I thought. *That's what I would be doing.*

At UCLA, I had determined that I would never again take losing in stride. I wanted to make losing the worst experience possible. I'd hit myself, bang my head against a wall, cry, scream, rip clothes apart, destroy nearby innocent objects, or whatever else I felt like doing. I figured that if I made losing the worst experience ever, I would never make that same mistake again. Good wrestlers must eliminate mistakes.

Then I would enter a period of almost depression that could last for a couple of weeks. I would become deeply introspective and try to determine why I lost so I could identify the mistake(s) I needed to eliminate. Then I would redouble my commitment and effort.

Losing flat-out sucked, and I made the time after a loss suck, too.

I learned far more from my losses than from my victories, because losses exposed mistakes I never wanted to make again.

Once eliminated from the Mongolia tournament, I started hanging out with the Korean wrestlers. They were friendly guys, and our teams would often go to the mess tent for meals together. I noticed early on several Korean wrestlers holding each other's hands. After I got to know the Koreans, some of them would run up to me, grab my hand, and hold it. I tried making hand motions and speaking in broken English to inform them that American men didn't do that. My message never got through, though, and they'd just smile, say something in Korean, shake their heads, and continue holding my hand.

One time I was sitting on a bench and the entire team came over. Those who could squeeze onto the bench near me took a seat. The two guys on either side of me had their arms around me. Their 105-pounder, who wound up winning his class, plopped down in my lap. I just accepted it as part of their culture. Or least I *hoped* it was part of their culture.

It saddened me to leave the Koreans at the end of our trip. I'm not sure why I got along so well with them, but they were fun to hang around despite the language barrier and were good people. I gave some of my jeans and US team gear to them, mostly to the one I had defeated 17–0 in my first match. He cried when we said good-bye to each other.

Our journey home began by taking the train from Mongolia northwest to Novosibirsk, Siberia, in Russia. I had gotten an ear infection from a cauliflower ear and my glands swelled up. We had no antibiotics with us, but I was able to trade a pair of jeans to the Russians in exchange for a couple of bottles of vodka to kill the pain.

Junior Worlds was my first international tournament, and even though I hadn't placed or wrestled particularly well, it was an amazing experience.

When we arrived back at John F. Kennedy International Airport, Dave and I hadn't showered for four days. Once we'd started traveling home, there was no place to clean up. Our only clothes were our unlaundered workout gear. Needless to say, our gear was dirty and smelly. On top of all that, I was sick. The two of us drew some strange looks walking through the terminal.

Dave turned to me and said, "If you're going to do this kind of stuff for a living, you've got to embrace adversity."

Dave and I had been trying to figure out what school we could leave UCLA for, and during our trip to the Junior Worlds, Dave told me we were going to the University of Oklahoma. I had no idea that's where he had wanted to go.

Oklahoma, although not as storied a program as its archrival, Oklahoma State University, still featured one of the nation's elite teams. The Sooners had won seven national championships, and at the time, only Oklahoma State had won more. The year before, Oklahoma had finished second at the Big 8 Conference tournament, behind Iowa State University and just ahead of OSU. The Sooners then placed fourth at the national tournament with four players honored as All-Americans. None of those four—Roger Frizzell, Andre Metzger, Isreal Sheppard, and Steve Williams—had graduated, so all would be returning for the 1981 season.

Jim Humphrey was an assistant coach at Oklahoma and one of the coaches on our Junior World team. Dave told Jim we were transferring to OU.

After our trip to Junior Worlds, Oklahoma head coach Stan Abel came to Palo Alto to recruit us. I wondered why he went through the hassle considering that Dave had already told his assistant that we were coming.

Stan and I met in my bedroom, and he launched into his standard recruiting pitch. He sounded like a car salesman making a speech he had repeated hundreds of times. Since I was the brother of Dave Schultz, I didn't really think that was necessary, but he continued.

For a moment after he had left, I thought, *Maybe I shouldn't go there.* But Stan turned out to be a good coach.

News of our decision didn't go over well at UCLA. We went back to pack all our belongings in the used Subaru we'd recently purchased and then went to say good-bye to Brady Hall. Dave and Brady decided to get in one more workout against each other before we left.

Brady got an overhook on Dave's arm and cranked Dave's

shoulder hard. After practice, Dave and Brady drove back to Brady's house.

Dave actually cried during the ride as he told Brady, "You tried to hurt me."

"You're damned right I tried to hurt you," Brady said. "Look at what you've done. I knew this was going to happen. That's why I didn't want you to come out here in the first place. You came out here and now you're leaving and taking Mark with you. I'm pissed!"

For once, I was glad to be Dave's younger and less responsible brother. Brady never held me responsible for leaving UCLA. It had never occurred to me that Brady would be mad. The program was in such chaos that I thought it was only natural that wrestlers would want out. Stability is the most important factor in success, and we were leaving the instability and disarray of UCLA so Dave and I could have a better opportunity to wrestle under the stability and tradition of OU's program.

All I had with me when we moved to Oklahoma was two bags of clothes. On the way, we stopped at California State University, Bakersfield, where a friend of ours, Joe Seay, was the coach. Joe tried to talk us into ending our trip right there and wrestling for him. Joe was building one of the best teams in the country and his offer was enticing, but the wrestling room was the smallest I had seen, with room for only one mat. I couldn't imagine how an entire team trained in there.

Dave and I talked about Joe's offer in our car and because we were fun-loving brothers, we decided to continue our discussion in a phone booth from which we would call the Oklahoma coaches if we changed our minds about going there. After we had weighed the pros and cons, Dave said, "Let's flip a coin. Heads we go to OU; tails we stay here."

The coin came up heads, but I think we would have driven on to Oklahoma even if it had been tails.

"I'm going to do a lot of sitting at OU," I told Dave during the drive. That was my way of saying I was going to need to conserve every last ounce of energy to make it as a wrestler there.

I knew Dave would win at Oklahoma, but I was uncertain how I would do. I was starting only my fourth year of wrestling and we were joining one of the nation's top recruiting classes.

Winning an NCAA team championship at UCLA would have been miraculous. At Oklahoma, championships were expected.

To survive in the OU wrestling room, I'd have to do a heckuva lot more than merely step it up a notch. I would have to sacrifice my life and train as hard as my body, mind, and soul would permit me. The greatest enemy I would face there was sitting in the passenger seat of our old Subaru and, to be honest, I didn't have a real good scouting report on myself. I still hadn't figured out who I was.

Failure was not an option. Yet on the other hand, I had no idea if I would be able to out-train, outsmart, outperform, and outsuffer everyone in my weight when the pressure was on and everything I was willing to sacrifice—my name, my reputation, my self-image, my flimsily positive attitude, *my life*—was on the line.

I adopted a philosophy of "do or die" heading into Oklahoma. I'd be doing everything and anything to conserve energy for my most focused attempt at becoming the greatest fighter on the planet. I would *have* to conserve energy if there was any chance of that happening.

But, still, I had serious doubts.

Was it even possible for me to be the best? Could I follow

through on my commitment to withstand everything without knowing what "everything" consisted of?

I didn't know the answer to any of those questions. I also didn't know that Oklahoma would become my personal hell on earth.

The first time I saw Norman, Oklahoma, was when we drove into town to start school there. I had visited Stillwater, the home of Oklahoma State, on a recruiting trip my senior year of high school, but that was in the spring. Summer in Oklahoma was a whole different story.

The very first day of practice, the entire team was led out to a duck pond behind the "jock dorms." We lined up and raced around a beaten-path course. Oh, my goodness! I thought I was running on the surface of the sun.

We both majored in exercise science, because those classes would take the least time away from wrestling. Dave and I took as many of the same classes as we could so if one of us was off wrestling or sick, the other could take notes and share them. Dave worked hard to overcome the academic challenge of having dyslexia. I finished with a 3.0 GPA at Oklahoma, and Dave's was actually higher than mine, but we squandered the educational opportunities we had. We both went to school to wrestle, not get an education. That was a huge mistake on our parts.

I almost could have passed for a deaf mute at OU. I didn't talk unless it was absolutely necessary or, on limited occasions, to make someone laugh. With my dad being a comedian, I thought if there was one best use for talking, it would be to make people laugh.

However, I never joked around with other wrestlers in my weight class. When you're on the wrestling mat, you have to turn into a selfish, greedy bastard and torture your opponent until either you or the final horn makes him give up. I learned real fast in the sport not to give away any friendship or trust to anyone in or around your weight. With wrestlers not around your weight—who you knew didn't have the potential to become "enemies" on your own team—it was acceptable to develop friendships. Actually, it was preferred, because you wanted greatness around you. You wanted others' greatness to rub off on you. If someone was great in wrestling, you had to respect him or you were disrespecting the very thing that you wanted to become.

But for anyone in or around my weight class, forget about it.

I worked hard at making myself as unapproachable as possible. I tried to always say less than the person I was talking to. When I did have to speak, it was at a low volume. I avoided nonwrestlers as much as I could, too, except for female students I wanted to get to know, of course. I frequently wore sunglasses and earphones so no one knew if I was watching them or could hear them. I looked down most of the time. I didn't want anyone to know what I was thinking or feeling.

I needed every advantage I could get with the quality of wrestlers around me at Oklahoma, and that included creating an aura of intimidation. I couldn't afford to show my human side, because as soon as others began to understand me, that aura of intimidation would start deteriorating. That hurt me in my relationships, especially with the opposite sex. But everything had to be sacrificed if I was to win.

The wrestlers lived on the same floor of the dorm, but I didn't think I could afford to show mercy, friendship, or trust. In the wrestling room, those would be used against me every time.

Dave was different. He became a merciless barbarian on the mat, but one step off the mat, he turned back into an angel. Later in his career, he learned to speak Russian so that he could communicate directly with the Russians and better understand how the world's top wrestlers thought. The Russian wrestlers and fans respected that to the point that at the Tbilisi tournament in Soviet Georgia, he could sit in the stands and talk to fans in Russian, go down to the mat and torture his next opponent, and then change clothes and go back up to the stands and continue visiting with the fans.

Now, outside of wrestling season, it was a different story for me. I partied like crazy when we weren't in season, but from November through the third weekend of March, there was no such things as "outside of wrestling." My whole world was wrestling, even when I left the room.

Because we had transferred, Dave and I had to sit out of competition our first year with the Sooners. I've seen some athletes during my long tenure in the sport turn that sit-out year into a year off, almost a vacation. Not me. I didn't think I would have been good enough to make the team consistently that year, so I determined to turn my redshirt year into an advantage.

Coaches Abel and Humphrey were a great combination. Coach Abel didn't get too deeply involved in the technical side of wrestling. He had been a two-time NCAA champion, but that was when technique wasn't as important as conditioning. Coach Humphrey, who was still competing as a wrestler, knew technique well and handled more of that side of coaching.

Competition for spots on the OU roster would be tough, and Coach Abel's strategy for piecing together a team was pretty cutthroat. He recruited a ton of talented guys, packed the room with them, and then let them beat on each other until the toughest came out on top. He was also smart with the scholarship money the NCAA allowed. He had all of us out-of-state wrestlers obtain Oklahoma driver's licenses and register to vote in Cleveland County so that we met the criteria for being Oklahoma residents and qualified for the less-expensive in-state tuition. Then he had us fill out requests for federal Pell Grants and made sure we put down a zero for earned income for the previous year. (That was accurate, but it was important enough for him to make sure we followed directions.) The Pell Grants covered the amount of the in-state tuition, and that freed up our scholarships for the new batch of incoming recruits. I wouldn't have had to wrestle to pay for school after my first year at OU.

Even looking toward the next year, I knew that my main competition on the OU roster was Isreal Sheppard, a chiseled 158-pounder who was tougher than nails. (Isreal's name was often misspelled as "Israel." I spelled his name wrong a bunch of times until the wrestling coach's secretary corrected me, and then I made sure I wrote it correctly every time.)

When I met Isreal, he was confident and brash and didn't mind attracting the attention of the coaches. Coach Abel seemed really pleased with Isreal at my weight. I knew my only option, as one of my mottos stated, was "kill or be killed."

Workouts with Isreal were superintense. The OU wrestling room wasn't as nice as would be expected of such an established program. There were three padded pillars in the center of the room, but one of the pillars was partially unpadded, leaving a small spot of bare wood exposed. Once, I tried to slam Isreal's head into that unpadded area but missed.

Isreal wore his hair in cornrows that felt like steel wool. When we wrestled, his cornrows would rub my face. Sometimes his hair would rub against my face so much that I'd flinch in the shower when water hit the raw spots. One day I noticed that the foam on top of the left side of my headgear was wearing away and the aluminum metal underneath the pad was barely poking through. That piece of aluminum was almost like a blade. The next time Isreal shot for my legs, I blocked him with my head and noticed that the bare aluminum had slightly cut him. I had found my answer to his cornrows. He didn't seem to braid his hair in cornrows as frequently after that.

I held an interesting view toward Isreal at the time. I cared nothing about him, because he was an enemy, yet he was one of the most valuable people in my life, because I could practice brutal moves against him without a shred of remorse. Going up against Isreal in practice as much as I did clearly helped me develop into a better wrestler.

Sometimes in our workouts, the team would work only on takedowns. I made up my mind that no matter who I was wrestling, I would never be the first one to say "I'm done." I also determined that regardless of who got the takedown, I would be first back to the center of the mat ready to start the next round. When I could get two or three guys to say "I'm done" in one day, I knew my strategies were working.

A constant part of Coach Abel's conditioning drills was running the stadium stairs at Owen Field, the football stadium. One

day after we had run to the top, just to prove to the other wrestlers—
and myself—that I wasn't scared of anything, I climbed over the
edge of the top of the stadium with one arm dangling over the wall.
When I knew that everyone else on the team had seen me, I climbed
back over. Then, of course, some of the others had to prove they
could do it, too.

Practices were so intense that afterward, we looked as if we were
competitors in some strange, clothed water sport. We'd be drenched
head to toe in sweat as if we had jumped into a pool. We could see
big wet spots on all the mats when we were done, and invariably a
fog floated above the room. When we left, our shoes squished as we
walked.

But I wanted more. Well, I didn't really want more, but I
needed more. After practice, I would do pushups, V-ups, body
lifts, wall sits, and frog hops. I'd secretly get in one extra workout
every day. I assumed my opponents, who were actually my teammates, wouldn't understand why I didn't get as tired during practice as they did, and that would destroy their confidence when
they faced me.

Each of my days was divided into two parts: before and after
practice. Before practice, I was all serious, dreading practice. I
probably looked as if I were headed to the gallows. After practice,
I was happy and relaxed, relieved practice was over.

One huge advantage I knew I held over Isreal that season was
that he was having to cut weight and under the pressure of competition. I wasn't. I worked that, especially not having to endure cutting, as much as I could. When I felt as if I was gaining a slight
edge on Isreal, I would use that edge to try to knock him down a
little further and pick up another slight edge on him. I had a year

before I'd have to earn a spot over him, and I was willing to persistently gain on him inch by inch.

As the season progressed, I felt that I was beginning to get the upper hand against Isreal, and from the way Coach Abel treated me, I believed he was taking notice.

Isreal placed third in the NCAA championships at 158. Fortunately, Coach Abel had plans other than pitting Isreal and me against each other at the same weight.

CHAPTER 6

National Champion!

It was as though a beam of light came down out of heaven, shined upon me, and revealed to me the secrets of wrestling.

I can only call the experience a revelation.

My and Dave's second year at Oklahoma marked the first season during which we could compete and the first time I weighed more than him. Coach had decided to redshirt Isreal for one season to wrestle at 158 and have me bulk up to 167.

My first tournament was the Great Plains Open in Nebraska, the same tournament at which Dave had defeated the two-time NCAA champion as a high school senior. I reached the 167 finals against Iowa's Mike DeAnna, the NCAA runner-up in 1979. I was ahead 3–1 or 4–1, and Mike and I were on our feet when the beam of light "appeared."

I stood straight up and, instead of shooting on me, Mike also stood straight up and just sort of stood there, as though he were wondering if he'd missed something like time running out or the ref stopping the match. I remember looking at Mike in that magical moment and thinking, *There is no way he can take me down.*

From that point on, everything I did in the match worked perfectly and I beat him 8–1 for my first win in a major open tournament. I was ready for everything coming my way in wrestling—except for Dave's secret move.

One time during practice, I was wrestling Dave. I shot in and he put me in a front headlock. I kept hold of his hands, waiting for him to spin behind. Then I would stand up and escape the take-down. But Dave didn't spin behind. Instead, he just kept me in the front headlock. The next thing I knew, I was dreaming that I was standing with cows in a pasture and looking skyward at birds and clouds. When I woke up, Dave was standing over me, his sweat dripping onto my face.

"You're pinned," he said with a huge *gotcha* smile.

I got up from the mat, ripped off my shirt, grabbed Dave by his ears, and head-butted him.

For months afterward, I would ask Dave to get me in that headlock again. Then I'd tell him I wanted to try it. We'd go back and forth, over and over, for months, until one day I knocked him out during a live practice. It was like my birthday, Christmas, and New Year's rolled into one.

Thus was born what I later called "the Schultz front head-lock." In our move, we would put the opponent's head under his armpit and squeeze the jugular vein to cut off the air and blood flow to his brain. That would knock him out. Then we would pin him and move him around to make it look as if he was conscious until he did come to again. Like me that day, our opponent wouldn't even know he had been pinned. The move gave us such a dominant advantage that wrestling's international governing body created a rule banning it.

Perry Hummel of Iowa State, the 1980 NCAA runner-up, was one of the toughest guys I ever faced. He was a sophomore like me, and over the next three years we squared off six times. We each won three times, and all six were tightly contested.

Our first meeting was in a dual at Iowa State. That was one of the craziest environments I wrestled in during college. All the close calls that day seemed to be going against our team, and the arena was filled with obnoxiously loud fans who called us every name in the book and then a few others. I've never heard more profanity from fans than in that dual.

Hummel and I were going at each other real good, with a lot of head-butts between us. He beat me 7–4, with the refs giving him four penalty points for me stalling. I thought I was getting hosed, and after the last two-point stalling call against me, I head-butted Hummel as hard as I could. I didn't care if I got thrown out of the match. I was pissed, knew at that point I was going to lose, and wanted to give Hummel something to think about for future matches.

I met up with Hummel again in the finals of the Big 8 Conference championships at Gallagher Hall on Oklahoma State's campus. I lost to him 6–4. We narrowly beat Iowa State for the conference team championship, but leaving the arena, I pulled my silver medal out of my bag and threw it onto the top of the arena. Later, I threw away the brand-new shoes I had worn in the conference tournament and went back to my old workout shoes.

I entered the NCAA championships at Princeton University ranked third at 167 pounds but drew a tough spot in the bracket. I beat Mike Sheets, a freshman from rival Oklahoma State, in the first round, but I could tell he was going to be very good very soon.

In the third round, I faced sixth-seeded John Reich from the US Naval Academy. Before the match, I kept hearing how great a rider Reich was. Because of that, I gave him too much credit. After a scoreless first period, he started the second period on top. I didn't escape from him. He rode me for about a minute before we went out of bounds next to my corner. Coach Abel grabbed me and yelled right into my face, "You get the hell out of there right now!" With just that one order, Coach shook me out of my sissy mentality.

That's it, I told myself. *I'm getting out.*

I took the down position and as soon as the ref blew his whistle, I exploded and had escaped in less than a second. At that moment, I realized that despite what I had been told about Reich, his ability to ride was nothing compared to my ability to escape. I beat him 15–9 and even got riding time on him despite the early advantage he had. That was the last time I put too much stock in what anyone told me about an opponent.

Defeating Reich advanced me to the semifinals against Perry Hummel. We went at each other real tough again, battling to a 4–4 tie in regulation. Then I beat him in overtime.

After that match, we all cut weight and went to Subway as a team for dinner. We had already clinched enough points for second place as a team, and Coach Abel was being congratulated. He pointed to me in line and said I was the one whose match had clinched second. It felt good to hear him say that, but frankly, I didn't care too much about the team score. Nothing mattered to me except the finals the next day, when I'd be facing Mike DeAnna for the third time that season.

The next morning, I told Coach I was going to stay at the hotel and rest while the others went to the arena for the early matches. Coach said he'd come get me and take me to the arena. About an hour and a half before the finals, I hadn't heard from Coach. I ran the twenty blocks to the arena and found Coach sitting in the corner of Roger Frizzell, who was wrestling for third place at 150.

"You left me at the hotel," I said to Coach. "I had to run here."

"Good job," he told me. "Get ready to wrestle."

The run served as a good warm-up for me, but I wondered at what point Coach would have remembered to come get me if I hadn't shown up.

Right before the finals began, there was a ceremonial parade of champions in which the wrestlers who would be meeting for the championships had to stand next to each other. Talk about uncomfortable. I didn't say a word to DeAnna.

Andre Metzger was the first from our team to wrestle for a championship, at 142, and he won his match. Dave's match was next.

I was warming up behind the bleachers while Dave wrestled Oklahoma State's Ricky Stewart, whom Dave had beaten pretty soundly in their two earlier meetings that season. I took a peek at the scoreboard to see that Dave had taken a 3–0 lead, then soon thereafter I heard the crowd roar and I knew that Dave had pinned Ricky for the title. I walked around from behind the seats to make my way to the mat and spotted Ricky running around the mat, arms raised. He had pinned Dave. I was stunned, because that had to be the upset of the year. I told myself I couldn't let the shock of Dave's loss get to me.

I took a 4–1 lead in the second period before the ref called me three times for stalling (one warning and two penalty points), slicing my lead to 4–3. I couldn't believe I was doing all the scoring and the ref was calling me for stalling. We had a full period and half of another to go, and the next stalling call would give Mike two points. The calls in that tournament had seemed to be going Iowa's way, and the ref was practically in my face while I wrestled. Sure enough, he raised his arm looking for confirmation from the mat judges to award a two-point stalling call against me. I immediately called timeout before the confirmation could come, went over to my corner, and lay down. Ron Tripp, one of our assistants, asked what was wrong. The ref was standing right there looking down at me, extremely interested in my answer.

"My knee," I said.

I had been wrestling with an injured left knee. Tripp started rubbing my right knee.

"Wrong knee," I told him.

"You turkey." Tripp replied, wrongly thinking I was faking an injury and it wouldn't have mattered which knee he was rubbing.

The stalling confirmation didn't come.

After the injury timeout, I walked back out to the mat and rode Mike for the duration of the period.

I started the third period down and escaped within seconds and took Mike down. He escaped and I took him down again. I won 10–4, with half of his points on stalling calls. I had three minutes and thirty seconds of riding time. To celebrate my first NCAA championship, I performed my customary backflip.

I went to a silk-screening store before we left for home and had a T-shirt printed that read NCAA CHAMP on the back. I wore the shirt on the plane ride home. No matter what would happen the rest of my career, at least my name would forever be on the list of national champions.

———

I went back to Palo Alto after the NCAAs, and Chris Horpel invited me to go to Newport Beach and relax with him and work out with some guys in that area. Things were different between us during that visit. Chris didn't seem to like me as much as before. I got this uncomfortable feeling that he considered himself superior to me, perhaps intellectually superior because he was a Stanford grad.

For some reason, Chris targeted my table manners. I had bad manners. Back at OU, I ate pretty much like a slob, tearing meat away from chicken and steak with my teeth as though I could be using those same teeth to tear away at my opponent's arms and legs. Forget manners at the table, I had an image to project, and that included making those around me aware that to me, food was fuel to be consumed, not something to be enjoyed.

Chris tried to teach me the fine art of dining. I could not have cared less about table manners at that point in my life. (I do now, I would like to add.) Plus, I felt that was Chris's way of trying to gain an advantage on me, to beat me. I didn't know why he would want to do that, but I was having none of it. The more he tried to teach me, the worse I made my manners. Chris gave up. I was satisfied that I had made my point.

After the Newport Beach trip, I went to Ashland for a while to relax and work out with Southern Oregon wrestlers. It just so happened that Iowa assistant coach J. Robinson was running one of his summer camps at the college and Ed Banach was there with him. I couldn't believe Ed was in my backyard!

I had grown to almost the same size as Ed. I worked out with him a few times and did pretty well against him, and that gave me a boost of confidence going into my junior year.

One day during the camp, I went into the Southern Oregon wrestling room and the entire team was working out. Everyone knew who I was. I had lived there and now I was back as the first NCAA Division I champ from Ashland.

Of course, they all wanted a shot at me. I gave it to them. All of them. At once.

I walked to the center of the mat and one by one the entire roster at every weight took turns trying to take me down. Thanks to that summer of poundings Dave had heaped on me, I had developed an almost impenetrable defense. With all due respect, there's a gap between NCAA Division I and NAIA wrestlers, and not one of those guys could have taken me down. I felt as if I could have stayed there all day and never been taken to the mat.

Southern Oregon coach Bob Rheim walked in sometime during all this and watched as wrestler after wrestler of his failed to conquer me. Apparently he had seen enough, because Rheim walked onto the mat waving his arms and yelled at me, "Get the hell out of here," then kicked me out of his wrestling room. It wasn't the first time.

Rheim had been one of the coaches who heard Dave call me a pot smoker when Dave was being recruited. After I had stopped smoking pot and started wrestling, I showed up at Southern Oregon's wrestling room to work out and Rheim called me a pot smoker in front of his team and told me to leave, saying, "We don't allow pot smokers in here."

I could only shake my head as I left under his orders for a second time.

"You're destroying my team's confidence!" he yelled as I was on my way out. I never returned to that room again, although years later, after Rheim had retired, we became friends.

I weighed in at 177 to start my junior year. Isreal Sheppard was back with us after his redshirt year, and to make the team stronger, Coach Abel put Isreal in the 158 slot, slid Dave up to 167, and placed me at 177.

That meant I wouldn't have to cut weight much and could focus instead on running workouts for conditioning.

Wrestling is a combination of technique, conditioning, and luck. Luck you can't do anything about. But technique and conditioning are all up to the wrestlers. Dave caused everyone in the sport to step up their commitment to technique, but conditioning remained the name of the game. Explosions require a huge amount of conditioning. A wrestler has to possess incredible conditioning to hit moves harder than, faster than, more often than, and before his opponent. Wrestling is not an easy sport, but the key to excelling is simple: Learn moves and condition like crazy. To acquire the conditioning required to win at the world-class level, I had to push myself to the absolute limits of my ability and endure pain day after day after day. Life had to become hell for me to be conditioned like I needed to be.

When an opponent was beating me, the only way I could come back was with a surge of energy. But that energy had to be channeled into scoring techniques, otherwise it would become wasted energy.

As a part of my exercise science major, a professor once tested my max VO2, which is the maximum volume of oxygen a body can consume. Mine was unbelievably low for a wrestler, or any athlete, for that matter. That meant my body didn't consume oxygen efficiently.

I desperately needed to improve my cardiovascular conditioning. Fortunately, for my junior season, the length of college matches was reduced from eight minutes to seven. Refs favored the more aerobic athletes on the mat, and I was an anaerobic wrestler. That year, freestyle matches were also cut back, from nine minutes to six. Reducing the length of matches was a significant benefit for me.

I started off the season by winning at the Great Plains tournament for the second consecutive year, but at one weight class higher. That qualified me to represent the United States in a Russian meet later in the year.

During a Wisconsin dual, I talked to an opponent during a match for the only time in my career. I was wrestling Dennis Limmex, who had been the top recruit out of high school at his weight. I was beating him pretty handily and caught him in a pinning combination called a "step-through crossface." I had him on his back, and he was bridging his back while I had my left arm wrapped around his head.

Because he was arched, his foot was within grabbing distance, and I grabbed it with my right hand and pulled it up high and arched his back even more so that his foot almost touched his head. Wrestlers call this "answering the phone" because you try to put your opponent's foot up against his head.

Limmex screamed.

"Pin yourself," I told him.

"I can't," he answered.

So I let up a little on the pressure. The turkey then tried to get out! So I pulled his foot up and almost had him answering the phone when he screamed louder. His coach, Russ Hellickson, ran out onto the mat and pulled me off his wrestler. Officially, I won by disqualification because of the coach's interference, but I didn't care how I won as long as I did.

For road trips, Coach Abel would stuff us like sardines into the school's Winnebago. We drove to Chicago, where I lost to Ed Banach, by a 5–4 score, for the fourth consecutive time in the finals of the Midlands tournament at Northwestern University. On the same road trip, I lost to a freshman from Kentucky whom I was leading 8–0. I turned him to his back and he didn't even reach for the back of my head. He just arched. That ref had been calling defensive pins that favored Kentucky. A defensive pin is when one wrestler is on bottom and the guy on top turns him to his back, and the wrestler on bottom reaches back and grabs his opponent's head.

The Kentucky freshman never grabbed my head, but the ref called another defensive pin and I lost. I got so angry that I threw my headgear and challenged the ref to a fight right there on the mat. I wouldn't back down from my threat, and that cost our team a two-point penalty.

That was a miserable road trip, and the ride in the crowded Winnebago wasn't much better.

From that road trip, I traveled to the Soviet Union for the Tbilisi tournament, which was considered the toughest tournament in the world. I finished fourth, but my mind was more back in the States than there.

I roomed with Syracuse wrestler Gene Mills, who was known as "Mean Gene the Pinning Machine." I woke up during the middle of one night and Gene was gone. I sat up in bed and started thinking about having to wrestle Ed Banach in the Iowa dual three days after I got home. Gene came back into the room from cutting weight and started washing his gear in the bathtub. He noticed me still sitting up in the bed in the near dark.

"Schultzy, what's wrong?" he asked.

"I . . . hate . . . Banach," was all I said.

Gene laughed.

I didn't really hate Ed, but I did hate the fact that he kept beating me and I couldn't figure out why.

My body was all screwed up timewise when I got back to Oklahoma from Russia. I woke up at 3:15 P.M., fifteen minutes after practice started, raced over to the gym, and unlocked my locker. Coach Abel came in and yelled at me for being late, locked my stuff back in the locker, and kicked me off the team.

I figured he was merely tense in anticipation of the Iowa dual, our biggest of the year.

Then he threw Dave and Metzger off the team, too, and left the locker room. It was actually hysterical watching Coach lose it like that. I unlocked my locker and took my gear out to go cut weight.

Coach never told us we were back on the team, but the next day he called our names when it was time to weigh in.

At the Iowa dual, Dave and I departed from our routine. Usually, we would pace behind the row of chairs next to where the wrestlers sat. I would start pacing longer before my match than anyone else I ever saw. After I had completed my college career, a wrestler told me he had given me the nickname "the Pacer." My pacing was my way of marking my territory. I didn't look at anyone as I walked back and forth, but I made sure everyone saw me, as though I was declaring, "I'm here, and this match is mine."

But that day, with me scheduled to face Ed, Dave suggested we instead go to a secluded room to get off the arena floor for a while. Dave found a room and sat against a wall. A kid, probably around nine or ten years old, walked into our room looking for a restroom. Dave pointed the kid down the hall. Years later, I heard from that boy. He had grown up and contacted me to ask if I remembered him coming into our room. I told him I did. He told me, "I'll never forget that moment. As soon as I walked in and saw you guys, I could feel the intensity in that room so thick that you could have cut it with a knife."

Dave's match was before mine, and he wrestled King Mueller. King had a heavily wrapped knee, and Dave beat him pretty bad. During the match, Dave had King's wrapped leg up on a high single and performed a brutal move I called a "knee-breaker." The *Amateur Wrestling News* ran a photo from that match right as Dave was taking King down. King's mouth was wide-open as he yelled, and all his fingers were sticking straight out as if he had been electrocuted.

My match with Ed was a barn burner. We exchanged the lead probably five or six times, and I was trailing 9–8 with ten seconds left. I hit Ed with a limp arm fireman's carry to a high-crotch and deposited him on his butt by running the pipe. I looked up into the arena to witness eleven thousand people simultaneously jumping out of their seats, screaming. My takedown came with two seconds left, and I won 10–9 to give Ed his first loss in two years.

Going into the heavyweight match to end the dual, we were tied 17–17 with Iowa. Our heavyweight was Steve Williams. Steve was a great heavyweight despite wrestling only two and a half months of the year. He was on a football scholarship and didn't join the wrestling team each year until after Christmas break. Steve wound up becoming a four-time NCAA All-American in wrestling, and he finished second at that year's NCAAs to the future great Olympic heavyweight Bruce Baumgartner. Not too shabby for a part-timer. It's scary to think about how dominant a wrestler Steve would have become if wrestling had been his main sport.

More important, Steve had a great heart. Whenever we had to cut weight a couple of days before a match, even though he didn't have to cut as a heavyweight, he'd put on plastics and sweats, run around the room with us, and get on the stationary bike just like us. He did it for one reason: He wanted to suffer along with us, his teammates. That tells you what kind of man Steve was.

Steve gained fame after college with a successful career as a professional wrestler, where he was better known by his ring name, Dr. Death. Steve died in 2009, at the age of forty-nine, from throat cancer. He had a heart of gold. I loved him, and I miss him.

At the Iowa dual, Steve faced off against Ed's twin brother, Lou. To give a good indication of what the part-timer Steve was up against that day, Lou won an NCAA championship during his career and took gold at 220 pounds in the 1984 Olympics.

Steve and Lou tied their match, and the dual ended in a 19–19 tie. It was one of the most exciting duals I ever participated in as a wrestler or as a coach.

At the Big 8 Conference, I beat Perry Hummel, again in overtime, and Dave finished second at 167 to Oklahoma State's Mike Sheets. We both had advanced to the NCAA tournament.

CHAPTER 7

Escape from Hell

Mark Schultz is a good athlete, but it takes more than being a good athlete to be a good wrestler. It takes mental toughness, and I'm mentally tougher than Mark Schultz." That's what Ed Banach was quoted as saying in *Amateur Wrestling News*'s preview of the national collegiate championship.

When the magazine's writer interviewed me for the same article and asked how I thought I would fare in the tournament, I said I didn't know but thought it would be like a footrace and come down to whoever was ahead at the very end.

When I read Banach's quote, I said to myself, *If we meet in the finals, one of us is going to die.*

The wrestling room at Iowa State was superhot. I was in there cutting weight, and the room was packed with seemingly everyone competing in the tournament, including the guys at my weight.

I made a point of not looking at anyone. Then a Stanford wrestler sat next to me, all happy and smiling, and tried to make small talk. I didn't acknowledge him, got up, and kept cutting. There was no time to socialize, and being happy even for a second could have messed up my psyche. I never hated any of my opponents, but because of my low max VO2, I had to generate anger within me and then channel that anger on the mat. Instead of, say, punching my opponent in the face, I would channel that anger into executing a scoring move. That was difficult on a regular basis, and at times it felt as if I were having to create magic during every match to win.

My closest match in the first three matches was an eight-point win in the quarterfinals. My opponent in the semifinals was none other than Perry Hummel. I beat him 2–1.

Ed Banach would be my opponent in the final. He had won three of his four matches by fall and the other by a score of 17–5.

In the fourth final on the last day of the tournament, Andre Metzger won at 142 pounds for the second consecutive year by defeating Iowa's Lennie Zalesky in their second consecutive NCAA finals matchup. Then in the match just ahead of mine, Dave won his first national championship by getting revenge for his Big 8 finals loss against Sheets.

With the next match on the schedule, I couldn't take time to celebrate Dave's win, but I was glad he had earned his own title in his senior year. I can't imagine what it would be like now if Dave hadn't won that one.

Right before my match, I was in the back warming up and wondering how it came to pass that someone had created an event as cruel as the NCAA Wrestling Championships. I felt so much pressure in those tournaments that it seemed inhumane. A few mats were rolled up in the corner, and on my way to the competition mat, I sat on those mats and prayed as hard as I could for God to please kill me immediately if I lost. I meant it.

Our match was televised on ABC's *Wide World of Sports*, and I believe it was the only match from the finals shown in its entirety. Al Michaels introduced our match as "the bout that everybody has anticipated." It was, because I had won a championship the year before and with Ed having won titles as a freshman and sophomore at a different weight class from mine, there was already talk about the possibility of his becoming the first person to win four NCAA championships.

I made a stupid move on an attempted throw almost two minutes into the match, and Ed caught me and scored on a take-down and a near fall to put me behind 4–0. Ed's lead was at 5–2 late in the first period when I tried a move I had never attempted but had watched Ben Peterson, an Olympic champion, pull off in a World Cup. From locked up in an upper-body tie, I lifted Ed off the mat by kneeing him in the inside thigh near his groin, then turned to the side and threw him on his back. I held Ed on his back for two seconds and scored four points to lead 6–5 after the first period. I increased my lead to 10–7 heading into the third and final period, but because I knew I had enough of a riding-time advantage to get the additional point, in effect I led by four points.

I had a 10–8 lead (not counting the anticipated riding-time point) with thirty seconds left. Ed would have to go for a four-point move, and when he went for the big throw with less than twenty seconds to go, I blocked it and scored a five-point move of my own to clinch the championship. I won 16–8.

Normally, I was exhausted after a match. But winning my second consecutive title, and beating Ed Banach to do so, gave me a huge adrenaline surge, and as soon as the horn sounded, I sprang to my feet and performed my trademark backflip. Dave and Andre ran out to the center of the mat to celebrate with me. I jumped into Metzger's arms and screamed at the top of my lungs toward the ceiling. When the ref raised my hand in victory, I jumped up and down, with the ref still holding my hand up high.

At the conclusion of the tournament, I was announced as the championships' Outstanding Wrestler.

Our team broke the record for points scored in an NCAA championship, but so did Iowa and Iowa State, and we finished third. Isreal Sheppard ended his Oklahoma career that year by placing fourth at 158. I owed a lot to Isreal. He was the one person who allowed me to focus my rage against another human being. It had been practically no holds barred with him in practice, and with no remorse. It was 100 percent pure rage and anger channeled into the science of wrestling. Isreal still probably has no idea how lucky I felt to have trained with him.

After the tournament, Ed came over to me and asked what weight I would be wrestling at the next year.

I told him 177.

"Good," he replied. "I'm going 190."

Mike Chapman, editor of the wrestling magazine *WIN*, ranked my match with Ed as the second-best match in NCAA history, behind only the 1970 NCAA finals when Larry Owings ended Dan Gable's 181-match winning streak.

I had so much adrenaline flowing through me that on the flight home, when we had a layover in Kansas, I went outside, found a secluded area near the passenger loading zone, and ran wind sprints in front of the terminal.

The following Monday, the OU student newspaper ran a front-page photo of Dave, Andre, and me celebrating at the tournament. We were the Sooners' three national champions.

Two weeks after the NCAA championship, I was asked to represent our country at the World Cup in Toledo, Ohio. I had planned on taking a break after the NCAAs, but I felt I was in great shape after the season and said I would compete. Gable was the coach, and I couldn't help but think that he would resent me for beating his guys in the finals two years in a row. But he didn't. Gable qualified as the "enemy" in my book, but I liked him anyway. I looked at him as someone who respected anyone who was tough, regardless of affiliation.

We were losing to the Russians at the World Cup when my turn came to wrestle Russian champion Vagit Kasibekov. I was making my way up the stairs when Gable said, "Now it's time for our big guns." I defeated the Russian 7–2, and all the Americans who followed me at the heavier weights won, too, and we won the World Cup.

And I had won the respect of the legendary Dan Gable.

The success of my first two seasons at Oklahoma filled my senior year with the most pressure I've ever felt in my life. Being an NCAA Division I wrestler presented enough problems on its own. Going through a Division I wrestling season has to be the most painful, pressure-packed experience in sports.

I didn't like competition. In fact, it wouldn't be too strong a statement to say that I hated it. Competition was the worst thing in the world, the most horrible, painful thing I had to suffer through. But I was stuck. I had to compete or I would be miserable for the rest of my life looking back and knowing I didn't fulfill my potential. I knew I had something special in me, like a God-given gift, when it came to wrestling.

Then add to that I was two-time defending NCAA champion and had been named the Outstanding Wrestler, and I had to deal with more pressure than at times I thought I could handle.

With my success at the 1982 NCAAs, for the first time in my career I believed that I was a pretty good wrestler—excluding the first months after my high school state title when I *thought* I was pretty good. Dave had taken care of that issue for me by pounding me on the mat all summer. I didn't need Dave to humble me going into my senior year, but I did need him to walk me through dealing with the pressure.

Dave was the only person who could help when I felt the strain of being a wrestler. He had an uncanny ability to get me to quit worrying about stuff. I'd be stressing about something, and he'd say, "Don't worry about it." That was it. Nothing fancier than that. But when Dave told me to stop worrying, I would. If someone else had said the exact same thing, it wouldn't have worked.

But I didn't see Dave as much as I had that year. He had married about a month before the 1982 NCAAs and moved into an apartment with his wife, Nancy. We still saw each other in the wrestling room, because Dave was helping as a coach and continuing to work out for freestyle competitions. But I wasn't able to just hang out with him as I had before, when we were roommates in the dorms.

Dave's having finished his college eligibility made a difference, too. Being fully devoted to freestyle with no dual meets to compete in, he no longer had to worry about making weight as often. He only had to cut once every couple of months before big meets. We lost that bond college wrestlers share over the constant demands to make weight. Then with him being married and not sharing a dorm room with me, we lost much of what we'd had in common at OU. I felt as if our lives had suddenly jerked off the same path and into different directions.

Andre Metzger, our other national champion in 1982, had also been a senior the season before. No other wrestler on the team could relate to the pressure to defend that I faced. Dave did his best to help when we did have time to talk, and Andre had become an assistant coach, too, so he was still around. But unless someone is actually going through the same pressure at the same time, it just isn't the same.

With our team losing two national champions, Coach Abel needed me to be a big winner for the team. The most points a wrestler could score for his team was six, with a pin, forfeit, injury default, or a disqualification. But I wasn't a big pinner. I would estimate that only about 10 percent of my wins in college came by pin. I felt overburdened from the pressure I was placing on myself to match my individual accomplishments from the previous two years. And now the coach and team needed me to be even better than I had been before!

For my own sake, I had to go out as a winner. I couldn't imagine anything worse than winning two national championships and then not winning my senior year. Given the choice, I would have opted to have not won the previous two years if it would have guaranteed a title as a senior. One title in my final chance would have meant more than two earlier ones.

To this day, I have recurring nightmares about my senior year. The details vary, but the way they play out tends to go something like this: I'm having to defend my back-to-back titles, it's two weeks out from the NCAAs, and I've forgotten to work out and am trying to figure out how to win without being in shape. I consider stabbing myself in the leg or crashing my car on purpose to get out of the tournament.

In some of my nightmares, I am at the tournament weighing in to wrestle the next day and I'm coming off an injury that has me out of shape. I have probably had that particular nightmare at least fifty times.

Every time I wake up from such a nightmare, I thank God it was only a dream.

Port Robertson was a former wrestling coach who worked in the OU athletic department as an administrator. I didn't know what his official title was, but to me he was "Lord of Discipline" and "Ruler of the Jock Dorms." Port liked me, and when I found out that a single room had opened in the dorm, I asked Port if I could have it. He gave it to me.

I spent every night after practice alone in my room. It was depressing. I had tried to stick to myself before, but I became more introverted that year. I bought a cheap black-and-white TV for my room to have as my company. I rarely talked to anyone in the dorm. I've never felt more alone and isolated than I did that year, and it was self-inflicted.

I started the season strong, including beating every opponent badly in a Las Vegas tournament, but I soon complicated my situation during an interview with one of Oklahoma's statewide TV stations.

I did few interviews in my time at OU, and I really hadn't

wanted to do any that year for sure. But the reporter was the daughter of a Sooners alum who had paid Dave and me to drive an RV to Dallas so he and his drinking buddies would have a place to hang out and drink the weekend of the annual Oklahoma-Texas football game. I agreed to the interview only to return the favor for the reporter's father.

I sat down for the interview and the cameraman placed his camera on a table. I hadn't seen him push any buttons, so I assumed the interview hadn't started. The reporter's first question was about how I liked OU. Another bad assumption on my part: I assumed she was just making some preinterview chitchat.

"I wish I would have gone somewhere like Iowa where the coach cared more about his athletes," I told her.

After I said that, the cameraman picked up his camera and turned the lights on. The interview lasted about forty-five minutes. The only part that made the news that night was what I had said about Coach Abel in what I believed to be an off-the-record comment.

I wasn't being totally serious with what I said about Coach. Part of it was me speaking out of my depression and prolonged frustration.

Coach Abel was in the middle of a difficult divorce and wrapped in his own little world at the time. The biggest impact I saw from his divorce process was that he wasn't able to spend the time I thought he needed to be spending with me, especially in light of how lonely I already felt.

I had no idea how consuming a divorce could be. Since then, I've had two myself and have discovered just how much one can dominate your time and distract from your regular activities.

My comment, predictably, created a firestorm. Alumni started calling Coach Abel to ask what was going on under his watch, and some were telling him they were going to stop donating money to his program.

Coach dragged me into his office the next day. "What the hell is wrong with you?! Is that the way you want it?!"

I was so into not displaying any weakness—and I also was a little ticked at him because I wrongly thought he was neglecting me—that I responded, "Yeah."

Our relationship grew cold instantly. I rarely talked to Coach after that.

My attitude and wrestling started going downhill. I began sporadically showing up in the wrestling room. I went back home to Oregon over Christmas and missed the Midlands tournament and three duals. My biggest threat to winning the national championship—at least as far as other wrestlers went—was Duane Goldman of Iowa. Goldman was a freshman, so we hadn't wrestled each other before, and I didn't want him to have any idea what to expect from me until we met in the NCAAs, if that was to be the case.

The team didn't matter to me. I was out for myself and felt that I was protecting my title, not fighting for another one. In my mind, I had nothing to gain and everything—and I mean everything—to lose.

I won the Big 8 championship in qualifying for my fourth NCAA tournament, in Oklahoma City that year. I came down with strep throat just as the tournament started. A media photographer took a picture of me warming up with my tongue sticking out, and my tongue was white, it was so dry.

I struggled in my first-round match, defeating unseeded Scott Giacobbe of Old Dominion University 8–5. In the second round, I faced number-twelve seed Bob Harr of Penn State. In the first round, I got him in the Schultz front headlock and choked him out, turned him over, and pinned him. But the refs only gave me a takedown. Harr woke up mad and spent the rest of the match attacking like crazy. I beat him 11–6 but had to deal with a pissed-off wrestler the entire match. The third round produced my only "easy" win, with a 15–4 defeat of unseeded Jeff Turner from Lehigh University.

I drew Ohio State's Ed Potokar in the semifinals. I was 25-0 that season with my reduced schedule. Ed had broken the Ohio State record for victories in a season with his 49-1 record. Winning our semifinal match would have given him fifty wins.

I led Potokar 4–2 in the third period, and both of his points had come for my being penalized for stalling by referee Pat Lovell. I was on top of Potokar with sixteen seconds to go and all I had to do was ride him out and I would be in the finals. But then Lovell hit me with *another* stalling call, giving Ed two points and tying the score at 4.

Lovell had been a heavyweight wrestler before becoming a ref. He was from the San Francisco Bay Area, like me, and we were friends. We'd even had lunch together at his home. Now I'll never forget Pat because of that last stalling call that tied the match. I'm not saying his call was wrong; I'm just saying I'll never forget it.

Pat's call stopped the match so we could go back to the center of the mat. Potokar was jumping up and down, superpumped. I, on the other hand, was almost scared out of my mind. We were tied and my opponent had yet to score a technical point. If Potokar managed to pull off an escape from the bottom, he would beat me 5–4 and my senior year and my life would be ruined.

When Pat blew the whistle to resume the match, Potokar exploded from the bottom. He was riding all the momentum of the late call that had tied the match. I was riding a bucking bronco.

Finally, Potokar stood up, broke my grip, and spun behind me. But right before the ref could call a two-point reversal, I did something I had never done: I squatted like a frog and dove straight backward, like a back dive off a diving board, hoping to grab hold of something. I hooked a finger into the loop of Potokar's shoelace, clawed my way up his leg, and held on like my life depended on maintaining that grip. The final seconds ticked off the clock and we went into overtime.

Potokar still couldn't manage a technical point in overtime, and with no stalling calls against me, I outscored him 6–0 in overtime to advance.

Goldman, the second seed and freshman sensation, defeated Perry Hummel in the other semifinal. Thanks to my Christmas in Oregon, I hadn't wrestled against Goldman, and that gave me an advantage going into the finals, in my opinion. The more often wrestlers face each other, the closer their matches tend to become. If I had wrestled Goldman previously, I think a certain amount of my aura could have been diminished merely by his getting onto the mat with me.

Maybe he wasn't thinking that way, but I was, and it gave me a psychological boost going back to the hotel the eve of our final.

Frankly, I needed every edge I could get because a memory of the NCAAs from my freshman year at UCLA kept haunting me. Mike Land was a senior at Iowa State and a defending national champion. In the 1979 finals, he faced a freshman from Lehigh named Darryl Burley. Land had won eighty-four consecutive matches, but in his last time on the mat in college, he lost to the freshman.

Now here I was, the senior defending champion everyone expected to win going up against a freshman in the finals.

So much for a good night's sleep.

A couple of hours before the finals started, I was sitting in my hotel room with Clinton Burke, our 134-pounder and the only other Sooner who would be wrestling for a championship. There was a knock on the door and Clinton opened it. We were only a half hour's drive from Norman, and all these friends of Clinton's came streaming into our room, laughing and drinking and smoking.

I'm sitting there on my bed thinking, *These people are going to kill us mentally.*

It was *way* too early to celebrate. Or be happy even. Being happy could ruin my mental state as I prepared for the match. Clinton seemed to have no intention of asking his friends to leave, so I grabbed my gear and headed to the arena much earlier than I had wanted to.

The commentator from *Wide World of Sports* was going around interviewing all the finalists at the arena. For me, that was no time to be talking. I gave one-word answers to his first three questions. Visibly frustrated, he said, "This is impossible. I can't do it." I got up and walked away to be by myself, just as I preferred.

Right before the first final, Clinton seemed to realize the enormity of wrestling in the finals. I could see him in the corner of the warm-up room looking all emotional. I wasn't sure, but it looked as though he was crying. Andre walked over to Clinton and told him he had to snap out of it. I couldn't be a part of that scene and stayed away from them. Clinton lost his match by two points. That left me as OU's only hope for a championship in 1983.

Coach Abel and Coach Humphrey had warned me about stalling. They said the refs thought I had been stalling too much in the tournament and had met and decided to show me no mercy in the finals. Then in the final moments before my match, Dave told me that the refs were going to be watching me very closely for stalling and wouldn't cut me any slack.

Jeez, did anyone else in the arena want to warn me about stalling?

From the moment Goldman and I met on the mat, I could sense he had already decided I was supposed to win. It's difficult to put into words, but there was something in his eyes and body language that gave it away.

Goldman's escape attempts seemed halfhearted, and he was easier to hold down than anyone I had beaten coming through the bracket. My only concern came from all those stalling warnings. I was called three times—the first as a warning and the next two for one point each. I didn't think Goldman would score on me otherwise, but locked in a close match and knowing the refs were paying extra attention to me, I was worried that a repeat of the semifinals match against Potokar would happen. It didn't, though, and with four minutes of riding time, I won 4–2 and for the third consecutive year defeated an Iowa Hawkeye to win the NCAA championship.

One year after taking part in one of the most exciting matches in college wrestling history, I had just won the most boring match of that year's finals. But I didn't care, because I had won. I had pulled off my biggest escape as a wrestler—the escape from the pressure and expectations that had weighed heavily on my chest for a full year.

I stood there with my arms outstretched like a bird. I finally felt released, unlatched from my burdens, free to fly away and leave behind all the junk that had accumulated to make my senior season pure hell.

Then I did something I'd done rarely during the season: I smiled.

I thanked God repeatedly.

Before taking the mat and winning my second championship, I had prayed that God would take my life if I lost. Now, one year later, and only six years after taking up the sport of wrestling, I stood there, soaking in the glory of being cheered as a three-time NCAA champion.

God could have taken my life right then and there, too, if he wanted and I would have died a happy person. There hadn't been many times in my life when I could have said that.

CHAPTER 8

Brothers, Olympians

There's that old expression about seeing the light at the end of the tunnel. Why doesn't anyone talk about what happens when you exit the tunnel?

My senior year had been my tunnel, and to help make it through, I had kept telling myself that there was a light at the end. If I came out on the other end with that third NCAA championship in hand, I thought I would retire and be happy the rest of my life. I would have been content with calling my senior year the final chapter and sending that book off to the printer.

But Dave had other plans for us.

Dave had won his championship as a senior and had earned All-American status all three seasons he was able to compete. But he didn't care too much for collegiate wrestling. He was better at freestyle wrestling. Collegiate, or folkstyle, wrestling required more of a control-oriented, grinding style. It favored super-conditioned athletes with strong upper bodies that allowed them to hold opponents on their back for near fall points and to accumulate riding time. Also, the option of the down position benefited wrestlers who could ride and escape.

Freestyle, however, did not have the down position or points for escapes and riding time. Freestyle featured more wrestling on your feet and favored wrestlers who were better at takedowns, throws, and turns. Dave was one of the best in the world at all three. Dave won eight freestyle national championships (plus two Greco-Roman) and was named the nation's top freestyle wrestler four times. Dave's body and wrestling style perfectly suited freestyle.

Dave tried to talk me into competing at the US Open, but I was so burned out from my senior season that I had no desire to go. At that point, I couldn't imagine putting my body and mind through another competition, but Dave wouldn't stop bugging me. He was not going to let me quit wrestling and convinced me to go with him that summer to try out in Iowa City for the United States' Worlds team. I went, not sure it was what I wanted to be doing, and we both made the team, with me defeating Duane Goldman again for my spot.

Dave and I graduated from Oklahoma with degrees in exercise science. I don't know how it is in most colleges now, but back then exercise science was a more academic way of saying PE. I used to joke that I actually was majoring in eligibility.

If we had gone the astrophysics route and had to study a lot more, we wouldn't have become nearly as good as wrestlers as we did. But wrestling, not education, was the reason we were at Oklahoma. Although jobs in astrophysics would have paid more after college.

Former college wrestlers who wanted to compete in freestyle had few options. The common route was to try to find an assistant coach's position at a college that would pay you poorly but at least give you a place to work out and provide wrestlers to work out against.

No such opportunity existed at Oklahoma. Coach Abel wouldn't hire us because he said we weren't team players. He was correct, at least in my case. My interview with the TV station didn't help our job prospects, either.

We did, however, receive an offer from Chris Horpel to coach with him at Stanford.

I had no ties to Oklahoma, and certainly no reason to stay. I gave the other wrestlers everything I possessed except for the clothes I could fit into one bag, hopped on my Honda 400 motorcycle, and split.

About half a mile west of Oklahoma City, I pulled over to the side of Interstate 40, shut off my bike, stepped off, and looked back toward the city skyline. I stood there for about twenty minutes reflecting on my time in that state, about my commitment to sacrifice my life there if that's what it would take to make it there. Dying trying would have been more acceptable than failing.

Do or die, right?

Four years later, I was still standing, winner of the national championship all three years I competed. I had won my final forty-four matches as a Sooner. By going 27-0 my last season in crimson and cream, I had broken the school record for most wins in an undefeated season, a record that stood for seventeen years. I had never lost a match at home and had avenged all my losses against my greatest opponents.

Satisfied that all my demons had been exorcised, I got back on my bike and headed home.

———

Dave and I were able to find a home owner who rented us rooms for a great price: our dad, who rented out rooms/apartments in his house. Dave and his wife took one room upstairs, and I had another. It was great to be back under the same roof as my brother.

The same living arrangements didn't go well when officials with the Amateur Athletic Union, which was nearing its end as the governing body of US wrestling, put me in the same hotel room as Dave and his wife at the 1983 World Championships in Kiev, Russia.

I'd had to get out when Clinton's friends crashed our hotel room the morning of the NCAAs a few months earlier, but I didn't have that option for the long stay in Kiev. I needed to be in my own room or in a room with a wrestler who didn't have his wife or girlfriend with him. This was the *World* Championships and we were the *United States of America*, not some piddling little country that was just happy to be there. I would have paid for my own room for the whole trip if I had had the money.

I needed a quiet room. I needed a room that I could make completely dark and where I could lie on a bed before each match and conserve energy to prepare for battle. I needed a room where I could get lots of rest between matches.

I wasn't given what I needed.

The eventual World Champion, Taymuraz Dzgoev of the Soviet Union, beat me by two measly points. I had a 2-2 record in Kiev and placed seventh.

Depressed over losing, I wondered if I would ever have another chance at a world title. I was just beginning freestyle and couldn't assume I would make another World or Olympic team.

Dave reached the finals of his weight and was trailing Taram Magomadov 4–0 early. For the first part of the match, I wanted Dave to lose, as though our hotel arrangements were his fault. But during his match, something in me snapped and I did a complete reversal. I knew Dave was better than his Russian opponent, and I jumped out of my chair, ran to the edge of the mat, and screamed at Dave, "Kill him!" Perhaps it was coincidence that this happened, but at that exact moment, the momentum of the match turned in Dave's favor and he launched a comeback to win 7–4.

I was happy for Dave but miserable that I had lost. I told Dave afterward that it wasn't fair for me to be put in his and his wife's room. I was mad, down, and feeling a little betrayed.

Even though Horpel hired Dave and me, I never understood Horpel's take on me. I had a strong impression that he aspired to make me inferior to Dave. After the '83 Worlds, I sensed Chris looked down on me as "Dave's less successful little brother." I didn't get it. I was a *three*-time NCAA champ. Dave had won once. But Dave was a World Champion, and Chris apparently put more stock in that because he would introduce Dave to people as a world champ but would say nothing about my college titles.

One time, our Stanford team went to Washington for a tournament. We were at a Stanford alum's house playing pool, and I missed an easy shot. Chris made some remark that ended with his calling me a has-been Chris hadn't won an NCAA championship, so I quickly shot back, "I'd rather be a has-been than a never-been."

Perhaps Horpel was trying to motivate me. I don't know. I just tried not to think about what I perceived as to how he treated me. I didn't want to let anyone get to me with their actions or words. "Forgive everyone of their sins" was my philosophy. Not for their sake, necessarily, but because I didn't want to get weighed down with any burdens I didn't have to carry. Simply competing supplied enough burdens of its own.

The next year, we went to the US Open in Stillwater, Oklahoma, and Dave and I both won national freestyle titles. I was driving the rental car back to the Oklahoma City airport. Horpel was in the passenger seat, and Dave was in the back.

"So," Chris said to me, "how does it feel to win the national championship?"

I was about to say, "Relieved," but before I could answer, the question entered my mind, *What is Chris expecting me to say?*

Did Chris think I would say I was happy? Heck yeah, I was happy. But if I told Chris that, he might think I wasn't expecting to win. If I'm not expecting to win, I'm not competing in the tournament. I went to the US Open to win. Dave was my main workout partner in the Stanford room. Pound for pound he was the greatest wrestler in the world, and we were pretty even in the room at that point. It shouldn't have been a surprise I had won. I wasn't surprised. Losing would have surprised me, because I fully expected to win. Then it came to me how I should answer Chris's question.

How did it feel?

"Natural."

Chris only laughed. The expression on his face indicated he hadn't expected me to say that, so I guess that was the best answer after all.

———

Back in our day, qualifying for the US Olympic team was a more difficult process than in recent years. I would need to wrestle in thirteen matches to make the team. We had to qualify for the qualifying tournament, as odd as that sounds. The US Open counted as a qualifying tournament, and that's where Dave and I earned the right to compete in the Olympic Qualifying Tournament. We both won there. The award presented to the top six placers in each of the weight classes was a tiny block of wood with the word *Participant* on it. That was my big prize for winning one of the toughest national tournaments of my life.

Modest award aside, winning placed Dave and me on top of the ladder for the Olympic Team Trials, which would decide who would represent the United States at the '84 Olympics in Los Angeles. In the ladder system, the fourth-, fifth-, and sixth-seeded wrestlers took part in a minitournament to determine who would fill the fourth spot. That person wrestled the third seed best-two-out-of-three for the right to take on the second seed in a best-of-three. As the top seed, I, like Dave, was able to wait for the survivor of those preliminary matches, and then wrestle best-of-three for the spot on the Olympic team.

In Dave's class, three-time world champ Lee Kemp advanced to the final. Dave swept him in two matches. That gave Dave wins against Kemp in the US Open and the qualifying tournament, all within a year of each other. I can't say that I was surprised, because Dave was that good in freestyle, but it was an impressive feat.

My opponent in the finals was Don Shuler. That was a rematch also, as I had beaten Don in the finals of the Open and the qualifier. I won the first match 7–2. Then Don beat me by the same score. In the third, and deciding, match, I won 4–2, earning a spot on the US Olympic team with my brother.

In May, three months before the Olympics, Soviet Union officials announced a boycott of the Games in Los Angeles. Thirteen other Eastern Bloc countries joined the boycott over the next several days. The Soviets cited concerns over inadequate security for its athletes in the United States.

Everybody in the world knew the Soviets' real reason was retaliation for President Jimmy Carter's decision to have the United States lead a sixty-two-nation boycott of the 1980 Moscow Olympics in protest of the Soviet Union's invasion of Afghanistan.

Wrestling figured to be one of the sports most affected, because the Russians and Bulgarians, who also chose not to come to Los Angeles, perennially fielded powerful wrestling teams.

Our sport is one of those that some sports fans pay attention to only every four years when the Olympics roll around. Because of the boycott, public sentiment was that the US team should clean up in freestyle. But what most didn't realize was that while the boycott certainly diminished the level of competition in general, that wasn't the case across the board.

My and Dave's weights, plus Barry Davis's at 125.5, still had worthy fields. Barry's class included two-time World Champion Hideaki Tomiyama of Japan. The only weight that I thought was more stacked than Barry's was Dave's at 163. He would have to contend with Martin Knosp, the 1981 world champ from West Germany. Dave's weight was as legit as in any other Olympics. My class,

180.5, included the reigning European champion, Reşit Karabacak of Turkey. The European Championship included the countries that boycotted the Olympics. I had my weight ranked as third toughest.

The depth might not have been that of a typical Olympics, but those three weights were still stout at the top. Despite the disparity in level of competition between the ten weight classes, expectations of American victories were the same across the classifications.

As far as I was concerned, the drop-off in talent for my weight because of the boycott was minimal, but the pressure to win had been ratcheted up three or four notches. There certainly were no guarantees with Karabacak in my class, but losing in the '84 Olympics would have been more humiliating than losing in any other Olympics.

A problem at the Olympic training camp complicated matters for me. I had asked my girlfriend, Terry, to join me there. Things were going well at first, and having her there had a calming effect on me. Terry was, to be blunt about it, hot. Really hot. She was so stunningly gorgeous that the other guys would go gaga over her. Apparently, some of the wrestlers' wives didn't like Terry being there and complained to the administrators of USA Wrestling, which had become the governing body of US wrestling. The wives contended that only wives, not fiancées and girlfriends, should be permitted at training camp.

The administrators assembled an informal meeting with the wrestlers, wives, and coaches about whether Terry should be permitted to stay. Dan Gable, our head coach, started the meeting by telling me, "There have been complaints that you and Terry are not married."

Who cares? I thought.

"We have determined that if you and Terry aren't married," Dan continued, "she has to leave."

"Okay, fine," I said. "We're married."

"That's it then," Gable replied.

Meeting adjourned, Terry stayed.

Between the growing expectations of the boycott and the distractions over Terry at a time when I needed to be nearing my peak in training, I felt as if the forces of the universe were conspiring against me.

CHAPTER 9

Golden Moment

The 1984 Olympics in Los Angeles was a return engagement, marking the first time the Summer Games had been held in the United States since Los Angeles had hosted the 1932 Olympics. Los Angeles had beat out New York City in winning the right to serve as the host city in the country's bid to bring the Olympics back to the United States. The two cities had served as bookends, though, for the Olympic torch relay, which would begin in New York City and last 82 days, trekking 9,000 miles through 33 different states before culminating in Los Angeles for the Opening Ceremony, where President Ronald Reagan would officially open the Games in his home state.

The boycott, of course, dominated much of the pre-Olympics talk. With the Soviet-led Eastern Bloc of countries not participating, the US team was expected to run away from the remaining competition in the medals standings.

Americans anticipated the Olympic debut of superstar sprinter and long jumper Carl Lewis. Diver Greg Louganis would finally receive his opportunity to follow up on his silver-medal performance in the 1976 Games in Montreal. Louganis had appeared primed to win a gold medal, if not two, at the 1980 Games before the US boycott. As far as international athletes, there was a lot of curiosity about West German swimmer Michael Gross, who, from images of his freakishly long arms coming out of the water, had picked up the nickname "the Albatross." And then there was the US men's basketball team that had won gold in all but two prior Olympics—in 1972 because of a controversial loss to the Soviets, and in 1980 when they were denied the opportunity because of the boycott. That was before the Dream Team days, when college athletes were still entrusted with the responsibility of maintaining dominance in the game invented in our country. Michael Jordan, Patrick Ewing, and Chris Mullin were on the '84 team, and all three would be part of the first Dream Team eight years later.

At a time when government spending for hosting Olympics was being scrutinized worldwide, the LA Games, under the leadership of Peter Ueberroth, was the first to be privately funded. Organizers bucked the trend of host nations building new venues for Olympics and then finding themselves stuck with trying to figure out what to do with the huge facilities after the Games ended. Although Los Angeles was the host city, venues already in place throughout Southern California were employed to host competitions.

Instead of building one Olympic Village to serve as the home of all the athletes, three villages were established on university campuses: the University of Southern California and UCLA in Los Angeles, and at the University of California, Santa Barbara, up the Pacific Coast.

The wrestlers were assigned to stay at USC. I remember noting a lot of pastel colors, for some reason, when we arrived. But other than that, I ignored much of what USC looked like for the Olympics, not to mention what was going around me. I was there to go to war, and that was it.

We had to get in line and walk through a metal detector to receive our credentials. The young lady who handed me my credentials had a media guide she was asking athletes to sign next to their picture. She opened to the page with my weight class. Chris Rinke, the Canadian ranked third, one spot behind me, had signed his photo.

"I see Rinke signed," I told her.

"Yeah," she said, "and he said he's going to win it. He was dead serious."

My face instantly warmed as blood sprinted to it. I could already tell these next two weeks weren't going to be fun. Up until that point, I had competed in only three international events: the 1982 World Cup, 1983 World Championships, and 1983 Pan Am Games. I had won the World Cup, but Rinke had beaten me at the Pan Ams the only time I had faced him.

The five-day freestyle Olympic tournament wouldn't begin until the Games' tenth of fifteen days of competition. The Greco-Roman portion started two days after the Opening Ceremony, which I couldn't even enjoy because of what waited ahead of me. I wished we could have traded places on the schedule with the Greco-Romans so I could have gotten the competing part out of the way and enjoyed life in the Olympic Village.

Greco-Roman was finished by the first full weekend. The United States had never medaled in Greco-Roman at the Olympics, but that year our guys won two gold medals (Jeff Blatnick and Steve Fraser), a silver, and a bronze. There was a lot of partying that Friday at the Olympic Village, with the wrestlers dancing around and all happy. I wanted to join in their celebration, but I wouldn't allow myself to because of the psychological damage it could cause if I showed too much happiness before competing.

Plus, their unprecedented success put more pressure on us in freestyle.

I spent most of my time leading up to our event training, eating, and sleeping to conserve energy. Free video games were set up in the Olympic Village for the athletes. You'd think those would be a source of fun, but they weren't for me.

I was playing a video boxing game when Stan Dziedzic, our team manager and a former Olympic bronze medalist and national team coach, started watching over my shoulder. My next opponent came up on the screen—Reşit Karabacak, "the Turk," who was ranked first in my weight class.

"Hey, Mark, there's the Turk," Stan joked.

I didn't laugh. In fact, I didn't react at all. Nothing was funny, nor would anything be funny, until I finished competing. I didn't talk about opponents or potential opponents ahead of matches, and I wasn't going to talk with Stan about Karabacak.

This is none of his business, I thought. *This is my life. This is something that's going to go down in history. Forever. Here he is making light of it, and this is serious business for me. If I lose to anybody, including the Turk, I won't get to call myself an Olympic champion.*

I ignored Stan, and he walked away. When I finished my game, I left and went back to my room.

Two days before our event, Dan Gable moved our team from the Olympic Village to a Motel 6 less than a mile from the wrestling venue, the Anaheim Convention Center. That way we wouldn't have to wait for buses, would have easy access to the scales, and could be in control of how and when we wanted to work out and cut weight.

The next day, my dear mom came to our hotel and asked if I wanted to go to Disneyland and get something to eat. One day from starting what had already taken on the feel of the most intense competition of my life and she thought I would actually consider going out to eat and having fun? Mom!

Weigh-ins took place two hours before the competition, and that was also when the draw for the tournament's two eight-man pools occurred. After each wrestler weighed, he reached into a bucket and pulled out a plastic egg. Inside the egg was his number for the tournament. I drew number 6, which meant I would wrestle against number 8 in the first round. The Turk drew number 8!

I was stunned. The first- and second-ranked wrestlers were going to meet in the first round. In two hours, I would be making my Olympic debut in what basically was the gold-medal match.

I was scared to death. I went back to my room and told my girlfriend about the draw.

"You look terrible," Terry told me.

Give Terry points for being honest. I just wished she hadn't been honest in that situation.

I stood in front of the mirror and looked like I always did after cutting to make weight. Wrestlers call that look "sucked," with hollow cheeks and eyes. I mumbled something to Terry like, "You just haven't seen me after weigh-ins lately."

I prayed I wouldn't feel as terrible in two hours as Terry said I looked. I plopped down on the corner of my bed and stared at the wall, sweating like a pig.

Good thing I didn't have to catch a team bus to the convention center. The way my luck was going, the bus probably would have run me over.

Facing the number one wrestler in the world in my weight in the first match, I knew I would have to perform my best immediately. In the first move of the match, the Turk underhooked my arm and followed with a limp arm to a single leg. I answered by grabbing him in a double wristlock. I had performed that move probably a thousand times with a guy's head on the inside trapped against my body. But I had watched a Cuban wrestler at the Pan Ams make that move with his opponent's head on the outside. I had only done the move that way a few times and only in practices. But this was *the* match of the tournament, right out of the gate.

It was either me or him. I chose me.

I locked his arm, threw the move to break his grip, elevated him in the groin with the arm he had between his legs, and threw him head over heels. I expected Karabacak to do a front roll, giving me two points. Instead, he landed on his head, unexpectedly halting all his momentum. I kept his left arm locked and it continued over his head. I felt and heard Karabacak's elbow pop. I knew right away he had broken a bone.

Thirty seconds into the match, I pinned him. The home crowd, not having heard Karabacak's elbow snap as I had, roared its approval. I raised my fists and walked off the mat, unsure of what to do, as the Turk remained on the floor and the ref calmly motioned for medical help.

That was a weird moment. It's unusual for that kind of injury

to occur during a match. I certainly hadn't tried to hurt Karabacak. The injury happened because of how he landed as I had his
arm locked. But then again, I couldn't show any weakness on the
mat. Wrestling is a man's game. Freak injuries—to you or your
opponent—are always possible. Inherent in wrestling is the mutual
agreement between opponents that they are about to attempt to
commit battery on each other. Every wrestler risks injury. I suffered more injuries in wrestling than I could count, including numerous broken bones. I think I wrestled injured more often than
uninjured.

When Karabacak got injured, I couldn't get out of my mind-
set because of what had happened to him. I still had four more
matches to go in the tournament.

I also knew the ramifications. The top-ranked wrestler had
just left the tournament; he wouldn't be able to wrestle his way
back to a chance at the gold medal.

In the match right before mine, Dave had hurt the knee of a
Yugoslavian while pinning him. Wrestling's international govern-
ing body is the Fédération Internationale des Luttes Associées
(FILA), or in English, the International Federation of Associated
Wrestling Styles.

The head of FILA, Milan Ercegan, happened to be from Yu-
goslavia. He had just watched, in back-to-back matches, the American Schultz brothers pin and send his fellow countryman to the
hospital and knock another competitor out of the tournament. He
assigned Head Official Mario Saletnik to watch my and Dave's
matches the rest of the tournament as a fourth official.

I defeated a wrestler from Italy in my next match in my group
later that night, under close scrutiny of the extra official. While wait-

ing to weigh in, I went up into the seats to join Mom in watching Dave. While I was up there, the public address announcer said, "Mark Schultz has been disqualified from the match against Turkey."

Mom started freaking out next to me.

"Oh, my God!" she exclaimed. "Oh, my God!"

"It doesn't mean anything," I told her, got up, and walked away.

Turkish officials had protested my victory, demanding that I be disqualified. Tape of the match was reviewed, and I was disqualified for "excessive brutality."

I knew there were two parts to the decision. First, did I win or lose the match? Second, would I be kicked out of the tournament? Because the announcer had only said I had been disqualified, I knew I could still wrestle and come back and win gold.

Technically, the Turks should not have been allowed to protest because they didn't file their protest until a couple of hours after the thirty-minute time limit for appeals had expired. In fact, FILA at first denied the Turks' request. Then FILA reconsidered and ruled to disqualify me. If the Turks had filed in time, I probably would have been booted from the tournament.

The move was illegal. I've never denied that. But it wasn't an intentional breaking of the rules, and I definitely was not aiming to injure Karabacak. I didn't talk to the media that night, but Gable gave a good explanation to reporters. With the arm at ninety degrees, he said, the move is legal. My hold started out legal. But the way the Turk landed caused me to take his arm past ninety degrees. At ninety-one degrees, the move became illegal and subject to the "excessive brutality" ruling.

I respected Dan. Even though I defeated three of his guys

from Iowa in the NCAA finals, I never got the feeling he didn't like me.

I didn't talk to Dan at the arena after the announcement was made. Dave did, though.

"They're trying to turn this into a sissy sport," my brother complained.

I heard that the Turkish government, I believe it was, had promised Karabacak money or property or something like that of value if he had won gold. He said in a Turkish newspaper article that I had fouled him. Years later, I was talking with a journalist who said he would be seeing Karabacak soon. I signed a T-shirt for Karabacak with a note saying I hadn't intended to hurt him and would like to be friends with him. I've never heard anything from the Turk, so I don't know if the shirt made it to him.

With the disqualification, I knew I couldn't lose either of my two remaining group matches and still have a shot at the gold-medal match. Chris Rinke, the confident autograph signer from Canada, was my next opponent.

After a 2–2 tie in the first period, I started the second period with a takedown and gut wrench. The ref gave me one point for the takedown and two points for the gut wrench. The scoreboard showed me with a 5–2 lead. In freestyle, if a match ends in a tie, the tiebreaker is known as criteria. If all the points are scored on one-pointers, the wrestler with the last point scored wins. But if any two-point moves are scored, the wrestler with the last two-pointer wins.

At that point, I had a three-point lead and had scored the last two-pointer. I could give Rinke three takedowns and still win on the criteria tiebreaker.

Down three points, Rinke started attacking me like crazy and I got called for my final stalling warning. I couldn't afford another stalling.

Then I looked over at the scoreboard and my lead was 4–2, not 5–2. The mat judges had reversed the ref's decision and awarded me one point, not two, for the gut wrench. That screwed up my calculations on what I needed to win. I thought I could give up two takedowns, instead of three, and still win on criteria. But I failed to take into account that with the subtracted point, all my scoring had come on one-pointers. If I gave up two takedowns, I would lose the tiebreaker.

While I was refiguring my mental math as we wrestled, the ref yelled, "Passive, rouge!" or "Stalling, red!" for the color of my singlet. In my confusion, Rinke exploded with the exact same underhook to a limp arm that Karabacak had used to gain control of my leg. But unlike the Turk, Rinke executed perfectly for the takedown. My lead shrank to 4–3.

That gave Rinke a huge energy burst. A full minute remained for him to get a takedown or a stalling call on me for the tie and, because of the tiebreaker, win. I was still thinking, however, that I could allow a takedown for a tie and win on the tiebreaker.

Rinke was on top, trying to turn me. He couldn't, and the ref stood us back to our feet. I had used all my stalling calls, and the ref yelled, "Passive, rouge!" again to warn me that he was about to call my final stalling penalty. Unlike most wrestlers I went against, Rinke opted for a standing restart. Rinke knew there would be a better chance to score on me from that position.

Not only had Rinke scouted me, but Jim Humphrey—one of our assistant coaches at Oklahoma—had been hired as the Canadian freestyle head coach. Jim knew better than anyone my style and how adept I had become at preventing opponents from turning me in the down position. It shook me to know that someone who knew me that well was in the opposing corner, and I'm sure Jim instructed Rinke to not have me start down.

I had to make a quick decision. I believed the refs had it out for the Schultz brothers and were looking for a way to get me out of the tournament. I had to do *something*. So I decided to shoot on Rinke's legs and let him take me down, which also would serve the effect of killing most of the remaining time. So I shot in without first setting up. It was a terrible shot. I barely touched his leg.

Rinke sprawled and locked his arms around my body in a front body lock. I was waiting for him to spin behind, but our positioning caused me to change my mind. I had a move in my repertoire that had been unstoppable, a "duck scoop." Instead of playing defensively, I decided to attack. I knew I could score with the duck scoop and that would give me even more time to stall if I needed to give away another takedown.

I tripoded up onto all fours with my head down. Rinke held on to his body lock just long enough for me to feel an opening. I exploded, throwing my head up and my hips down as hard as I could. At that exact moment, Rinke felt the attack and let go of his grip. But it was too late. I spun behind him in half a second: 5–3; time ran out; I won despite the confusion.

I then won an uneventful match, 16–5, against a wrestler from New Zealand to advance to the gold-medal match.

D ave's gold-medal match was the night before mine, against
Martin Knosp, the 1981 World Champion who had defeated
Lee Kemp in the last Worlds.

The refs were keeping a close eye for the Schultz front headlock, and the special off-the-mat judge had warned Dave three
times in his previous match for holds around his opponent's neck.
His opponent was warned once for the same thing, so it was that
kind of match.

Every time Dave locked up Knosp in a headlock, the ref broke
it up. One time, the ref stepped in and broke up a headlock by
Dave and Knosp fell to his back as if he were choking, trying to
draw a penalty against Dave. It didn't work.

With Dave having to wrestle without one of his best weapons,
he broke a 1–1 tie with 1:37 remaining with a single point and
then added two more scores, including a takedown with ten seconds left for a 4–1 win.

I watched Dave win, but I wasn't able to enjoy his gold-medal
victory. I had too much pressure on my shoulders, and all I could
afford to do with my final match the next day was focus on what
I had to do to avoid losing.

My last opponent was Hideyuki Nagashima from Japan,
who advanced out of Group A. I had watched him in one match
and, honestly, wasn't impressed. With the Turk, me, and Rinke,
the top three wrestlers all had drawn into Group B. I knew if I
could just keep my head together for one final match, I could take
home the gold.

Right on the first whistle, I shot Nagashima and caught him

in the face with an accidental head-butt. Three seconds in, he took a brief timeout to recover. Before the match, I had decided which techniques I would use against Nagashima. A football forearm shiver to a high-crotch followed by an inside leg trip took him down, and then a gut wrench gave me a quick 4–0 lead.

Nagashima put me in a tough spot only once, when he attempted a headlock that slipped off. Other than that, I controlled the entire match, which wasn't an entire match. A minute and fifty-nine seconds into the first round, the match ended on technical superiority with me leading 13–0.

Backflip!

I was a little winded as the ref raised my hand in victory. We didn't even wrestle two minutes, but I had scored eight points in twenty-six seconds on a flurry of moves. I was not, however, too tired for my trademark backflip. After the ref raised my hand, I pumped my fist one time to the American partisan crowd, embraced Nagashima, and shook hands with his coaches, I walked over to my corner and did another backflip. Why not? An Olympic gold medal has to be worth two flips, doesn't it?

With my victory, Dave and I became the first brothers in US wrestling history to win Olympic gold medals. But only because Lou Banach won gold one match after mine. Like Dave, his brother Ed had won gold the previous day.

I wish I could say I was overjoyed to win. But that wouldn't be accurate. The TV broadcast of that match is on YouTube, and when I have watched it, I've noticed that I never smiled before TV broke away for commercial. The strongest emotion I felt was relief. Not exactly a gold-medal moment athletes dream of, but the weight of the world had just been lifted off me.

The medals ceremony was actually rather odd. What separates the gold medalist from the winners of silver and bronze is that only the gold medalist hears his national anthem played. In college, I would get emotional hearing the anthem when it was played before matches. I used that emotion as a way to get psyched up. With my low max VO2, I had to find ways to create adrenaline, and anything I could use to create more emotion was a tool I needed in my belt. But at the Olympics, hearing the anthem after I was finished wrestling was completely different from my routine. As the anthem played, and the home crowd sang along, and the Stars and Stripes was raised in the arena, I didn't know what to feel.

I first realized the significance of that last match in a bathroom, of all places. Just as in the moments after winning the 1978 California state championship, I retreated to a bathroom to have a few minutes alone. My path to gold in the Olympic tournament was different, not to mention more interesting, than other wrestlers' because of the disqualification and being forced to come back from an early loss. I don't know if this is still the case, but I was told that I was one of only two men in Olympic wrestling history to lose a match and still win gold.

When I looked at myself in the bathroom mirror, I saw the recipient of a miracle. There had been the disqualification and the controversy surrounding that match, followed by the close scrutiny Dave and I were under in the rest of our matches. Then it had taken everything I could call up from within myself physically and mentally to defeat Chris Rinke. He was gunning for me hard.

Then there were the comparisons to Dave. I knew before the tournament, as did many others, that he was going to win gold.

Dave was the only reigning World Champion at the Games, and he was very good in 1984. No one in the world, whether he had come to Los Angeles or not, could have beaten him that year.

But I didn't think that Dave believed I was going to win. I didn't know if I was going to win, either. That had been an inconsistent year for me. Sometimes the great Mark Schultz would show up, sometimes the lousy one would. And on our sport's biggest stage, carrying the overbearing burdens of the expectations of the once-every-four-years US wrestling audience, I had kept the lousy Mark Schultz from popping up from wherever he had been showing himself without warning.

Before leaving that bathroom, there was one thing I knew for sure: God had blessed me with a miracle.

Dave and I didn't have a conversation that night about both of us winning. We knew each other so well, we were so in sync with each other, that neither of us needed to share our thoughts to know that the other was relieved to survive that tournament with a gold medal to show for his perseverance in the fight.

Now, I did have a celebration that night. Dave had his wife with him. I had my girlfriend with me, and Terry, a group of her friends, and I partied that night. We partied hard, too. If there were an Olympic gold medal for celebrating, we would have won it!

A large group of US medalists went on a three-city tour with parades and parties, and Dave and I were included. I wouldn't have gone without Dave, but the tour turned out to be a blast. There were no rules on the flights. We didn't have to buckle our seat belts, for one. On one takeoff, while the nose of the plane was higher than the tail, one athlete I didn't know stood on a magazine at the front of the plane and "surfed" down the aisle. A volleyball player shook up a bottle of champagne and started spraying people. When he got me and Terry wet, I pushed him to the floor in fun.

At one parade, I rode in a car with gymnast Mary Lou Retton, who'd won five medals, including gold for the individual all-around. Mary Lou was really nice, and getting to meet her and spend a little bit of time with her was cool. As a former gymnast and as the winner of a wrestling gold medal, I had an appreciation for how amazingly she performed in winning five medals.

I want to say that parade was in Dallas. We were riding in the second convertible behind the first car with some city official. When we came to the point along the parade route where we were supposed to stop briefly, the city official got out of his car and walked back to ours. He didn't say anything to Mary Lou or to me. Instead, he walked directly to Terry and said, "I've just got to ask who you are." I'm telling you, Terry was good-looking enough to stop a parade.

Being a gold medalist afforded me the opportunity to meet other great athletes, such as gymnast Peter Vidmar and track star Edwin Moses. I also met then–New York City mayor Ed Koch.

My biggest thrill, however, came when President Reagan and his wife, Nancy, met with medalists at the Beverly Hills Hilton.

Bob DeProspero, a member of the Secret Service, had a son, Bobby, who had been a wrestler at Oklahoma while Dave and I were there. Mr. DeProspero was the head of security under Reagan, and when the athletes were lining up to meet the Reagans, Mr. DeProspero spotted Dave and me in the middle of the line and

CHAPTER 10

Erasing the Asterisk

I didn't get into wrestling to win medals.

Dan Gable once said, "Gold medals aren't really made of gold. They're made of sweat, determination, and a hard-to-find alloy called guts." Wrestling is not fun. I've heard countless wrestlers through the years talk about how much they enjoy the sport. Not me. I never felt that way when I wrestled. My philosophy was that if I was having fun, I wasn't working hard enough.

For me, the sport provided the way for me to become a great fighter. I wanted to fight and defeat the best wrestlers in the world, and the medals served as proof that I was becoming the person I wanted to be.

The status that comes from earning an Olympic gold medal is unparalleled in wrestling, although the other medalists and I in '84 had to deal with questions about the merits of our accomplishments. Sometimes the questions appeared to be a deliberate attempt to take some of the shine off our medals.

In wrestling, the United States won its first four Olympic medals ever in Greco-Roman. In freestyle, we won seven of the ten gold medals plus two silvers. The seven golds tied the record for most wrestling gold medalists from one country in a modern Olympics.

When Dan was asked about the boycott's effect, he claimed that we still would have won at least four weight classes if the Soviets and Bulgarians hadn't stayed home. No doubt, we had a strong team that year. It's just that we didn't have an opportunity to prove how strong. I've often been asked how we would have fared against a full field at those Games, and I still struggle to come up with a good answer. I don't really know how it would have turned out if the Russians and Bulgarians had participated, and we'll never know.

I do know, though, that the boycotted Olympics resulted in a brighter spotlight than normal shining on the next World Championships because all the top wrestlers would be there.

Before that came the '85 World Cup in Toledo, Ohio, which had been billed as featuring the best teams from each continent, except that South America was not represented. I beat Chris Rinke 10–0 in advancing to the finals against Vladimir Modosyan, a four-time Tbilisi champion. Modosyan was the toughest opponent I ever wrestled against. And the hairiest. His body was covered with so much hair that I called him "Hairy Guy."

Modosyan beat me 9–1. Dave won his finals match, but the Soviets defeated us 7–3 for the team championship.

I received a plaque for placing second to Modosyan. Leaving the University of Toledo's Centennial Hall, I held the plaque in my hand like a discus, spun once, and heaved it into the Ottawa River. I was wrestling with the Sunkist Kids club at the time, and the next week, club president Art Martori called and asked if I wanted a rematch with Modosyan. We met again during a dual in a mostly empty high school gym near Chicago, and I beat him 8–1.

The year 1985 was the best of my career. The loss to Modosyan was my only one that year.

Here, at the 1982 NCAA championships in Ames, Iowa, I'm going through my pre-match routine before defeating Ed Banach to win the second of my three collegiate national championships. I was named Outstanding Wrestler at that year's meet.

Mark Schultz

Mark Schultz

With Dave, left, overlooking Stanford University, where we worked together as assistant coaches after completing our college careers.

Steve Brown

Performing my backflip at the 1984 Summer Olympics after winning the gold-medal match by technical superiority over Japan's Hideyuki Nagashima.

AP

I didn't know what to feel, other than relief, after receiving my Olympic gold medal.

Dave and I were the first US brothers to win wrestling gold medals in the Olympics—by only a few minutes. We later became the only brothers in US wrestling history to each win World and Olympic championships.

Winning Olympic medals gave Dave and me the opportunity to meet President Ronald Reagan and his wife, Nancy. This photo was taken before I accidentally kissed Mrs. Reagan on the lips!

John du Pont had this poster made of me after I won the 1987 World Championship as a member of Team Foxcatcher. John wanted to use my name and my championship to promote his team.

John du Pont in the trophy room of the mansion on the Foxcatcher estate. After his mother passed away, John had his awards placed in more prominent positions than his mother's. But most of the trophies in the room came from his mother's breeding of Welsh ponies and championship beagles for competition.

Mark Schultz

My brother, my coach, and my friend. That easy smile of Dave's made him popular all around the world.

AP

Dave in a lighter moment with John du Pont inside the state-of-the-art Foxcatcher National Training Center that John paid to have built on his property.

An aerial view of John du Pont's mansion in Newtown Square, Pennsylvania. Imagine going through the financial struggles I faced while trying to continue my wrestling career and seeing this home from a helicopter when I flew in to interview with John for the Villanova job.

John du Pont steps out of a police van after murdering Dave and being arrested at the conclusion of his forty-eight-hour standoff at his mansion.

Du Pont after being declared unfit to stand trial.

Defeating Gary "Big Daddy" Goodridge at UFC IX in 1996 provided the career-ending victory that had been missing since the disheartening end to my wrestling career at the 1988 Olympics.

This is what a fifty-three-year-old Olympic wrestling champion looks like. Do I look like I'm still ready to go?

I did come close to losing in an unusual situation at the US Open after my luggage got lost by the airline. Bobby Douglas, the Sunkist Kids coach whose book on takedowns I had memorized as a high school wrestler, gave me two options: wait for my gear, which I needed to cut weight in order to compete at 180.5 pounds, or take the twenty bucks he was offering me, go eat, and wrestle up a weight at 198. I didn't know if my luggage would show up in time, so I opted to wrestle up even though I weighed 187.

My opponent in the finals was Bill Scherr, the runner-up the year before. I led Bill 4–2 with about thirty seconds remaining when I attempted a fireman's carry. It was a stupid move to try at that point in the match, and he made me pay for my mistake, catching my arm and throwing me on my back to tie the score. Bill would have won on a criteria tiebreaker, so with fifteen seconds on the clock, I hit every move I could think of. As we were going out of bounds with five or six seconds left, I spun behind him for the winning point.

The much-anticipated World Championships, with every nation that boycotted the '84 Olympics competing, were held October 1985 in Budapest, Hungary. I had been hearing for more than a year how we weren't real Olympic champions because of the boycott. There was no special designation in the official list of champions to denote the boycott, but there were plenty of critics who had mentally placed asterisks beside some of our names. Mine included.

During the eleven-hour trip overseas, I prayed the plane would crash so I wouldn't have to deal with the pressure. I prayed that more times than I care to admit on the way to big competitions.

I had doubts about my ability to win in Hungary. I knew I was good enough and had solved the inconsistency that had been a concern leading up to the Olympics, but wrestling was so violent and there was so much pressure. Good wrestlers choked all the time, it seemed, and in my mind I could put together a list of wrestlers who had lost when they shouldn't have. It was one of those scenarios where, going in, I hoped for the best and prepared for the worst.

Sometimes you do get what you hope for.

I defeated Bulgarian Alexander Nanev, a three-time runner-up in the World Championships, 10–5 in the finals. Earlier, I had beaten a Soviet, Aleksandr Tambovtsev, 1–0. With victories against the best wrestlers from the two best teams not to compete in Los Angeles, my Olympic gold medal shined brighter than ever.

I was one of two Americans to win in Hungary, with Scherr taking the 198 title. Dave was one of two Americans to place second, but his World Championship in '83 and mine that year made us the only '84 Olympic gold-medal winners to also be world champs. In addition, Dave and I became the only US brothers to win world and Olympic titles—a feat accomplished only by two other Soviet brother combinations.

Winning the '85 world title silenced the critics who had been saying I was not good enough to win at an Olympics with the Russians and Bulgarians. It partially silenced the critic within me, too.

I was on a real high when Dave and I returned from Hungary to our jobs at Stanford. My first day back in the Stanford wrestling room, the entire team clapped and cheered for me. Finally, Chris

Horpel could no longer remind me that my brother was a world champ and I wasn't.

That first day, Chris called me into his office. He didn't congratulate me on my new title. He didn't apologize for treating me as lesser than Dave. He didn't promote me or give me a raise from my ten-thousand-dollar-a-year salary after two years of working for him.

He fired me.

There went the great day I was enjoying.

I sat there stunned. Confused. *Pissed*.

Was Chris jealous? Was he trying to prove his authority over me? I didn't know.

I didn't know what to say other than, "Okay, fine."

"You can work out here," he told me, "but I can't pay you."

I got out of my chair and turned to leave his office. As I reached his door, he added, "Oh, yeah, I'm going to need the keys to the car back."

Brad Hightower was one of the Stanford wrestlers I had taken under my wing. His dad owned a car dealership and wanted to express his appreciation by giving me a badly needed Toyota Tercel. In order to write the car off, though, he had to donate it to a charity and officially designated the car as a gift to the Stanford wrestling program. The car wasn't legally mine, but it was given for me to use.

Chris gave the car to Dave's wife. She wasn't a Stanford employee, but he gave the keys to Dave to give to Nancy. That created a weird dynamic because Dave, Nancy, and I were renting rooms in our dad's home. We were all under the same roof, and I had to look out the windows every day and see Dave's wife getting in and out of "my" car.

That sucked.

The only reason Horpel gave me for firing me was that he couldn't afford me. I wasn't a yes-man. Dave wasn't, either, but he had the ability, which I never developed, to express himself while staying within the lines. Maybe that was a factor. I don't know. But after I was let go, Horpel gave my salary to Dave, doubling his pay to twenty thousand dollars per year. So much for the affordability reason.

Dave got my money, and his wife got my car.

I felt betrayed by my own brother. I never asked him about it, but he had to have known I was going to get fired. That's not the kind of thing that happens without someone in Dave's position being made aware of the plans. Dave must have consented to my being fired, even if reluctantly. But for a decision that major, how could he have kept it from his brother?

Our situations were different. Dave had a wife and son, Alexander, by that point. He needed more money than I did, and I was pretty desperate for money. USA Wrestling sure wasn't helping us.

My firing cut one of the cords between Dave and me. It stung badly. I thought he and Horpel were against me. I felt isolated and alone. I got real serious and became sensitive and oppositional to everyone around me. Anyone who had an opinion to share with me didn't need to waste his time, because I didn't care.

Dave and I continued to practice against each other in the room, and I got cutthroat with him. I was ready to fight him every time we stepped onto the mat. I targeted his crotch. That's the opponent's center of gravity and a man's most vulnerable area. Once I started attacking his crotch, I began taking Dave down at will.

Horpel seemed surprised at how easily I was taking Dave down. Going after Dave's crotch made me a better wrestler because in attacking the crotch I realized how I was getting my hips directly under his center of gravity instead of off to one side. That gave me an awareness regarding my center of gravity that I put to use against everyone I wrestled after that.

Despite everything that happened with my firing, I still loved Dave. He still was my brother, and nothing was going to come between us. I couldn't forget all he had done in helping me develop into the man I had become. But my getting fired, and assuming Dave at least knew what was happening, changed me. I became more independent from Dave. I quit looking to him to be my leader.

To replace my lost income, I took time off from training to put together a bunch of wrestling clinics. I had a directory of high school wrestling coaches, and I would pick out a particular area and call coaches in that area to book clinics. Luckily, I was one of only two reigning World Champions in the United States. Wrestlers may not have received much publicity outside of Olympic years, but inside our sport, my name meant something. I could tell as soon as I identified myself if a coach would invite me to put on a clinic based on how he reacted to my name.

I needed a car, though, to drive to my clinics and contacted Brad Hightower's father. He sold me a light blue 1982 Camaro Berlinetta (with a cruise control that didn't work well) for seven thousand dollars. That wiped out my savings. My "Victory Tour"— that's what I called my clinics—and my Berlinetta took me to different parts of the country.

The clinics brought in twenty-four thousand dollars in three months. It would have taken me more than two years to make that much at Stanford. But putting on clinics was hard. The travel became a grind. More important, the 1986 US Open and World trials were coming up, and I needed a stable training environment to begin preparing for those.

I started looking for coaching jobs, and Marlin Grahn offered me a position at Portland State University. Marlin had defeated me at the 1979 Far West Open, while I was at UCLA, and we became friends for life. Marlin said he could pay me fifteen thousand dollars. But there weren't many good workout partners there, and I turned down his offer.

Chris Horpel did wonderful things for me. His help while I was in high school was instrumental in my becoming a successful wrestler. But his firing me at Stanford felt like a betrayal. He has made attempts to discuss it since, but I haven't wanted to talk to him about it. He knows what he did, and I don't see any need to relive it.

There hasn't been anyone in my life who has helped me *and* hurt me as much as Chris did.

I won the 1986 US Open, defeating Mike Sheets 8–6 with four gut wrenches in the finals. Sheets had won at 180.5 the previous year when I wrestled up a weight. After the tournament, my frustration over having to compete while living in near poverty boiled over. I found Gary Kurdelmeier, USA Wrestling's executive director, and got in his face.

"You need to change the meaning of the word *amateur* so we can make money and keep our amateur status like other sports," I told him. We would watch athletes in other sports receive media attention and secure endorsement deals because their sports promoted and marketed them. Their sports not only allowed them to make money off their success and retain their amateur status to compete in the Olympics, but they also put them in position to do so. Those other sports seemed to genuinely care about their athletes.

"No one can stop you," I told Kurdelmeier. "You are a monopoly in the US."

Kurdelmeier disagreed, and I was close to doing something that would have gotten me in trouble when my former OU teammate Dan Chaid grabbed me and dragged me away.

I was sick of it. Some athletes decided to cash in after they won an Olympic gold medal. That's not a criticism. They could choose their path, and more power to them. For my part, I wanted to keep competing.

They gave some wrestlers small stipends that didn't come remotely close to covering financial needs. They were more like a small amount for administrators to give up in exchange for being able to say they were helping us financially. With as little as they were sending us, they could not claim they were doing *all* they could to help us financially.

I couldn't tell you what kind of money USA Wrestling brought in, but I do know that they were hosting hundreds of tournaments each year and made a lot of money off entry fees. And before you could enter a tournament, you had to purchase a twenty-five-dollar membership card. But little of what USA Wrestling made went to the wrestlers. I remember that in 1983, when I placed seventh at the World Championships, US wrestlers who placed in the top seven received $1,500. Dave won the World Championship that year, and I think he received $5,000. I don't know if the money came from an Olympic development fund, from USA Wrestling, or from the United States Olympic Committee through USA Wrestling. My $1,500 didn't make much of a dent in my living expenses. Whatever USA Wrestling brought in, it seemed like barely any of it went to the wrestlers and it certainly didn't help my financial situation.

We had to train year-round to be competitive on the international stage, while teams like the Russians were fully financially supported by their government. We were competing against, essentially, "professional amateurs." Yet there were not many decent-paying jobs that could give us the flexible schedule we needed. It was either make a living or keep competing. Doing both was not an option.

That's why so many of us took low-paying jobs as assistant coaches in colleges. Others took volunteer coaching positions so they could at least train and then found some other way to get by. It felt like when we did manage to win, despite USA Wrestling's lack of support, the administrators showed up to take credit for whatever they could and then they went back to their comfortable lives while we went back to our low-paying jobs and small apartments.

After Nationals, I returned to Palo Alto to begin training for the '86 Worlds. That's when I met a guy who wanted to be my manager. He invited me to visit with him, and he had the largest office in the largest building in Palo Alto. I told him how I was trying to promote myself and make more money so I could continue competing.

"That's what I do," he told me. "You ought to let me do it for you."

He said he was worth millions and would promote me for 50 percent of everything he made for me.

I figured it was worth a shot. I needed money, and although 50 percent was a big cut, I was willing to give up half of whatever someone else could bring in for me because I didn't think I could bring in anything for myself. I didn't have time to try to market and promote myself while training. I had to keep winning to be marketable, but I couldn't make myself marketable and continue winning. I needed someone to manage me, and I didn't have anybody who could. Plus, if the guy didn't make any money for me, I figured, half of zero was zero.

The guy turned out to be a crook. He didn't bring in one penny for me, but he wanted money from me anyway. When I told him I was done with him, he said I owed him 50 percent of what I had made from my clinics, even though he had done absolutely no work related to them. When I told him what I thought of his demand, he threatened to sue me. I had to pay for a lawyer so I wouldn't have to give that bum anything. Hiring a lawyer didn't help my finances any.

I was wrestling great, at a real high point in my career with Olympic and World championships in successive years. But being fired had not only left me feeling insulted, it had also thrown me into financial desperation. I lost my health insurance when I lost my job. I was used to wrestling without insurance, but I had never liked it. Without income, I was one freak injury in a violent sport from being wiped out financially.

USA Wrestling was not supporting me. There was no athlete residency program, as there is now, that would allow me to live and train at the Olympic Training Center in Colorado Springs. My only option was to train at Stanford and live off the money I'd made doing the clinics. But dealing legally with my "manager" had cut into my savings, and I didn't know how much longer I could go without finding some source of income.

I was looking for anything I could do to remove some of the financial pressure so I could train undistracted. My desperation made me an easy target.

PART TWO

Destroying a Champion

CHAPTER 11

Just "Coach"

There wasn't much privacy in the apartment I rented in my dad's house. My apartment on the second floor was more like a hallway. There were stairs at the back of house, but it was easier for Dave, Nancy, and whoever was renting out the third upstairs room at the time to go back and forth from downstairs and their apartments by walking through my room than to use the stairs and walk outside around to the front.

Sharing upstairs with others and having them passing through my apartment made getting good sleep difficult. But rent was high in the Palo Alto area, and Dad gave us a break on the rent even though I didn't want charity. I tried twice to have a roommate to split rent with me, but that took away even more of the little privacy I did have. Without a roommate, most of my low salary went to paying my rent of $550 a month and taxes, leaving not much money for food. As much as I loved being in the same house as my dad and Dave, my living conditions were uncomfortable.

Between the US Open and the World Team Trials, I was in my apartment waiting for practice when I received a phone call from someone identifying himself as a chief surgeon for something at Stanford University Medical Center. He told me that I would be receiving a phone call from a man named John du Pont. He told me that du Pont was a bigwig heavy hitter, and he wanted to vouch for du Pont before we talked.

I had never heard of this du Pont guy before and the doctor didn't give me a hint what he wanted with me.

I was curious why the guy had called and why a chief surgeon would need to vouch for du Pont. I wondered if something was wrong or off with du Pont. What made the call stranger was that the surgeon didn't come across as comfortable calling me. But I figured, *What the hell? I don't have anything else going for me.*

Later that afternoon, du Pont called and introduced himself as starting an NCAA Division I wrestling program from scratch at Villanova University outside Philadelphia, and he wanted to talk to me about coming there as an assistant coach.

"How much would it take to bring you here?" he asked.

The figure $24,000 was in my head. If I had known then what I would soon learn about du Pont, I would have said $300,000, and he probably would have said okay. But $24,000 would have been more than Dave was making at Stanford even after having my salary added to his, and I wasn't looking for anything more than an average assistant's job in a stable environment. So that was the amount I gave du Pont.

Du Pont said he would get back to me.

It turned out that du Pont had first called Dave. Dave had that reputation as one of the greatest technicians and greatest wrestlers in the world, and he was well-liked. Dave knew how to be true to himself while still saying and doing the right things that would help him climb the ladder of USA Wrestling. Dave had the ability to be honest while not offending the powers that be. When Dave spoke, even if he was offering criticism, his sincerity couldn't be questioned.

Unlike me, with my preference to stay alone and not share my secrets, Dave gave his time to everybody. If kids asked him to show them moves, he would. I would spend time with kids, too, and show them basic moves, but Dave was better at all that than me. Plus, because he had been wrestling longer, he had more moves to share. In my mind, I hadn't stockpiled enough moves to be giving any away.

Because of Dave's friendliness and willingness to share, he became highly thought of throughout the wrestling community in the United States and around the world. He enjoyed volunteering his time to speak to school classes, especially his kids', about his Olympic experiences. He thought nothing of giving his medals and trophies to family members and friends as gifts. When other wrestlers asked Dave to show them some of his moves, he gladly and unselfishly taught them. Dave loved people and gave of his time freely, and time is the most valuable thing we have to give others. Overseas, learning to speak Russian had earned Dave the respect of Russian wrestlers and endeared him to Russian fans. Dave was probably more recognized and appreciated in Europe than in our country.

Dave's name came to du Pont's mind when he decided to build a program at Villanova. But Dave had just accepted his raise from my salary and that pretty well locked him in at Stanford for at least the next year. Dave gave du Pont my name, though.

After our first conversation, du Pont called the next day and said he could pay me the salary I had requested.

I wanted more information from him, though. Schools were eliminating wrestling programs, not adding them.

Du Pont was vague in his answers, causing me to determine

he didn't know everything he needed to know to start a program. But nothing he said surprised me or made me think he had a questionable motive.

I wanted to get more of a feel for du Pont, though, and had him call me over the next few days so I could try to get a better gauge on him.

As I learned that he was a big-hitting millionaire, I liked the idea that someone with that kind of money was coming into the sport. Art Martori had started the Sunkist Kids Wrestling Club, and I had wrestled for him, but Art had mostly paid for expenses for his wrestlers to compete. His club provided little backing for actual training and living costs. Based on what du Pont led me to believe, although speaking mostly in vague terms, I thought he was going to become the first multijillionaire who would come into the sport with a commitment to compete at the highest level regardless of cost.

Over our next couple of phone conversations, though, I got a feeling that he was hiding something. He didn't seem forthcoming with information, and I could not figure out why. That made me cautious, but again, nothing came up in our talks that was a red flag on the guy.

In fact, the more we talked, the more I got the sense that he increasingly liked the idea of my coaching at Villanova. However, I wasn't becoming more and more interested in going to Villanova. I kept having this thought that there was something a little off about du Pont, but I couldn't quite identify it over the phone.

But still, he had money—lots and lots and lots of money—and seemed seriously interested in wrestling. With du Pont's financial backing, I thought Villanova was on the verge of building the next

East Coast college wrestling dynasty. And if I could make more than twice the money I had made at Stanford while being able to train in a stable environment, then du Pont's money could provide the means for me to accomplish what I wanted in my wrestling career. I told him we could meet two weeks later at the World Team Trials in Indiana if he wanted. He said he would meet me there.

To cut weight for the trials, I was running around the University of Indiana track when another wrestler, Rob Calabrese, caught up to me. Rob lived in Media, Pennsylvania, about ten miles from du Pont's estate. I asked Rob what he thought about du Pont and Villanova starting a program, and he called it "an unbelievable situation" and "an incredible opportunity."

A guy named Chuck Yarnall, a young wrestling coach at the private school du Pont had attended near Philadelphia, took me to meet du Pont at his hotel. Walking toward du Pont's room, I was expecting that I would be able to get a quick read on him once I saw him in person. As long as he wasn't too much of a loser, I assumed, I would be fine.

When Yarnall opened the door, I stared at a loser. Du Pont, in his late forties, was sitting in a chair, looking like Richie Rich all grown up and hooked on drugs. My gut reaction was a feeling of revulsion. Du Pont looked like a spoiled rich kid. I had lived with delayed gratification for so long that it was revolting to see the personification of the opposite of everything I was and believed to be true. I could tell right away that du Pont and I weren't just different from each other; we were complete opposites.

Du Pont's hair was the first thing I noticed about him physically. It looked as if he had borrowed Ronald McDonald's bottle of hair color to dye his hair but hadn't maintained it. Gray roots extended about an inch from his scalp before the bright red took over. His hair was parted in the middle and dandruff was plastered on his head along the part. Not regular dandruff, but thick, thick dandruff. It looked as though he hadn't washed his hair in months.

He was wearing a T-shirt and shorts, and he had one leg wrapped or in a cast from what I think was a knee surgery, with a black sock and a tennis shoe on the other foot. Thick varicose veins popped out from his bare leg. I wondered why a millionaire hadn't had those taken care of. If I'd had his money, I would have looked like Mark Harmon. (Remember, this was 1986.) Du Pont was thin, with twigs for arms. But his belly looked as if he had swallowed a basketball.

Then when we were introduced and he smiled, du Pont's teeth were dark yellow and caked with food. I wanted to ask him if he had looked in a mirror recently.

Some kind of drink sat on the table next to him, and when he started to talk, he obviously was either drunk or stoned off his ass. He babbled in a slurred voice. I had trouble making out what he was saying, except when he called me "pal." Over and over. As he kept talking, he would interrupt himself to ask, "You understand what I'm saying?" I didn't.

I was correct—I was able to get a quick read on du Pont, and I could not have walked into that room and met a bigger loser if I had designed one based on the worst characteristics of the worst people I'd met. I had met and been around quirky people before, but none like du Pont. The guy didn't even attempt to look clean and sober to meet me. Du Pont's appearance and actions were, simply, odd. He seemed harmless but seriously, seriously off.

I knew right then and there that the one question I needed to get answered would be how involved he would be in Villanova's program. If he was going to fund the program and I wouldn't have to see him or talk to him, no problem. But if he was going to be anywhere near the wrestling room, this job interview was done.

"What will your position be at Villanova?" I asked.

His answer wasn't very specific. He said he might come into the office every once in a while to see how things were going or if we needed anything, but other than that he was going to be referred to in the media guide as simply "Coach." Not "Head Coach," not "Assistant Coach." Just "Coach."

My gut was telling me to walk away. But the potential benefits seemed great. And what risk was there? If for whatever reason Villanova didn't work out, I could just walk away. I didn't have any better options at the time, that was for sure.

I should have trusted my gut. Or had du Pont write on a signed sheet of paper what his role would be. Instead, I told him I was interested and would talk with him again after the trials.

I defeated two-time NCAA champion Mike Sheets in two straight matches to make the '86 World Team. With a few weeks until the World Championships, I made arrangements to travel to Philadelphia for a firsthand look at the Villanova job.

John's helicopter pilot, a Vietnam veteran named Larry Shemley, met me at the airport. Waiting for my baggage to drop onto the carousel, Larry and I had a pleasant conversation. I liked Larry, and with his being a vet, he had my immediate respect. I asked Larry about the program du Pont was creating.

"I think you'll like it," Larry said.

Larry gave me an aerial tour of historical sites like Valley Forge and Gettysburg. If the tour was designed to impress the hell out of me, it worked.

I had no knowledge of the estate where du Pont lived. We were flying in the helicopter over the city of Philadelphia with all these houses snapped snugly together. Then everything opened up into what looked like a national park. Right in the middle was the mansion that was the centerpiece of the estate, with several other buildings on the estate that turned out to be other homes.

The mansion looked as if it had three stories, because the basement level was visible from ground level and the entrance to the first floor stood at the top of about twenty stairs or so. The landscaping was immaculate, thanks, I later learned, to a team of landscapers who worked around the clock to maintain the property.

If he lives here, I thought as Larry lowered us toward the helipad, *we can do anything we want at Villanova. We can dominate the NCAAs in five years.*

My optimism and energy were off the charts. I had finally found the brass ring!

John met me outside and took me over to Villanova. The wrestling room was in the Butler Annex, and the space was larger than any I had ever seen for a wrestling team. John said we would have to share it with the baseball team initially, but that it would soon be exclusively ours. He had it all planned out, with offices overlooking the mats. One of the offices would be mine. At Stanford, I not only didn't have an office, I also didn't have a desk or a phone.

"How long until the room is ours?" I asked.

Du Pont responded with another vague answer, then added

that because he had donated a bunch of money to the school, it probably would happen before the season started or soon thereafter. I took that to mean October or November.

That was the year after Villanova's men's basketball team, coached by Rollie Massimino, had stunned Georgetown in the finals to win the 1985 NCAA National Championship. Du Pont walked me over to the basketball arena, named John E. du Pont Pavilion. His name was in big letters on the front of the building. Then we stopped by the school's swimming complex, which was also named for him.

Holy crap, I thought. *This guy must have more money than God.*

Compared to two buildings bearing his name, giving the old annex to the wrestling program seemed like nothing. John made it sound like having a wrestling-only space was merely an administrative detail awaiting final approval.

The job had tremendous potential. Du Pont was willing to pay me what I considered good money for an assistant wrestling coach. He said he'd pretty much stay out of the way. And, having competed uninsured in the Olympics and World Championships, I would have health insurance again. I also could recruit my own workout partners. Although I wouldn't be with Dave, I could round up some tough guys to make me a better wrestler.

I accepted the job despite a foreboding sense that many things about the job and du Pont were not as they appeared.

After I informed Dave that I was leaving Palo Alto for Villanova, he decided to also leave to become an assistant at the University of Wisconsin-Madison. I didn't ask Dave why he was leaving; he had appeared to have it made at Stanford. He had twice the salary he'd had before, with cheap rent at Dad's place; he and Nancy had the free Tercel; and Stanford provided him with health insurance.

Maybe he was mad at Horpel for firing me. Maybe he was leaving as an act of loyalty to me. Maybe without me there to push him as a workout partner, there was no reason to stay. Wisconsin had a strong team with more-than-competent partners.

Whatever the reason for Dave leaving, David Lee followed him to Wisconsin. Lee was Stanford's best wrestler and had come to Palo Alto because of Dave. I entered the wrestling office to catch the end of a heated exchange between Dave and Horpel over Lee's following Dave.

Chris said the best thing for Lee would be to remain at Stanford.

"No, it isn't," a calm but defiant Dave countered.

That was good enough for me. I walked out on the first time I had seen Dave and Chris get into it like that.

I loved it!

The '86 World Championships were a nightmare. Between getting fired by Horpel, my financial problems, the manager/crook who tried to rip me off, and the job search, I had been through a ton of distractions over the past year. It all caught up with me there in Budapest.

I lost my first match to some lousy Hungarian. It was his only victory in the tournament. I came back and kept winning, though, to advance to the semifinals, where I would meet Alexander Nanev, the Bulgarian I had defeated in the finals the previous year.

The 1986 tournament was the only year FILA turned the scoreboard away from wrestlers and more toward the crowd. FILA's goal was to prevent wrestlers from stalling late in matches. If wrestlers couldn't see the score, FILA's theory held, they would wrestle hard all the way through matches. FILA went back to the previous way because wrestlers delayed matches by stepping out of bounds and taking the long route back to the center of the mat so they could read the scoreboard.

The scoreboard was still visible from the mat, but only from a certain place and at a certain angle.

I was trailing Nanev by one point with time running out. I shot several times and finally got the takedown. Then I gut-wrenched him. As I was getting up to my feet, I tried to catch a glimpse of the score. I couldn't see it. So I looked to my corner for some kind of signal from my coaches.

J. Robinson, our head coach, yelled, "Go! Go! Go!"

Shit! I'm behind!

I took a lousy, desperate shot with ten seconds left. There was nothing there to grab. Nanev took me down to—I didn't realize this when it happened—tie the score 4–4. I lost on a criteria tie-breaker.

An hour later, I was sitting, dejected, in the hotel lobby and Bruce Baumgartner, our heavyweight, came over to talk to me.

"Why did you shoot?" Bruce asked.

"Because I was losing."

"No, you weren't," Bruce said.

I returned to Palo Alto angry, not only over losing at Worlds but also because of how I had lost. Knowing I was about to leave home didn't brighten my mood any. I hated having to move away

from my dad, and Philadelphia was all the way on the other side
of the country.

I was still in shock about being forced out. My parents had
both graduated from Stanford. My grandfather taught at Stanford,
and my grandmother worked there as a doctor. I had been born at
Stanford's hospital. When I had left Oklahoma for Palo Alto, I felt
as if I had finally made it home again. But because Horpel had
fired me, I was having to head cross-country to the East Coast. Just
like when I'd had to leave Palo Alto to move to Oregon, I felt as if
I was being kicked out of my home.

I wanted to get in one last workout in the Stanford wrestling
room, and it had to be with Dave. I think it was the best I ever
wrestled him. Dave had to have known how bad I felt about moving away. At the end of our workout, he was using me to drill some
headlocks. He stopped and looked directly into my eyes.

"I haven't told you that I love you in a long time," he said. "I do."

Then he kissed me on the cheek.

CHAPTER 12

A Man and His Program in Disarray

John du Pont was the richest man I've ever met. And the most miserable. There are some things in life you just can't buy, but John du Pont tried anyway. I would soon learn that he wasn't just difficult or strange—he was manipulative in a way I'd never experienced before. His money allowed him to have a power over people that was anything but healthy.

He believed that everyone had a price, and he wanted to see what each person's price was.

That was a fact I'd see in action almost immediately.

I paid about eight hundred dollars per month to rent a one-bedroom apartment in a middle-class, blue-collar neighborhood three miles from the Villanova campus. I had a couch and a lounge chair in the living room and a desk in my bedroom. The coin-operated washer and dryer were in the same building, and all in all, I had a pretty good setup in a clean apartment complex.

But compared to the chalet that du Pont lived in on the estate, it was like taking up residence in a cramped utility room.

Shortly after I had moved to Villanova, du Pont called me at my apartment and asked me to come over to the chalet. His home was state-of-the-art, capable of being locked down like a fortress with steel blinds that rolled down over the windows. Those blinds closed so tightly that rooms would go pitch-dark when they were rolled down even in the middle of a bright, sunny day. Stepping down from the foyer into the living room, the first thing that caught my eye was a white fur, like a polar bear's, draped over the couch. Among the pictures on the living room walls was one of du Pont shaking hands with President Gerald Ford.

A few people were in the living room when I walked in, including two guys who were some kind of Washington, DC, dignitaries or advisors or fund-raisers. They might even have been John's "fixers," who were brought in when John faced legal problems. I didn't care enough to find out. Another guy was Bob, who John later told me was an event organizer. John liked to host awards ceremonies for himself, complete with awards he paid to have made at a local trophy shop, and it must have been Bob's job to organize those events. A secretary to John, named Victor, was also there.

Du Pont was more drunk off his ass than usual, and I could tell by the expression on those men's faces that John had been running them through the wringer. He had the ability to suck the life out of people.

The guy from Washington spotted me after I walked in and said, "Oh, thank God you're here." I think he was hoping I was there to relieve him of his duties of having to babysit John.

I walked over to the fireplace along the right wall and turned around to notice almost all of the eyes in the room were on me, like I was supposed to do something. I was standing there trying to figure out what was going on when du Pont said to me across the room, "Thank God you're here, *pal!*" Whenever he called me "pal," I wasn't sure how to take it because he would say it in a weird, sarcastic, half-friendly, half-accusatory way.

Du Pont started crawling on his hands and knees across the floor toward me, and when he reached my feet, he grabbed me around the waist as though he wanted to wrestle. Then he began clawing his way up my body. I don't recall seeing du Pont drunker than he was that night. The other people in the room knew how he was, but they seemed to be in disbelief that this so-called member of American royalty had stooped to this level of behavior. I grabbed him, pushed him off me, and headed directly toward the door as the two guys from Washington begged me to stay longer.

I thanked God, too, when I had made it outside. *Thank God he's not at Villanova and I won't have to deal with him very much.*

"Get it in writing." That's the lesson I learned from working for du Pont at Villanova.

The first few weeks, John was true to his word and stayed away, not coming into our offices at all. Chuck Yarnall, the high school coach who had introduced me to du Pont at the Indiana hotel, was our head coach. We didn't have the Butler Annex to ourselves yet, but that day was coming.

Or so we were led to believe.

It wasn't too long before du Pont started dropping by the office. He was always drunk or on drugs, or both, spitting as he spoke. When he talked to me, I tried to keep enough distance between us so that his spit wouldn't land on me.

He once came and plopped down in my office, and said, "I'm really craving blueberries right now."

Seriously? I'm trying to get stuff done before practice and he's interrupting me because he's craving blueberries?

"If I had a basket of blueberries right now, I would eat them all up. Yum, yum, yum!"

What is he doing here?

"You understand what I'm saying?"

Even when I understand what he's saying, I don't understand what he's saying.

He was always asking, "You understand what I'm saying?" That must have been his way of forcing people to acknowledge him.

Within a couple of months, du Pont was there every day. Always on something. Always wasting my time with his endless talking, interfering with what I needed to do with Chuck to get our program up and running the way we wanted.

As John sat in my office and talked about nothing, I'd be thinking, *Why did you bring me here? I thought you wanted me to coach, and now I can't because of the amount of my time you waste.*

He didn't need an assistant wrestling coach to listen to him talk; he needed to be spending his time with a psychiatrist.

There was no structure to the job, and as far as I could tell, John answered to no one on campus. The money he had donated plus the rest he had pledged for the athletic facilities seemed to keep Villanova's president quiet. I never saw anything that indicated the athletic director was doing anything more than looking the other way.

Du Pont may have been listed as a generic "Coach," but it was John's program. Chuck was the most powerless head coach in NCAA Division I, regardless of sport.

John did whatever he wanted, and I answered to him and only him.

The idea that Villanova would provide the stability I needed quickly evaporated. In fact, that place became the epitome of instability.

When John was in the office, whatever he wanted me to do was my job description for the day. Instead of actually doing work, he would delegate authority, usually to the person who got stuck listening to his alcohol- and drug-induced chatter.

You understand what I'm saying?

Chuck might be in charge one day and me the next. Deciding who was in charge for that day, or for that hour, was John's way of displaying his power.

A local television station came out to do a story on Villanova's new wrestling team and focused on John's role. There was one scene of John swimming in the swimming complex named for him. He got out of the pool, soaking wet, and the camera followed him into the John E. du Pont Pavilion, where right in the middle of men's basketball practice, he walked up to Coach Massimino, grabbed a basketball out of the coach's hands, and started talking into the camera as water dripped off him onto the court. John was showing everyone how much access he had at Villanova and how he could do whatever he wanted.

We didn't have much of a team to begin with. It's difficult enough to start a program with all-new wrestlers anyway. But John and Chuck couldn't attract good wrestlers. We basically started off with a nothing team. John and Chuck had resorted to walking around campus looking for guys wearing high school wrestling T-shirts. If he had wrestled in high school, he could have a spot on the team.

After a few weeks Chuck said to me, "John said to tell you that you're in charge of recruiting from now on."

That pissed me off because I was just getting into the part of the year when I would ramp up my training for the 1987 World Championships, and now I was having the extremely time-consuming and difficult role of recruiting dumped on me.

I sold my wrestling credentials to recruits. Du Pont certainly didn't have the look or personality to talk them into coming without flaunting his money, but I had my Olympic gold medal and World Championship to tout. It didn't take long to learn the recruits were looking for coaches they could count on. But I didn't have any authority. I figured out that if I didn't say I was planning to stay at Villanova for five years, the recruits would scratch us off their list of possible schools. Five more years? Forget it. If not for the upcoming '87 Worlds, I would already have quit.

By the spring, we still didn't have the Butler Annex to ourselves. Wrestling requires a wrestling room. You can't have a legitimate Division I program without your own room.

We had to roll out the mats every day before practice and then roll them up after practice. It took us half an hour to roll them out and tape them down, then another half hour to put the mats away. At first, I was involved in that process every day. That was cutting into the coaching work I needed to be doing, so we hired some of our wrestlers as a mat crew and paid them to take care of the mats.

It takes a while for mats to flatten out when you're having to roll them out every day, so we had to deal with ripples in our mats. We would be preparing our guys for the next dual and one of them would trip over a ripple. That was so small-time.

I kept asking du Pont when we were going to have our own room.

"Soon," he'd say, and that was as specific as he would get.

After about three months of that crap, we started taking our wrestlers to John's estate to work out. He had converted his indoor pistol range into a wrestling room. However, shooting ranges need to have a really low ceiling so bullets don't ricochet. We didn't have to roll the mats up and down at the farm, but wrestlers couldn't lift anyone high over their heads or they would hit the ceiling. We actually changed our wrestling style to emphasize more low-level shots because of those ceilings.

We had to tell potential recruits that the wrestling room would be there the year they were coming. I didn't know if that would prove true, but "soon" doesn't excite recruits.

John did find a way to impress recruits, though. It required obliterating NCAA rules, but he did it. Recruits were flown in on private jets and his helicopter, and they were put up in an expensive hotel with unlimited room service. Meals consisted of lobster, cracked crab, and champagne. John's philosophy was to screw the NCAA's rules limiting how much money could be spent on each recruit's visit. The kids were high school recruits, and they didn't know all the rules that we were supposed to be following. They were getting a good deal, and I think they went along with du Pont's ways because they didn't know any better.

The athletic officials at Villanova, however, did know the

rules. I don't think they ever really wanted a wrestling program, but they were willing to tolerate our presence because du Pont had pledged so much money for the basketball arena and swimming complex. I think they were embarrassed that du Pont was part of the athletic program, but to my knowledge, they did not complain about or look into our recruiting practices.

John had a bad habit of offering full scholarships to every recruit we brought in. NCAA rules allowed for a total of 9.9 scholarships per year in wrestling. A typical team would have thirty players on the complete roster, and very few, if any, would be on a full ride. As Coach Abel had demonstrated at Oklahoma, filling a roster with 9.9 scholarships required creativity.

Each recruit's finances had to be taken into consideration. Each one's ability had to be evaluated to determine which recruits were most important to add to the program. The ones who filled the biggest needs and offered the most to the program received the larger shares of scholarships. At least that's the way it worked at real programs.

When John got involved in recruiting—which was pretty much all the time—he would tell a kid he had a full ride if he wanted it. I had no idea how he planned on paying for those scholarships. Not financially, but on paper where it wouldn't look as if NCAA rules were being violated.

The first year, there was one kid who was one of the first he gave a scholarship to. I'm sorry to say this, but the kid didn't deserve a scholarship. Nothing personal, he just wasn't a Division I–level wrestler. He was receiving free tuition, and I wouldn't have offered him even free books to be on our team.

We talked about how we needed his scholarship money to give

to others who could help the team. Du Pont told me to get rid of the guy. *He* had given the kid the scholarship and told *me* to yank his free tuition away from him!

I didn't know how to do that. We had a meeting to talk about it, and du Pont told me to write down the reasons to remove him from the scholarship. I made a list about half a page long and handed it to John. He signed his name at the bottom without even reading it.

I felt bad for the kid. I was the one who had pointed out that his being on scholarship was hurting us. Fortunately, the university stepped in and kept him on a nonathletic scholarship.

That situation should have never occurred, and it happened because the program was poorly run.

When I took over recruiting, I tried to build a team and John kept ruining it. I had to find ways to discourage him from getting involved in recruiting. Of course, I couldn't just tell him to butt out, because it was his program and he had free run of the place.

Chuck Yarnall didn't last a year. The university announced that Chuck had resigned in February 1987, with no reason given. He actually had been fired. By me. Because du Pont told me to do it.

Yes, an assistant coach fired the head coach. That's the way things worked in du Pont's program.

My involvement in Chuck's dismissal is one of the biggest regrets of my life. Chuck was a really good guy. I liked him a lot.

Du Pont was in the hospital recovering from a surgery and wanted me to come see him.

First, he called Mark Spitz on the phone while I was there. Mark won nine Olympic gold medals in swimming and had trained with the Santa Clara club. John had gotten to know him during that period when he was concentrating on swimming.

Judging from what I could hear on John's side of the conversation, it sounded like a phone call that Spitz wasn't too thrilled about receiving. Du Pont gave me the phone at one point to have me talk to Spitz. Mark said practically nothing to me, as if he was wondering why John had handed the phone to me.

I think the primary purpose of the call was for du Pont to show off to me.

After the call, John wanted to talk wrestling.

"Do you want to be the head coach at Villanova?" John asked.

I told him I didn't, and I'm pretty sure he knew that before he asked. There's no way I would have taken Chuck's job after watching John's meddlesome ways. Plus, Chuck was the head coach.

"I don't think Chuck can be the coach," John said.

Honestly, as someone who liked Chuck, I have to say that du Pont should not have hired him as head coach. He was a high school coach. Chuck, who was thirty, would have made an excellent administrator, but he didn't have the credentials to be a Division I coach.

I've always speculated that was why du Pont hired him as Villanova's first coach. He wanted someone in the top job whom he could control. John wanted to be the head coach, but he didn't want to have to do all the head coach's work. John didn't want to have to be there every day scheduling practices and working the mats and doing all the tedious work required to run a program. He had no interest in learning the NCAA rules regarding recruiting.

I couldn't have pointed to one part of a typical Division I coach's job description that du Pont could have carried out. I mean, he couldn't even grasp the simple concept of dividing and offering scholarships. But he wanted to be treated like the head coach and, probably more important, to feel that he was the head coach. In a media interview the previous fall, John had referred to himself as the head coach.

From his hospital bed, du Pont told me that he would be leaving town soon and that when he returned, he wanted Chuck gone and that I was the one to fire him.

I should have told John I wouldn't do it. I should have left with Chuck.

I can't remember how I told Chuck he was fired. I'm glad I can't remember because it pains me enough more than two decades later to know that I did fire him. I wish I could erase that awful moment from my life. I should have made John do his own dirty work. I don't even think he would have had the guts to do it. He was so weak that he would latch on to strong personalities and hide behind them, using them to get done what he wanted done.

The university's handling of Chuck's departure was telling. A school spokesman told reporters that the wrestling coaches understood all along that although Yarnall held the title of head coach, du Pont would function as the team's head coach. What a bunch of bull. I never had that understanding, or I wouldn't have gone to Villanova in the first place.

The school's athletic director, Ted Aceto, said in a released statement, "Du Pont is and always has been our head wrestling coach. Chuck Yarnall's title had been co–head coach. John du Pont will continue as our head wrestling coach."

It appeared that something fishy was going on behind the scenes, as that was all breaking news to me.

I felt trapped at Villanova for two reasons: I needed the money, and the 1987 World Championships were just a few months away and I couldn't disrupt my training. I wouldn't have been able to find workout partners as I had there.

But beyond then, I saw little to be optimistic about.

I couldn't count on USA Wrestling for support and would have to be a college coach to keep training and competing. But wrestling jobs were growing increasingly scarce. Title IX was signed into law in 1972 to end sex discrimination in education. In athletics, that meant leveling the playing field for men and women so that both genders would have equal opportunities.

I assume the hope behind Title IX was to increase the number of opportunities for women up to the level men enjoyed. However, the way it played out more often than not was that the funding and opportunities for men decreased. In some cases, greatly decreased. Wrestling, with much higher participation among men than women at all levels of the sport, was one of the hardest-hit sports at the collegiate level.

Wrestling programs across the country were being swept out to help meet the requirements of Title IX. Fewer programs meant fewer jobs. Fewer jobs meant more coaches holding on to the jobs they were fortunate enough to hold. I was a twenty-six-year-old assistant coach, and there were too many older, experienced, former head coaches looking for jobs.

When I had come to tight spots in my life, I would look to

joining the military as an option. I considered that again. The military had a special wrestling team, and if you were a good enough wrestler, you could fulfill your duties by representing the military in wrestling competitions. But the military had never become a plan A because of my memories growing up, watching Vietnam vets come home. They were wounded and disabled, yet our own American citizens were calling them "baby killers" and the government seemed to be neglecting them.

The thought came to me that I could leave Villanova, pick a school I liked, move to be near that school, and then go on welfare. Based on the way I had been raised, that wasn't an option I would seriously consider.

I was stuck, and with all pretense removed in the wave of Chuck's departure, John was free to be the official and undisputed head coach of Villanova wrestling.

But he couldn't run the program. I couldn't, either, because he was constantly in my office, drunk, telling those stupid, pointless stories. I think it was more important to John that I humored him than that I tried to make the program successful.

We traveled together for the last few matches of the season. He would have delirium tremens, and I would sit there and look at that miserable wretch I was with and think, *I can't wait for this season to end. This is my last year at Villanova.*

John had to have sensed my frustration. How could he not have? Toward the end of my first year, he asked if I wanted to bring in a workout partner. I knew the perfect guy: Dan Chaid. Dan had been a high school wrestler in California whom Dave and I had gotten to know and help train. Dan was an eighth-grader my junior year and was in the stands when Dave won the state championship as a senior. Dan wound up winning two state championships of his own.

Dan followed us to Oklahoma to wrestle, where he was a four-time All-American and won the 1985 NCAAs at 190 pounds. He had worked one year as an assistant at Arizona State when John hired him and provided him housing. Dan was made an assistant coach whose job description basically consisted of two things: coming to practices and training with me.

I n going to Villanova, I had been made a part of du Pont's Team Foxcatcher. Du Pont had established his team, named for his father's Foxcatcher Farm stable of Thoroughbred racehorses, to financially support athletes in swimming, modern pentathlon, and triathlon. He decided to add wrestling, and I was the second wrestler to join behind Rob Calabrese. Everything about the name Foxcatcher and being a part of the team had felt wrong in my gut.

After I came aboard, John quickly began adding to his team more world-class wrestlers who had been struggling to get by on shoestring budgets.

Dave joined du Pont's club after the 1986 Worlds and while he was coaching at Wisconsin. Du Pont paid Dave to be a Foxcatcher wrestler and assistant coach to go along with the salary Dave was drawing from Wisconsin. Knowing that Dave had no intention of leaving Wisconsin, I didn't see any need to warn him about joining Foxcatcher. At that point, John was paying Dave what amounted to a second salary. But wanting to prevent a repeat of the mess at Stanford, I negotiated a deal with John by which he would never pay one of us an amount different from the other's or give one of us a lesser title than the other's. That turned out to be a shrewd move on my part.

Without telling the Foxcatcher wrestlers, du Pont scheduled a dual meet against the Bulgarian national team. I think he scheduled the meet to screw with me, because I would have to wrestle again against Alexander Nanev, whom I could count on running into in the bracket of just about every World Championships. I believed I held an edge over Nanev and wrestling him with another Worlds coming up could benefit only him. Videotape was becoming more popular at the time, and I didn't want to have a match with him on tape that he could study to try to close the gap between us.

John insisted that I wrestle Nanev, and I repeatedly told him I didn't want to. I didn't wrestle in dual meets after college except the one opportunity I had to get revenge on Vladimir Modosyan in Chicago. But Dave agreed to participate in the Bulgarian dual, and that trapped me into having to wrestle, too.

I don't talk about competitions or opponents beforehand. Once that dual was in place, though, du Pont wouldn't shut up about it. Every other sentence out of his mouth was, "The Bulgarians are coming!" It bothered me, and he knew it. I tried to avoid John even more than usual, spending as much time alone in my apartment as I could.

The day of the dual, Calabrese and I crashed our cars into each other's on the way to the gym. We were messing around driving in circles to get our minds off the dual. I was preoccupied with the rage I felt over John's trapping me into wrestling against Nanev, and we had a fender bender. Rob got mad at me, and that incident about finished me off mentally for the dual.

I lost to Nanev 1–0 in a next-to-nothing match. I didn't try to win. I didn't care to show him anything in a stupid dual that amounted to no more than an exhibition, especially with Worlds coming up.

The match most fans wanted to see was Valentin Jordanov, who had won two of his six World Championships at that point, against Ed Giese at 114.5 pounds. By the time Giese's career had wrapped up, he had placed twelve times at Nationals in freestyle and Greco-Roman, and had been a five-time finalist for the US World Team. Jordanov defeated Giese.

That dual marked the start of a friendship between Dave and Jordanov.

Du Pont kept badgering me to let him sit in my corner during my competitions, but I kept telling him no. I let Chris Horpel sit in my corner at big tournaments after he fired me, with no choice but to forgive him as I'd had to forgive everyone so I wouldn't have to carry that extra burden. Chris was a good coach, and it helped me to have him there. But du Pont—forget about it. He had nothing to contribute. He just wanted to be seen in my corner and then take credit later for anything I won.

John hired a camera crew to shoot video of him at the 1987 World Championships in Clermont-Ferrand, France. John was having a documentary made about himself called *Quest for the Best*, which later aired on the Discovery Channel. Everywhere John went at Worlds, his camera guys followed him.

Later, after we had returned to the States, John flew some of us with him to South Carolina, where he fired the starting gun for a triathlon. His film crew was trailing him there, too. They wanted video of me talking about what a great leader John was. I tried to put them off, but they kept coming back to me. They must have really wanted that sound bite, because they were persistent in asking. I found a way to meet both of our desires. I got drunk and then told them du Pont was great, blah, blah, blah. I was so drunk that they couldn't use the footage in the final product.

In one of my early matches in France, I went up against West German Reiner Trik, who had placed fourth at the '84 Olympics. I had the lead, and he shot on my legs. I grabbed a double wrist-lock, the same move with which I had broken the Turk's arm in the Olympics. I didn't hurt Trik, but the refs must not have liked my making that move, because with about ten seconds left in the match, they cautioned me for stalling.

That loss put me in a spot where the only way I could advance to the finals would be to pin, caution out, or shut out the defending World Champion, Vladimir Modosyan of the Soviet Union.

I went outside the arena to just get away, and one of John's cameramen came out and handed me a beer. I had never consumed alcohol during a tournament, but I drank that beer. I didn't think it would matter, because if Modosyan simply scored a point against me, I wouldn't wrestle for the championship.

Bruce Baumgartner walked up to me.

"You can do it," he said.

"No, I can't," I told him.

"Oh, yeah," Bruce said. "I forgot about the power of negative reinforcement."

The first period against Modosyan was scoreless. In the second period, I took him down with about a minute left for a 1–0 lead. That was the only point of the match. I couldn't believe that I had shut out Modosyan.

I advanced to face Nanev for the second time in a Worlds finals match and beat him 2–1 to win my second World Championship. Lee Kemp had won three World Championships from 1978 to 1982, and with my two world titles and my Olympic gold, I tied Lee for the most wrestling world titles won by an American. We even received an entry in the *Guinness Book of World Records* for our feats.

After winning Worlds, I had to take the required drug test. The testers told me I could drink beer, water, or soda if that would help me produce a urine sample. I asked for beer. Then Ri Jae-sik, the 105-pound champion from North Korea, came into the room to take his drug test. He asked for a beer, too. We kept drinking beers and got hammered.

Neither had any idea what the other was saying in our native languages, but that didn't stop us from laughing our asses off. When the testers asked if we were ready to pee into the cup, we both said no so we could drink more beer. I had to pee badly, but I wasn't going to cut off the supply of free beer. Finally, I couldn't hold it in any longer. I filled up three cups with pee running over onto my hand, and I spilled my first cup on one of the testers. Good thing I had filled those other two cups.

Immediately after we returned from my becoming the first American wrestler to win the Olympics and two World Championships, John wanted to make a Team Foxcatcher poster with me, Foxcatcher's first World Champion, as the poster boy. John wanted to send a poster to every college program in the country as evidence that his team was on the wrestling-world map and had to be contended with. I took part in a photo shoot with me acting as if I had just won the title, wearing Team Foxcatcher's red-and-white singlet with yellow trim, oil on my body to make me appear sweaty, head down, index fingers raised, with a large American flag behind me.

Emblazoned right beneath my red wrestling shoes, on one of the white stripes of the flag, in all caps, were the words TEAM FOXCATCHER. I'd bet that was John's favorite part of the poster. I had a mixed reaction when I first saw the poster. It was quite a compliment to have such a huge poster made of me, and I liked the way I looked. On the other hand, I loathed seeing TEAM FOX-CATCHER under me and on my singlet. I resented being portrayed as giving credit to the team, and thus John, for my accomplishment, because that was exactly what John was trying to buy.

Du Pont was taking credit for my success while at the same time trying to ruin my career.

CHAPTER 13

At All Costs

John du Pont was a collector. When he was younger, he had collected seashells, birds, and bird eggs and stored them upstairs in the mansion. It wasn't just any collection—he had traveled to the Philippines, Samoa, the Fiji islands, and Australia, among other places, accumulating hundreds of thousands of seashells and more than forty thousand specimens of birds.

He took me once to view his collection at the Delaware Museum of Natural History, which he had paid to build. When du Pont's father died in 1965, John received his family inheritance, reported to be in the range of $50 million to $80 million. With that money, he was able to fulfill his long-held plans to build the museum, which opened in 1972, to display his collection.

I experienced a strange mix of emotions being there with John.

On one hand I felt sick because the building was filled with dead animals he had collected, stuffed, labeled, and stored. On the other hand, I felt bad for him because that collection obviously had been a huge part of his life. That museum was one of John's most sacred places, and although I thought his primary reason for taking me there was to impress me, I did appreciate John's revealing a part of himself that he hadn't showed me before.

I was more saddened than impressed. That trip to the museum was a window into John's soul, and it didn't seem filled with philanthropy, kindness, and generosity. Instead, his soul seemed dark, small, and cramped.

There had been many things in my life I had not had the money to buy, but I had learned that you didn't need currency to find confidence, happiness, loyalty, brotherhood . . . and love. Du Pont had none of those. He had the money to buy just about any material possession he could have wanted, but despite his best efforts, he had failed to obtain the things he yearned for the most. And he had made himself morally bankrupt in trying.

That all the animals in his museum were dead and stuffed made perfect sense to me. He didn't have to feed them, he didn't have to maintain them. All he had to do was collect them. He killed them, owned them, controlled them, and hung them on walls for other people to admire.

Now, I realized, he was collecting wrestlers. We were his newest trophies. We had become his objects to control with his ancestors' money, and we were more fun to play with than his seashells and birds because we were collectables that he could manipulate. If you didn't want to be displayed on his wall, he threatened to ruin you.

I discovered during the '87 Worlds that the conditions for me at Villanova were about to sink even lower. I heard that du Pont had offered Andre Metzger, my and Dave's teammate at Oklahoma, a coaching job and that Andre had accepted.

Andre placed third at Worlds at 149.5 pounds. He had permitted John to sit in his corner during his matches, and John's camera crew was there to record every second of it.

I felt as if Dave, Andre, and I were brothers at OU. We'd had our picture on the front page of the newspaper the year all three of us won NCAA championships. But when du Pont hired Andre, that proved to be the beginning of the end for me at Villanova.

John had already suspiciously rejected my recommendation for a hire. He wanted a coach for the middleweights, and I told him about Bill Nugent, the Outstanding Wrestler at the 1985 US Open at 149.5 pounds. Bill was coaching a clinic in Pennsylvania, and I suggested he come to Villanova to meet John.

I introduced Bill to John as "the best middleweight in the nation last year."

Normally, I would bring a recruit over to John's house and he would offer the kid the world. Not only did he not offer Bill anything, but when Bill left, du Pont told me, "Never make a recommendation to me again." Looking back, I suspect John didn't like the fact that Bill and I were friends, because I later came to the realization that John wanted someone in place whom he could use against me.

After Worlds, I asked John for a five-thousand-dollar raise. He turned me down. With Andre also on staff, I sensed John had worked himself into a position where he didn't have to have me around anymore. "Now I've got two foxes in the henhouse," John boasted to me.

I had been the coach with all the wrestling skins, but Andre sported a solid résumé. Ever the manipulator, John could use Andre as leverage against me. He could run me out of there with a moment's notice and still have a big-name assistant to attract recruits *and* give him credibility in the wrestling community.

Du Pont did wind up giving me a raise going into my second

year, but when he wanted to give one to me, instead of when I had asked for it. In other words, on his terms.

He bumped my salary up to thirty thousand dollars, although he changed how he paid me. The first year, he paid my full salary up front. The second year, he paid the coaches in thirds. I assumed he thought that as long as we had money still coming instead of having already received the full amount, he could better keep control over us.

Actually, John didn't pay me directly. I had a contract that paid me one dollar per year so I could receive insurance coverage through the university. The rest of the money from John was routed through a trust fund at USA Wrestling. My accountant checked with USA Wrestling and was told the money would be considered a scholarship and, thus, tax exempt. USA Wrestling later dropped the trust fund program, though, and said that what they had told my accountant was incorrect. I ended up having to pay more than six thousand dollars in back taxes and penalties to the IRS.

Our second season was the first for which we had been able to put in a full recruiting effort. We were able to attract some good talent. Most of the recruits had been state champions in high school. But the program was in such disarray that we weren't going to win no matter who we signed.

Other than du Pont's presence, the lack of a devoted wrestling room was the biggest hurdle we were unable to overcome. By that, I mean a wrestling room on campus that had ceilings higher than a shooting range's.

"Soon" never materialized.

But then again, "soon" always came from the lips of the guy

who also said he wouldn't be around except to drop in and see if we needed anything.

I got so fed up with not knowing where I stood that I wrote up a proposal for the program with rules, job descriptions, and a chain of command. I took my proposal to John and asked him to read it, make any changes he wanted, and sign it. He refused. If we had established any structure, he couldn't have been the dictator.

As if the writing on the wall wasn't enough of a message when Andre came aboard, the letterheads he had printed spelled out clearly what was going on. Stacks of letterheads were delivered to our office, and John's name was at the very top with the title of head coach. Andre's was right below John's name as assistant coach. Down at the very bottom of the page were the other assistant coaches—Chaid, Calabrese, Glenn Goodman, Bill Hyman, and me. My phone number was the one listed. In other words, if there was anything that needed to be done, call me, but John and Andre were the marquee names.

"Did you approve this?" I asked John.

"No, I didn't," he answered.

Then when the guy from the printer came in to collect for the job, du Pont said he wasn't going to pay him and the two got into an argument that ended only when the guy got flustered and walked out.

John smiled when he left. Here was this multimillionaire acting as if he had won some big victory by not paying for stationery.

It wasn't about the money with John, even though that's what people focused on with him. For John, it was about control, and his money gave him control over others.

I made a deal with du Pont to let me run a wrestling camp at Villanova. Many college coaches today put on camps, and often they have permission to run camps written into their contracts. Camps provide a variety of benefits. They promote your program, they're a good way to teach your sport to younger athletes, they're good community relations, and they bring in extra income that can be used to supplement a coach's salary or be placed right back into the program for scholarships or equipment.

John hooked me up with someone who he said could put together a camp brochure that would be mailed out to every high school coach and wrestler in Pennsylvania. The guy came into the office and he was disheveled, unshaven, and overweight, and his eyes aimed in different directions. The brochures came out fine, though. Somehow.

Calabrese, Hyman, and a couple of other friends helped as camp instructors, and we drew about eighty kids. Not bad for a camp's first year. We made $8,000 in that one week. A week later, du Pont asked me, "What are we going to do about the cost of the brochures?"

Turned out his guy had charged $7,500. I wound up splitting the cost with du Pont and when all was said and done, we netted only about half of the $8,000.

Another time, I bought a few office supplies at the student union. They were on my desk when John found out I had made the purchases, and he picked up a paper clip and looked at it long enough for me to stop what I was doing and look at him.

"Do you know how much this cost?" he asked. "This cost a nickel. You know how much a nickel is?"

He made a big freaking deal out of a nickel, and then he took some of us on a Learjet to fly off to South Carolina so he could fire the starting gun for that triathlon. Then we got back into the jet and flew home.

Du Pont would drop thousands, tens of thousands, of dollars in a heartbeat if it would bring him attention, and then he would turn around and nickel-and-dime us just to remind us we were dependent upon him.

He provided us with meal tickets to eat at a cafeteria across from the field house. Then one day he decided to take them away, no explanation given. The upside, though, was that if he didn't know we would be eating at the cafeteria, he couldn't join us for lunch.

His table manners were horrendous. He would talk with his mouth wide-open as he ate, as though there was nothing in his mouth. Once, I got stuck sitting directly across from him and he was spraying food and spit all over the table, my food, and my clothes. It was so disgusting that I couldn't touch my food. I got up and left right in the middle of the meal.

Du Pont's meddling carried over to the mat. At one dual meet, he sat next to me on the bench. I was shouting moves to one of our wrestlers and John started arguing with me right there in the corner about which moves our guy should be doing and what I should be telling him to do. I looked over at him and let my eyes tell him, *You're an idiot.*

Nothing good happened when du Pont was around.

He came to a practice on his farm dressed as a cop and started waving a gun around. The wrestlers scattered. I just stood there and looked at him. He was trying to act like a big man. Nobody thought du Pont would shoot, much less kill, another person. Why would anyone with his money, power, and influence risk losing all that to live in a prison cell? John was unstable, but he was not insane.

What was more disturbing was the wrestling move he claimed to have created. He called it the "Foxcatcher Five." Basically, it was him grabbing someone's balls with five fingers.

His idea came from a story I had told about a match I had in college against Don Shuler. Don and I wrestled five times, and he was the guy I had to beat in the finals of the Olympic trials to make the '84 Olympic team. Don was one of the few guys to put me on my back in college, and I think he might have been the only person who didn't lose to me in Oklahoma's home arena.

The first time we wrestled was at home, and I was leading 4–0 in the third period. Don reversed me to my back and tried to pin me. He received two points for the reversal and had me on my back getting pinned. Holding an opponent on his back for two seconds was worth two points and three points were awarded for holding him for five seconds.

I was on my back scrambling like crazy trying to get Don off me because three points would have given him the win. He had me in a tight hold and I felt his groin press down hard on the palm of my hand, trapping my hand against the mat. I had to free my hand or lose. I squeezed Don's balls for a fraction of a second. He yelled and popped off me like a champagne cork. I spun belly down. Don complained to the ref, but the ref hadn't seen the quick squeeze and instructed him, "Keep wrestling." The match ended in a 4–4 tie.

John had a tendency to not pay close attention to other people's stories, but that one captured his attention. From that, John came up with his Foxcatcher Five. He was overly proud of his "move" and loved to tell people about it, even women. Whenever he would talk about it, he'd laugh and attempt to make a big joke out of it.

During my summer camp at Villanova, I was sitting on a stage and he came up to me and made a claw with one hand and said, "The Foxcatcher Fiiiiiive." He moved his hand toward my balls. I stared at him like, *Touch me and you're dead.* He didn't touch me. But he did put his move on other Villanova coaches and wrestlers.

One wrestler came and told me about John grabbing him. He was nervous about telling me, saying half-jokingly, "Yeah, that Foxcatcher Five. John got me. Ha-ha."

I should have reported John to the athletic director. That was another one of my "should haves" at Villanova. The sexual abuse scandal involving a Penn State football coach a few years ago has dramatically changed attitudes toward reporting and disciplining for such abuse. I don't know what would have happened back then if I had told the athletic director. But if that incident had happened today, post–Penn State scandal, du Pont would have been disassociated with Villanova and his name taken off the buildings before the university president could have asked him, "You understand what I'm saying?"

That would have abruptly ended du Pont's reign on campus. Who knows what else that might have stopped.

———

The clock started ticking the night of a party at my apartment. We put together a group of female students called the Mat Cats. (Villanova's nickname was the Wildcats.) It was common for wrestling programs, and other sports in colleges, to have a support group like that. Their basic function was to assist and cheer for the team. They kept score and stats during matches, helped with water, cheered, that type of stuff.

We recruited seven of the most beautiful girls on campus, took them to the mall, and bought them blouses with a wildcat on the back, Armani shirts, nylons, shoes, socks, earrings, bracelets, perfume, and anything else that looked or smelled good on them. Recruits liked seeing spirit groups like the Mat Cats on their visits to various schools, so they also helped us with our recruiting.

I threw a party to celebrate someone's birthday, my World Championship, the recruiting class we had brought in, and probably another thing or two I've forgotten about. Basically, we wanted to have a party. The Mat Cats were among the invited guests. Word got out about the party, and some of our wrestlers who were underage showed up. There was alcohol there, but I wasn't going to kick out the underage ones who showed up.

It was just a regular college party. It wasn't really a problem, but Metzger made it into one.

The next day, I walked into the Butler Annex with Dan. John and Andre were with the team, and Andre was telling the wrestlers they shouldn't have gone to our party. While I listened, John kept looking at Dan and me with this goofy grin on his face.

John walked out, and Dan and I followed him. I grabbed John by the arm and said, "What the hell do you think you're doing?"

John yelled at me, "You back me and I'll back you!"

"That's it!" Dan shouted back. "I'm out of here!"

Dan was on his way out when I grabbed him and John by the wrists and took them into a locker room and unloaded on John.

When I had finished, John looked at me and said, "I'm going to ruin your career."

That was one time he would make good on his word.

Du Pont sent me to Oregon on a recruiting trip in December 1987. I spent Christmas at my mother's house, and on Christmas Day, while we were opening presents, John called me.

"You're fired," he told me. "Don't come back on campus because the police are looking for you." Then he hung up. The police weren't looking for me. He was just trying to scare me to keep me away for a while.

He didn't give a reason for firing me and never gave me one after I got back to Philadelphia.

After I did return to Philadelphia following the holidays, I found out that du Pont had flown the team on a Learjet to wrestle in Puerto Rico. The trip was not on our schedule. The trip also, it was later reported, violated NCAA rules because the team did not wrestle enough times to comply with established rules for such trips. They wrestled only once in Puerto Rico. Basically, it was just a free minivacation for the team, and they wrestled one time so they could try to justify the trip.

Rob and Dan came to my apartment to tell me about the trip, and they said du Pont had wrestled against José Betancourt, who had competed on the Puerto Rican team at the '84 Games. José let du Pont win. That got John to apparently feel all tough because he ordered the Puerto Rican coach to pick up John's bags and put them on his plane, as if the coach was his servant.

"I don't care who you are," the coach snapped at du Pont. "I'm going to kick your ass!"

That scared du Pont, and he ran to board the plane and told everyone else with the team to hurry up, too.

John wanted credit. He *needed* credit to make up for what he had failed to accomplish.

In 1987, he wrote a book titled *Off the Mat: Building Winners in Life*. I overheard him dictating some of it into a tape recorder. He was zonked out of his mind, drunk. It was a joke, and what he was dictating made no sense whatsoever. I heard he paid to have the book published and given free to college coaches around the country.

He asked me to write the foreword. I reluctantly wrote one but made sure not to give him credit for anything I had achieved. Years later, I read the foreword. My name was on it, but it wasn't what I had written because it gave credit to John for my success.

I had never considered the possibility of someone creating awards to be presented to himself. Being around John gave me plenty of opportunities to see how he pulled it off.

He had me speak at one of his awards banquets. I wasn't going to say anything that would make John look good, so I got up and talked about winning my Olympic gold medal and kept the subject focused on me rather than John. I tried to be as funny as I could about myself and had the room laughing.

I was followed to the podium by a guy I didn't know who had been sitting next to John. Apparently, John had anticipated some of what I would say and had hired this guy to come in and say things that contradicted my speech. I wanted to get up and punch the guy out when he said, "Winning a gold medal means nothing."

One of the funniest stories about John's "awards" involved the Citizen/Athletes Foundation he created. No one I knew of ever figured out what the Citizen/Athletes Foundation was created to accomplish. Other than a special night and award for John, of course.

I didn't even like the name of the foundation. I wasn't a citizen/athlete. I was all athlete!

Du Pont had pens, stationery, cuff links, shirts, ties, and pins made up with the foundation's name on them. For the big banquet in Washington, DC, he hired a professional football player to deliver the keynote address.

The important people were given seats up front. The Villanova wrestlers and coaches sat at the back end of a narrow hallway. Technically, we weren't even in the banquet room. But we could see the football player as he spoke, and it was comical listening to him move from story to story trying to make a point coordinated with a subject that had not been defined.

The player would have been just as effective if he had stood up there and read us the back of a cereal box. I wondered what was going through his mind, other than, *I just have to get through this to collect my check.* Not that it mattered anyway. The whole event was a ruse to give du Pont another of his own awards and boost his name in public.

After the football player, another guy got up to present du Pont with his award. I've never attempted this, but it must be difficult to, with a straight face, say good things about a man who was receiving an award he had made up for the sole reason of giving it to himself. From the way the guy struggled with the presentation, it looked difficult.

When du Pont received the award, I didn't clap. I just sat there and stared at the farce of a scene. Du Pont thanked a billion people no one had heard of and tried to sound like a wrestling expert.

At the end of his acceptance speech, he addressed us in the back of the room/hallway. He obviously had been drinking and paused several times to try to create drama. Then he blurted out, "Practice tomorrow at seven A.M.!" Of course, he wouldn't be there. He would never get up that early for practice.

He walked around the room after the ceremony, stumbling often, going from one guest to another, sometimes accidentally spitting in their faces, so he could receive congratulations that were as fake as his latest award.

CHAPTER 14

Protest at the Olympics

Moving to Villanova was supposed to bring the stability I had been looking for since finishing my college career. But now I had lost my job, and being around du Pont was sapping my will to compete. Getting away from du Pont's influence was my best bet to win gold at the Seoul Olympics, but I couldn't for financial and training reasons. Things were going so badly for me that even a normally routine procedure to fix my eyesight went terribly wrong.

My nearsightedness had contributed to my loss at the 1986 World Championships because I was unable to see the scoreboard after FILA had changed its angle to the mat. I had thought about getting eye surgery to eliminate the problem. John had fired me but I still had health insurance, and I thought that would be a good time to have the surgery.

But the procedure didn't fix the problem. I was still near-sighted and had slits in my eyes for nothing. I was taking painkillers for the severe pain. But I was having to think about my future at the same time, too. There was no chance of finding another college job that time of the year. Plus, the trials for the World Championships were a few months away. I was in great shape and probably more confident than I had ever been in my career. I couldn't afford to let this opportunity slip.

Joining the military became an option again, but basic training would run through the trials and I didn't think the military would let me skip out to compete in them. Yet my money wouldn't last long enough that I could keep training without income.

I went over to John's house. He was drunk and babbling incoherently, then started freaking out and yelling and screaming. I couldn't tell what had him so upset, but he kept asking, "You understand what I'm saying?" "You understand what I'm saying?" "You understand what I'm saying?"

I told John that I didn't care if I coached at Villanova anymore, I just wanted to keep working out with Dan Chaid. John said he would think about it, and I went back to my apartment.

John started calling me every day.

"You can stay," he'd say. "But you have to move onto the farm if you do."

That didn't make sense. He had fired me from Villanova but wanted me to live on his farm? Rent-free?

He kept offering, though, and even told me that if I would trade in my Camaro, he would replace it with a Lincoln Grand Marquis. Financially, I had few options. Not having to pay rent would alleviate a big financial burden. So about three or four weeks after getting fired, I moved out of my apartment and into the chalet on his estate. John's mother lived in the mansion and he lived in both the mansion and the chalet, but he spent more time in the mansion. I assumed—I hoped—he would stay in the mansion more when I moved into the chalet, but he didn't.

The mansion was old and in need of repair. The chalet was new. In addition to the fortresslike steel blinds, it had a kitchen with the most modern appliances available, a fully stocked bar and a nice piano in the living room, a Jacuzzi room, and bedrooms on opposite ends of the place. My bedroom was surprisingly small, and the mattress was too soft. It was like sleeping on a hammock. That's fitting, because I never felt comfortable in the house. The chalet appeared much nicer, but my apartment was a significantly better place to live.

I moved in prepared to make a quick exit if necessary. Other than my clothes, I took little more than two bags of workout gear with me and a pin collection I had won after winning the '87 Worlds, with pins from all the countries in the tournament. I rented a storage unit to hold the rest of my possessions, including all my medals and awards. I wasn't going to consider his place my home, and I didn't want John to see any of my awards because I didn't want him looking at them and thinking he had helped me win even one of them.

The timeline is a little fuzzy for me all these years later, but after I had left Villanova and moved onto the farm, Metzger and du Pont had a falling out. Sometime during that period, I was talking on the phone with Hal Miles, a good friend who was head coach at Virginia State. I told Hal that du Pont should have started a freestyle program instead of an NCAA program because freestyle wouldn't have required following NCAA rules.

I didn't know until du Pont walked into my office after the call that he was listening to my end of the conversation.

"Should we drop the program?" John asked.

"Honestly," I told him, "we shouldn't have started it."

"That's it," John said. "We're dropping it."

Metzger left the program in January or February. I was no longer part of the program and only went to Villanova to pick up wrestlers to work out with me in the wrestling room at the farm.

After the season, university officials announced the program was folding because of facilities, which meant the lack of a private wrestling room. I wasn't around the university after being fired, so I have no knowledge of the university's role in the closing of the program, but I do know that after du Pont overheard my phone call, he decided the program would be dropped.

The program needed to be put out of its misery. It was never a legitimate program. It was just du Pont and his money. Nothing more, nothing less.

Villanova's administrators liked du Pont's money and had been willing to tolerate him for his money. John wanted to have a wrestling team there, so they gave him an office and said he could have a team. But the program was doomed from the beginning because the administrators never gave us a wrestling room. If they were serious about having a wrestling program, they would have given us the Butler Annex. It would have been a minor concession considering the money John had donated to them. They didn't really want wrestling on their campus, though. They didn't really want du Pont on their campus, either. Who would? The guy was a disaster.

I get that it must be tough growing up rich, not knowing whether people like you because of your money or because of who you are. But it seemed like nobody at Villanova made any meaningful efforts to put any kind of controls or organization into the wrestling program. The program violated NCAA rules regarding recruiting. They left John alone and he took full advantage.

I felt bad for our wrestlers. I remembered what it was like my freshman year at UCLA when there was turmoil in that program. The mess associated with Villanova's wrestling program went far beyond what I experienced at UCLA. It had to be stressful for the wrestlers to go through all the crap in the program and then have their wrestling careers yanked out from under them.

I couldn't remember our record, but I recently came across an old newspaper article that said the program won eight out of thirty matches in its two years of existence. I was surprised to read we had done that well.

We were able to bring some good wrestlers in for the second year. Tom Rogers placed third in conference our second season. Lyndon Campbell wrestled at Cal State Fullerton after Villanova's program folded, and he qualified for the NCAAs three times there. But even with good wrestlers in place, the program was so bad it was a no-win situation. As far as I know, the rest of the wrestlers' careers ended along with the program. Fortunately, they were able to stay at Villanova because the university honored their scholarships for up to four years.

With the Villanova program folded, John turned his attention to amateur wrestling. He made his first donation to USA Wrestling that year, for $100,000. He gave another $100,000 the following year. From 1989 through 1995, he donated $400,000 per year.

He became an at-large member of USA Wrestling's board of directors. His name began appearing in the titles of the US freestyle national championship and World Team Trials. The team's warm-up suits bore his name. In 1991, John was named USA Wrestling's Man of the Year, with the picture of a smiling John appearing on the cover of *USA Wrestler* magazine.

If his goal was to buy access and power, he achieved it.

——

After I moved onto the farm, one of my first orders of business was to do something about du Pont's hair. He still had the same style as when I'd first met him—parted down the middle with long, gray roots beneath that Ronald McDonald red color.

I kept my head shaved and offered to give him a shave like mine. I offered not for his benefit, but mine. I don't think he cared how he looked, and I just couldn't look at that ugly hair any longer.

He agreed to let me cut his hair. I have to say, the new style didn't look too bad. The shave improved his appearance significantly, but as long as he was on alcohol and drugs, he was always going to look like a bumbling fool.

John had undergone multiple knee surgeries, and in addition to being an alcoholic he was hooked on prescription medication. He would come to Villanova and blame his lack of balance on pain pills he took for the various injuries he had suffered, including both knees and his back. He blamed the knee braces he often wore for causing him to stumble. But he was both drunk and on pills. I don't know exactly at what point this took place, because I didn't see it until I moved to the farm, but cocaine became his preferred drug.

It sounds odd to say, but switching to cocaine was better for him. It was like the movie *Flight* with Denzel Washington, whose character would get drunk and they would sober him up by giving him cocaine. That's the effect cocaine had on du Pont. After he had been on cocaine for a while, he became more coherent.

While I was living on the farm—and not while I was coaching at Villanova—John asked me if I knew where to get cocaine. I
had done coke once or twice at parties before moving to Villanova
when someone had given me some. (Coke was too expensive for me
to buy.) I told John I knew a guy who had some, and John gave me
fifteen hundred dollars to buy some for him. I picked some up, and
we did coke two or three times together. The last time I did coke
was in 1989. I took too much and my knees buckled and my heart
started racing. That scared me enough to get me to stop.

One night, John showed me what looked to be a kilo of coke
in a dresser drawer. Because of all he had done for the local police,
he had an official badge. I witnessed him using the badge once to
get into the Pennsylvania state wrestling championships. He did
not have a ticket and, despite all his money, he didn't want to pay
a few bucks to purchase one. So he flashed his badge and walked
right on in.

I guess he had even used the badge to get into the police's
evidence vault because the bag of cocaine read EVIDENCE in bright
orange letters. John shoved a straw into the bag and took the biggest hit of coke I have ever seen anyone take. It was so big a hit that
I feared something bad could happen to him.

"What do you want me to do if something happens, call 911?"
I asked him, just in case.

"No," he said. "Call my lawyer."

There was never a period when I was around John that he was
not on something, whether it was alcohol, prescription meds, or
cocaine.

————

The role John's mother played in his life received a lot of publicity after my brother's murder. John seemed to be a mama's boy. He was the only one of the four du Pont children who didn't leave the estate to have a family of his own. I didn't have much occasion to talk with his mother, so I knew little about her personality.

She died in mid-August 1988 at the age of ninety-one. John took over his mother's decision-making role for the estate, and he seemed comfortable with the step up in power. John changed the name of the estate from Lisiter Hall Farm to Foxcatcher Farm. I had never known anyone to call the place by its official name. Everyone I knew had been calling it Foxcatcher or, simply, "the farm."

After his mother's funeral, John had the mansion remodeled. His "awards," athletic trophies, sports posters, and photos of him with celebrities were given places of prominence over his mother's mementos.

The death of John's mother has been frequently cited as a turning point in John's life. His family members have said that when John's mom died, his mental condition began deteriorating. I left for the Olympics that September and spent about two months after the Olympics living at the farm before moving away, so that's not a long period of time. But I didn't see any change in his mental condition immediately after his mother died.

I did not see anything different about him at all, and he didn't say much to me about her death. From my dealings with him, it was almost as though her death didn't happen.

The Olympics were to begin in mid-September in Seoul. I was actually ready to retire before then because my association with du Pont had drained the motivation out of me. I was tired physically, mentally, and emotionally. The only way out was to quit wrestling. But I couldn't quit.

I had won the '87 World Championship and was ranked as the favorite to win the Olympics and become the first American to win two Olympic gold medals in wrestling since George Mehnert in 1904 and 1908. And 1904 was the first Summer Games to include freestyle, and only the US team had competed that year.

Expectations were through the roof, and if the people who held those expectations could have spent just a couple of days with me when du Pont was around, they would have seen how unrealistic their confidence in me was.

Part of me thinks John wanted me to lose because he had never been a winner and didn't want me to win. Another part of me thinks John wanted me to win so he could take credit for my success. Whichever was his true motivation, he wouldn't stop distracting me.

I told him to leave me alone so I could focus.

He didn't.

I told him I was going to have a T-shirt made that read SHUT UP AND LEAVE ME ALONE. He showed up with a box shortly thereafter. Inside were two T-shirts bearing that statement. One was for me, one for him. What I had intended to be my message to him, he made our message to the world. That demonstrated how John perceived himself: special and above others. In his mind, nothing applied to him, and he was royalty and could do whatever he pleased.

I was as unmotivated as I had ever been going into the Olympic qualifier in Topeka, Kansas, in mid-May. Mike Sheets beat me in the final match on a defensive pin. It was my first loss to an American in five years.

Going into the final wrestle-offs the next month in Pensacola, Florida, featuring the top six in each class, I was seeded second behind Sheets.

In my first match of a best-of-three, I was leading NCAA champion Rico Chapparelli 5–0, but mentally I'd had it. Rico came back and beat me badly, 16–8, and I simply didn't care. I was done and ready to retire. If being around the likes of John du Pont was the only way I could compete, I could no longer do it. I went back to my hotel room, disgusted that I had allowed myself to be cornered into this seemingly impossible situation with no apparent solution. I destroyed everything in the room that wasn't bolted down and with my head smashed a mirror to which I had taped the message "No prisoners." I decided to forfeit out of the tournament, and ordered a ton of food from room service.

Hal Miles came to my room. He was the only person who had come to Florida solely for my benefit, and we had a long, serious talk. He told me I needed to quit thinking about the refs. Refs didn't like my style. I defended myself with an almost impenetrable defense and then exploded on opponents, and for some reason, refs were always hard on me because of that. I was angry and depressed that night, and Hal listened to me as I poured my heart out. I told him it felt like everyone and everything was working against me. He told me that he was there for me and what the rest of world does shouldn't matter to me.

"God gave Mark Schultz a haven where you can go and the world can't touch you. That's the mat," he told me. "You make the world pay. You let the world know that once they walk out on that mat with Mark Schultz, their ass is in your world and you will decide who lives and dies. You're the best in the world."

"What do you expect from me?" I asked Hal.

"Be the type of man who is on his death bed and if the ones you love needed you to take a deep breath, get up, and go do what you've got to do, you would do it and then come back, lie down, let it out, and die. But don't you *dare* die until you do what you've got to do. If you can't do that, then you ain't a damn man!"

I got up off the bed and Hal ran out of the door. The intensity in my room was thick. But more than anything he told me, it was his letting me know that he was there for me, whether I won or lost, that straightened out my thinking.

I unretired before telling anyone other than Hal of my plans. But with a loss to Rico, the only way I could get a shot at Sheets for the Olympic team spot was to beat Rico two straight the next night. I overhauled my wrestling philosophy for those matches. If that was going to be my last competition in my home country, I would wrestle for the first time the way I wanted to and damn the refs. I would attack my opponent's groin and turn the matches into real fights with no regard for potential calls by any referee who might have it in for me.

If this is the way I'm going to be remembered by Americans, I thought, *then they're going to remember me for the explosive violence I could put behind my athletic ability and for the creative technician I had become.*

I pinned Rico twice, once with one second left in the match, and went to the scales.

I was twelve pounds over the weight limit!

I had enjoyed too much of the room service during my brief retirement. I had only ninety minutes to make weight. Sheets followed me to the scale, made weight, and must have figured he would make the team by forfeit.

I've never heard of anyone dropping twelve pounds in ninety

minutes. I puked up the first pound and a half. Then I put on four layers of sweats and ran around the arena for twenty minutes. I knew I would have to do more to lose the weight, so I dragged a stationary bicycle right in front of the arena's doors so everyone would pass by me as they exited. A small crowd formed around me, including wrestlers who started rooting for me. I was riding the bike like a madman. Dave was right there beside me the entire time, encouraging me, pushing me, sticking ice up my nostrils to cool my airways without my taking in any liquids.

With ten seconds to make weight, I got on the scale. Someone told me they saw Sheets at a restaurant, and when he learned I had made weight, he spat out his food. That was the most weight I had ever lost in so short a time.

I swept Mike the next day by scores of 6–2 and 13–1, with the score of the final match proving to myself and the wrestling community just how good I had become. Dave lost in the 163 finals to Kenny Monday, a three-time All-American at Oklahoma State who would go on to win gold in the '88 Olympics. Andre lost the 149.5 spot to Nate Carr, a three-time NCAA champion from Iowa State and eventual bronze medalist in Seoul.

Bruce Baumgartner and I were the only Americans from the '84 Olympics to qualify for the '88 team. Coach Jim Humphrey said he would be disappointed if our team didn't leave Seoul with five gold medals. He was counting on me to win one of those. We won only two, and I placed sixth. I retired after the Olympics. I quit before they were over.

I won my first five preliminary matches, including victories over the second-, fourth-, and fifth-place finishers at the previous World Championships.

I started by beating Alexander Nanev, my opponent from that stupid dual du Pont had set up, 4–0 despite injuring my right knee. Then I took care of Reiner Trik. The match was stopped with more than a minute remaining and me leading 16–1.

On the second day, Andrzej Radomski of Poland and I were tied 0–0 after the first period, but I turned it on to defeat him 8–1. Then I pinned Victor Kodei of Nigeria at 1:41. The pin came after I had jumped to a 5–0 lead. That night, I pinned East German Hans Gstoettner at 2:02 to move to 5-0 in the tournament.

On the next-to-last day of the 1988 Olympics, on the last day of my wrestling career, I lost 7–3 to the Soviets' Aleksandr Tambovtsev. Necmi Gençalp of Turkey would be my opponent in the semifinals. With just the one loss, I still could have wrestled back for a chance at the gold medal.

But I couldn't do it. I didn't *want* to do it.

I had always said that it would be important to end my career with a big victory. That's why as a senior at Oklahoma I couldn't stand the idea of not winning the NCAA championship in my last year as a collegian. But on that day as I contemplated how I could live the rest of my life if I didn't go out a winner, as a two-time gold medalist, there was only one scenario that seemed worse than losing.

Winning.

There were times when I would have given my life to win. Or even for just the opportunity to win.

"Do or die," right?

I had worked too hard for too long with no support. And now that I had found the person who could provide me the support, he demanded everything I valued about myself in return.

It just wasn't worth it.

I could not win for Foxcatcher. I could not give du Pont the credibility and status that would come from his team's producing an Olympic champion. I couldn't let him use me one more time.

The Turk beat me 14–0. I let him win. There were plenty of times during that match when I could have scored, but I didn't try. I didn't care. I had quit before that match began. I forfeited the next match, to determine fifth and sixth places, and got on the first available flight home.

The media reported that I had walked away with a knee injury. My knee was hurt, sure. But in reality, I had walked out in protest. My loss was a protest against USA Wrestling. Against the whole system, really. Throwing that match, and by a score as ugly as 14–0, was my statement: This is what happens when you don't support us. This is the state of our sport right now.

Throughout my career, I'd had to figure out a way to defeat everyone in the world—to create that "magic" in every match. Once I had reached the top of the world, I realized the difference between winning a world title and placing second was razor thin. I definitely wasn't an emotionally fragile wrestler, but there was a sort of fragile nature within me, in that I was vulnerable to having my training routines disrupted. I needed and coveted stability. It was the one thing I needed most to succeed. My dad had provided me with stability. So had Dave. UCLA wasn't stable, Oklahoma was. Getting fired at Stanford disrupted my stability and led to my moving to Villanova.

Du Pont and Foxcatcher certainly weren't stable environments. I could have won two or three more world titles if I had landed in a stable program. I could have competed for at least another five years if USA Wrestling had provided me with a measly ten thousand dollars a year. I could have made that work. I *had* made that work before.

But instead, guys like me, with incredible skill and potential and drive and motivation, were having to stoop to rely on a lowlife like John du Pont to survive. Team Foxcatcher had become basically the only place where wrestlers could survive financially while competing, and as long as du Pont was getting the recognition he wanted, and USA Wrestling was getting the money it wanted, then all of us wrestlers weren't going to get what we deserved: respect and a fair chance in the fight for survival.

Du Pont kept using my name to gain power and credibility in the wrestling world. If I had won the gold medal, it would have solidified his status in the sport and led people to believe that he was a harmless benefactor. That would have been a lie.

Du Pont used to say that he was going to remove all the financial obstacles so I could focus only on wrestling. He didn't include that he would then replace all those financial obstacles with one gigantic, insurmountable obstacle: himself. I couldn't stomach the thought of du Pont's being pointed to as a good example, as a good leader. He was far from either. There was a reason he was having to pay people to say all those nice things about him that he so desperately wanted to hear.

He had threatened to ruin my career that one day in the locker room. He did it, too, the son of a bitch.

I just couldn't give him the credibility he wanted more than anything. I couldn't do it anymore. I couldn't take it anymore.

And after twenty-seven years of fighting and scrapping for everything I had accomplished and become, the only way I could fight back was to drop my impenetrable defense and fight no more.

CHAPTER 15

A New Home, a New Life

I never competed as a wrestler again. I had won an Olympic gold medal and two World Championships. No other American wrestler could claim that combination. I had won the US Open four times, the NCAA championship three times. Yet I felt I had not fulfilled my potential.

I wished I were a Russian, because their elite wrestlers were paid to train and compete. They were not forced to fight to survive; they were allowed to flourish. And they certainly didn't have to rely on the likes of John du Pont.

Dave, still in Wisconsin, also stepped away from competition, retiring for a year to take on the role of national coach for USA Wrestling. National coach was an unpaid position usually held for only one year so that different coaches could receive the honor of leading the national team. But if Dave had wanted to keep that title for more than a year, I think he had enough clout with USA Wrestling that he could have remained the coach.

I had planned all along to leave Foxcatcher after the Olympics, but the farm did offer me one thing after I returned from Seoul: a place to hide. I felt depressed knowing that not only was my career complete but I had also come up short of what I should have been able to accomplish. I wanted out of Foxcatcher and as far away from du Pont as I could get, but at the same time I wanted

to be someplace where I wouldn't have to face questions about the
'88 Olympics. I typically withdrew from people anyway after a big
loss. After my biggest loss—what I knew was my last loss—I didn't
know how long I would want to hide. I asked my girlfriend to
come stay with me at the farm for a while.

Du Pont had a key to my house and would walk in uninvited.
I had no privacy whatsoever. After my girlfriend had been there
about a week, John freaked out for some unknown reason and
came into my room waving a gun around and pointing it toward
us. That terrified my girlfriend, and I jumped in front of her. John
didn't scare me. I never felt threatened by him. He was just a weak
man trying to make up for lack of confidence and low self-esteem.

John left and came back with a videotape.

"I want to show you something," he told us as he inserted the
tape into the VCR.

The video was of a surveillance van that could shoot a laser
onto a window and hear people in the house via the window's vi-
brations. My girlfriend and I just sat there and watched. It was
weird, as though he was trying to tell me that not only was there
no privacy, safety, or autonomy on the farm, but there also was
none anywhere we could go. But again, I blew it off as another
empty threat from a weak man.

I decided right then that I needed to accelerate my plans to
leave before the end of the year.

One time I went into the main office and one of his family
members, whom I believed to be a sister, was there. I was talking
to her when John entered the room. He was trying to be extra nice
to her. I think he offered her something to eat. She flashed him a

"drop dead" look and snapped, "Don't try anything on me, John. I am not corruptible!"

I think she might have been sending a message to me about John being a corrupt manipulator.

John tried to portray himself as a philanthropist, but in truth, what he gave to others were actually purchases for himself. Whenever he gave away money, it was always in exchange for fame or recognition. He was egotistical and charged by an unearned sense of entitlement.

He had the pavilion and swim center named for him at Villanova, although he never paid the full amount he had pledged. A donation to nearby Crozer-Chester Medical Center resulted in the John E. du Pont Trauma Center with his name out front in big, easy-to-see letters. The public knew about those gifts.

Yet I remember one time when a woman privately called John and asked if she could bring orphans to the farm to play in the swimming pool. John declined, saying, "We're not bringing the have-nots out here to see what the haves have."

The atmosphere on the farm changed for the rest of my time there, and things just kept getting worse and worse. When the Team Foxcatcher poster of me had been made, he asked me to sign one for his kitchen wall. I had written something on it that I thought gave him more credit than he deserved. I decided to take the poster out of the frame and replaced it with a poster with no writing on it. Du Pont told me he had known about my switch but didn't say anything about it because he understood why. Then he took the poster off the wall, placed it on the kitchen table, and asked me to sign it, "To my mentor and coach."

I refused. That could not have been further from the truth. I had a long list of unkind names I would have written on that poster—and they would have been true—before I would have lied and called him my mentor and coach.

About that same time, we had a conversation in which John told me a story that I haven't heard anywhere else.

We were in the kitchen and John offered to make me a sandwich.

"Okay," I said.

"I'm going to make a sandwich," he told me.

As he moved about the kitchen putting the sandwich together, he kept repeating that he was going to make me a sandwich as though it was a big deal.

I started eating the sandwich, and John said, "You know, Mark, when I was younger, I was riding a horse, and that horse threw me onto a fence and I straddled the fence. My testicles became infected and they had to cut my balls off. The ones I have are plastic, and I have to take testosterone shots every day. Some days I forget."

I looked closely into John's eyes as he told the story. In a rarity with him, there was no deception or ulterior motive present. I could tell it was painful for him to share that story, and in a way I felt honored that he was sharing it with me.

I believed the story because it made things I had noticed about John suddenly make sense. He had androgynous characteristics. He could act feminine. His hair was thick. He had emotional issues and a lack of confidence. Maybe that was why he drank so much. I imagined that would be tough to live with. That was the one time I felt genuine pity for John.

Back then, and much more so after Dave was killed, there was

---

speculation that John was gay. I had my suspicions, but I never observed at Villanova or in my time living on the farm anything that would cause me to say he was a homosexual. I never knew of any relationships he had with guys.

There weren't many women around John, either. There was one girlfriend of his that I recall, and she walked around like she wanted to use John's money to become a movie star. She liked the fact that John was into wrestling and had all these well-built men around. But other than that, I never noted John to be particularly friendly toward women.

He did tell me once that he had been married and divorced.

In 1983, he was married, briefly, to an occupational therapist. She was not from wealth like John. Their wedding was du Pont in every way, with five hundred guests, uniformed trumpeters, and fireworks. The marriage lasted only a few months.

Although she had signed a prenuptial agreement, she filed a lawsuit against him. The lawsuit was settled without terms being disclosed, but one of the interesting bits of information to come out of the case was the fact that du Pont's worth was estimated at $46.2 million. That sounded like a lot until 1987, when *Forbes* magazine listed du Pont as being worth $200 million.

Years later, his ex-wife would reveal odd and abusive behavior she witnessed while married to du Pont, including his excessive drinking, throwing her into a fireplace, trying to shove her out of a car, and threatening to kill her with a knife. On one occasion, she claimed, du Pont held a gun to her head, called her a Russian spy, and said that Russian spies got shot.

When I knew it was time to leave, I called Dave and asked if he could come to Pennsylvania to help me finish packing and load what I had placed in storage. Later that day, I was standing on the porch and John walked up to me.

"Dave's coming," I told him.

John got inexplicably pissed.

"Now you're going to team up against me, two against one?" he yelled at me.

"No, I just want to see Dave."

"Okay, big boy," he said. "Now it's just you against me."

I relished that possibility.

"You want some of me?" I asked. "Try it and I'll bust your head open."

John got scared and left. Then he came back to say, "You just taught me a lesson. Thanks." He immediately turned back around and walked off again.

I don't know what the lesson was, but he left me there on the porch upset that I had made such a huge mistake in coming to be a part of Team Foxcatcher in the first place

Dave arrived the next day. John and his attorney immediately asked Dave to come over to see them at the main house, and they didn't want me to accompany him. I was angry that John and his attorney had gotten hold of Dave before I could talk with him.

Dave looked a little bothered after the meeting at the mansion. He told me he didn't want me to break my ties with John because he was still on John's payroll. According to the deal I had made with John, he would pay Dave and me the same amount as long as one of us was competing for his team. Dave then suggested I should sign a poster or something for John before I left. I didn't want to, but I did for Dave's sake. I don't remember what I wrote on it.

That night in the chalet, Dave wanted to talk but John wanted everyone to go to sleep. The next morning, my wallet was missing. After I canceled all my credit cards, John handed me my wallet and said his secretary, Victor, had found it on the floor of a room I had already thoroughly checked. I think John hid it to delay my departure or to see what I was going to do before I left.

Dave left to return to Wisconsin, and I loaded up the last bit of my stuff. Du Pont had his head of security watch me leave to make sure I didn't steal anything. It was December 1988, and after a year of living on the farm, I wanted out of Pennsylvania and away from John du Pont. For good.

I had lost everything to that demon, including the happiness I had worked so diligently to regain after losing it as a kid. I got in my car and peeled out, leaving a long skid mark over the front of the lawn outside his mansion.

I had no plans for where to go from Foxcatcher. As I drove west, the idea of being near Wayne Baughman drew me to Colorado Springs, Colorado. I didn't know him well at the time, but I knew all about him. Every good wrestler knew about Wayne.

He was head wrestling coach at the US Air Force Academy in Colorado Springs. The city also was home to USA Wrestling, Athletes in Action, the US Olympic Training Center, and the National Judo Institute. Colorado Springs seemed like the place for me.

Wayne was wrestling at Oklahoma the year I was born. He won one NCAA championship and earned All-American honors three times. As an amateur wrestler, he won sixteen national championships and never placed lower than third in twenty-five national tournament appearances. He also competed in three Olympics and eight World Championships.

He had taken over the Air Force program less than a year earlier. He was also an epic runner, logging five miles every morning, and he competed in a few one-hundred-mile races.

Wayne had recently written a book titled *Wrestling On and Off the Mat*, similar to the name of du Pont's book. But comparing his book to du Pont's was like comparing Wayne to John as a person: much better and completely different. Wayne was the epitome of masculinity and strength.

Respect was the first word I would think of when asked about Wayne. Pretty much the entire wrestling community felt that way about Wayne, lifting him up as a model of integrity.

I volunteered to be an assistant to Wayne at the academy and bought a small house from him. He'll never know how much his allowing me to hang around helped me slowly work my way back mentally to where I was before leaving Palo Alto for Villanova. The normalcy I found in Colorado Springs opened my eyes to just how manipulative du Pont had been. I felt as though I had escaped from a cult.

One day I was sitting at home watching the Discovery Channel when that documentary came on that John had paid to have made about himself. They showed du Pont doing all these coaching things, like teaching kids simple moves and blowing whistles at practice. At the very end, they showed me standing on the awards stand at the 1987 World Championships, bent over to have my gold medal placed around my neck. As soon I stood up straight, *The*

John du Pont Story appeared superimposed on the screen over me as if he were the reason I had won. The words were so large I couldn't even see my face. Seeing that made me sick to my stomach.

The takeover is finally complete, I thought. *He destroyed my career and has climbed up to the top of USA Wrestling.*

But he couldn't stay there for long. I think everyone in wrestling knew that du Pont didn't belong in the sport. He had nothing to offer but money, but his donations bought him time to climb the political ladders of USA Wrestling and FILA. Even though he received Man of the Year awards from USA Wrestling and *Amateur Wrestling News*, most of the wrestlers had strong disdain for du Pont. If he hadn't slowly begun to lose interest in the sport, they would have pushed him out. Even John could not have stayed in a sport in which everyone hated him. The odd thing was that being in the wrestling community was the closest I think he ever felt to being accepted.

My contempt for du Pont ran so deep within me that partly because of that documentary, I thought about killing him in 1989. Growing up, I had been taught the path to success consisted of working hard, making sacrifices, suffering, being honest, and not taking shortcuts. Watching John rise in power in wrestling convinced me those were all lies. People in wrestling stuck their hands out in exchange for giving John what he wanted. His greatest ability was being able to meet every one of their prices. I couldn't have felt lower than when I saw his name appear over my image on the documentary he had paid to have made and aired. That served as the final reminder that he had taken advantage of all my pain and suffering to gain prestige and power, and then ruined my career. I wanted revenge.

I bought a miniature crossbow and placed a plastic milk jug on a stick and imagined the jug was du Pont's head. I practiced enough to where I was good at hitting the jug from fifty feet, which I knew was the distance from a group of bushes at his mansion to a person walking up the steps from the driveway.

I planned to sell everything I owned, drop out of society, drive to Newtown Square, sleep in a car to avoid motel receipts and witnesses, hide in the bushes outside the mansion, and wait for du Pont.

I would shoot him in the head with an arrow as he walked up the steps. As he lay dying on the steps, I would calmly walk up to him so he would know in his final minute alive that I was the one who had shot him. But I would be careful not to get so close to him that any of his blood would get on me. He would beg for his life as he watched me grab another arrow. He'd apologize profusely. "I'm sorry for everything! Please! Pal! Please! No! Don't! Ple—"

Take that!

Each time he would beg, I would sink another arrow into him until the last one would be planted directly into his throat or an eye.

If I got caught and questioned later, my alibi would be that I had been on a camping trip. I would drive to Brazil, change my name, and have a kid with a Brazilian woman so that as a parent of a Brazilian, I could avoid deportation.

D ave and I stayed in constant contact. He had taken a break from competition, and after I had been in Colorado Springs for a few months, he called to tell me he was thinking about leaving his assistant's job at Wisconsin.

"John called me and offered me a job coaching at Foxcatcher," he told me. "I'm thinking I might take it and start competing again."

"Okay," I said, "but I don't think you know what you're getting yourself into. But if that's what you want to do, make sure any deal you make with John is in writing, especially the details of your job description and where you stand in the chain of command. Or you'll get screwed."

A short while after I talked with Dave, John called and told me Dave had accepted the job and that he hadn't forgotten the deal I had negotiated with him.

"I'm going to pay you the same as I pay Dave—no more, no less," John told me. "And neither one of you will have authority over the other. You're both coaches for Foxcatcher."

John paid me forty thousand dollars per year even though I had left. More important was the health insurance that came from being on the payroll.

I feared Dave's move to Foxcatcher would subject him to the same sabotaging of a career that I experienced. But living on the farm wasn't as bad for Dave as it had been for me, because he had two major advantages I had not had when I had lived there.

First, he had a family with him to provide support. By that time, Dave and Nancy had also had a daughter, Danielle (named for Dan Chaid), to go with Alexander (named for legendary Soviet wrestler Aleksandr Medved).

His second advantage was that by that time, numerous other wrestlers were living and training at Foxcatcher. Off my name and accomplishments, du Pont's team had grown in prestige and created an attraction to his farm that allowed him to add to a wrestling collection that would come to include top wrestlers like Dave, Chaid, Rob Calabrese, Dave Lee, and Valentin Jordanov, and coaches Greg Strobel and Jim Humphrey.

At least for Dave, the presence of other wrestlers meant there were plenty of other people for du Pont to bug. The only times Dave had to talk to John were when John came to practices, and that wasn't every day.

At Foxcatcher, Dave never lacked for workout partners, such as Kevin Jackson (a future Olympic champion) and Royce Alger (winner of two NCAA championships). Other wrestlers were flown in from time to time to train with Dave. He was never short of bodies to beat on.

I visited Dave at the farm in 1989, and he seemed to be doing pretty well there. He, Nancy, and the kids lived in a two-story house—maybe twenty-five hundred square feet—on the far side of the estate, a full mile removed from the mansion. The entire corner of the eight hundred acres basically was their backyard. There was a forest nearby where he would go hunting. Dave was really into guns and knew how to clean and cut up deer to make steaks and jerky.

Du Pont's farm already had the gym that he had used during his pentathlon days, with the Olympic-size pool and the ceramic mural of John competing in the five pentathlons. Next to that gym, du Pont had just built the largest wrestling facility in the country. The Foxcatcher National Training Center covered fourteen thousand square feet at a cost of six hundred thousand dollars. From one end to the other, the facility had three full-size, Sarneige-brand mats—the same type used in the Olympics. There also were coaches' offices, showers, lockers, a training room, and a video room. I had never seen a wrestling gym so well equipped and maintained.

At the back end was John's office, away from the other offices. THE EAGLE'S NEST was engraved in a plaque on his office door. Inside were a desk and a big round bed. All around the base of the bed were sticks to make the bed/nest look as though it had been put together by an eagle. John liked for others to call him "Eagle," because he constantly referred to himself as "the Golden Eagle of America."

While being around Wayne Baughman had helped me return to a good place mentally, being in Colorado Springs didn't provide the stable environment I desired. After a year there, the academy hadn't hired me full-time as I had hoped. I was working every day without compensation, my back was starting to go out on me, and I had a long commute to the academy. USA Wrestling wouldn't hire me to work at its headquarters, either.

I was lonely, and I moved back to Ashland for a woman.

I had met Kristy at a bar in Ashland after the 1985 World Championships. All I knew about her before I walked into the bar was that my friends had told me she was a wrestling trainer at Southern Oregon. But based on the physical attributes they described to me, I had to see her. I couldn't afford to marry her then and went back to my job and training at Stanford without her.

Kristy and I married in 1989, bought a truck and a trailer, put everything we had in it, and took off for Utah because I had read that Park City, Utah, offered the most vertical drop in snow skiing for the money. We skied there for a few weeks and then drove about an hour south into Provo, and the cleanliness of the town grabbed us. We stopped there and the people we came into contact with were friendly. We parked our trailer in a Shopko parking lot, and I disconnected the truck to drive over to the campus of Brigham Young University.

Pulling up to the campus, I was struck by the mountains standing tall in the background. We sure hadn't had that kind of view at Oklahoma! The campus was even cleaner than the city. As soon as I stepped onto the campus, Provo was where I wanted to live.

I asked the first person I saw where the gym was. After he told me, I asked why he had come to BYU.

"Actually, I came here to wrestle," he said.

He was trying to impress me by sounding as if he was a member of BYU's wrestling team. I introduced myself. I think he was embarrassed knowing that I would be going to the wrestling room, where I later watched him compete in an intramural tournament.

Walking toward the wrestling room in the Smith Fieldhouse, right between the field house and the Richards Building, I spotted a four-point mule deer.

This is the greatest campus on earth, I thought.

I spent eleven years at BYU and never saw another mule deer on campus.

I came up with the great idea of grabbing a wrestling brochure to see the picture and name of the coach—Alan Albright—and research who some of his best wrestlers were so I could walk up to him as if I'd known him all my life and say, "Hey, Alan. How's Rick Evans doing this year?"

The wrestling team was on a road trip, and when they returned I met Alan and asked if I could work out there. Not only did he allow me to work out, but he also gave me a locker and gear, and access to the weight room. Alan and I hit it off right away, and we remain good friends.

After I had worked out a few times, Alan told me he was considering retiring from college coaching in a few years and said he might be able to help set me up to take over when he left. It was like a dream come true thinking about the possibility of securing a Division I wrestling head coach's position.

I officially became an assistant coach there in 1991 and was hired as head coach in 1994, when Alan left to coach at a high school south of Provo.

Utah was also the site of four momentous occasions in my life. Three were the birth of son, Mark David, and daughters, Kelli and Sarah Jessica. The fourth was my conversion into the Church of Jesus Christ of Latter-day Saints.

I moved to Provo with preconceived notions about Mormons. Coach Albright didn't tell me I was wrong—he showed the error in my thinking by how he lived.

I had attended a Nazarene church early in my life and did not have a good experience. From that point on, I had not been a member of any religion and vowed to trash anyone who claimed membership in the one true church. I could not accept that all churches were true, because some of their beliefs conflicted.

After I had been around BYU for a while, Alan started talking to me about how the Book of Mormon was the cornerstone of the LDS Church. He would make claims about the Book of Mormon being true, and I would challenge him. Alan had an answer to every challenge.

I would ask questions of Alan and Corey Veach, another BYU assistant. A friend gave me some anti-Mormon literature to read, and Alan had Peter Sorenson, an English professor at the school, point out where the literature was flawed.

All my questions were being answered, and all the answers I had heard about what was wrong with Mormonism were being refuted. Then Alan informed me that Joseph Smith, founder of the LDS movement, was a wrestler. If that turned out to be true, I told myself, then I would probably be willing to read the Book of Mormon. I researched, and it was true. In my research, I could not find an account of his losing a match to anyone.

On September 22, 1991, Alan baptized me into the LDS Church.

In 1993, I was sitting at home in Provo when a guy I didn't know called and said, "The best jujitsu fighter in the world is in town. Do you want to fight him?"

I had heard of jujitsu but didn't know anything about it. I thought the call was part of a joke.

"What are the rules?" I asked.

"There are no rules!" he said.

I scrapped the notion that this was a joke. *If there are no rules,* I wondered, *would we be trying to kill each other? Is this going to be a fight to the death?*

I couldn't back down from that challenge.

This was right before the 1993 NCAA championships, and I wouldn't be able to meet this jujitsu guy until our team returned home.

"Tell him to be in the BYU wrestling room a week from Thursday," I told the caller.

I was nervous for the next week. I was working on a master's degree but couldn't concentrate on my assignments. I didn't tell anyone what was going on, but when the big day arrived, there was a small group of people in the room, some with video cameras.

My first sight on the mat was Alan wrestling some guy who looked as if he belonged in the movie *Kumite*, with the front of his head shaved and his hair pulled into a long braid. Alan was on his feet and the guy was on his butt, scooting into Alan and trying to hook Alan's feet with his.

If this is all it is, I thought, *it's no big deal.*

When the people saw I had walked in, the action stopped.

The guy got up, came toward me, and introduced himself as Rickson Gracie.

"Are you the guy?" he asked.

"Yeah, I'm the guy. Are you the guy?"

"Yeah, I'm the guy," he said.

We had established that each of us was "the guy."

Rickson was a Brazilian jujitsu expert and had the cauliflower ears of a wrestler. Seeing his ears, I had no doubt he was tough.

"What I do," he explained, "is elbow, knee, punch, and kick, but we're not going to do any of that today. We're going to grapple and try to get each other in submission holds and chokes until one of us taps out."

Oh, good. No homicide today.

I was pretty happy with that plan.

Rickson stood there in front of me, in no stance.

"Come on," he said.

I shot in, took him down, and had him in a cradle for probably twenty minutes. I wondered why the guy seemed so content to let me hold him down.

I didn't know any submission holds and made things up as I went. Based on what I had learned from two weeks of training with the US national judo team while I lived in Colorado Springs, I kept my chin down and elbows in. But that's about all I knew, because submission holds were against wrestling's rules.

My grip gave out, and Rickson escaped and tried different chokes and armlocks on me. Then he tried a move called a "triangle," or a figure-four in wrestling, and I couldn't get out of it and had to tap out when my air supply got cut off.

Our wrestlers watching from the bench were laughing at me. If I hadn't just had my air flow cut off, I would have gone over to the bench and kicked some serious ass.

"Can we do it again?" I asked Rickson.

I was on top of him again for another twenty frustrating minutes before tiring and allowing Rickson to reverse me. As a wrestler my natural reaction was to go belly down so I wouldn't get pinned. He immediately pulled my chin up and did a rear naked choke to tap me out again.

Rickson told me I was the toughest guy he had ever gone up against and joked that he would retire if I learned jujitsu.

Though humiliated, I learned a valuable lesson that day. I had never practiced submission holds because they were against NCAA and Olympic rules. The rules of wrestling instead pushed me toward conditioning and staying on top of an opponent, but there was no reason to learn techniques that would make people submit. I didn't get into wrestling to win matches. I got into wrestling because I believed it was the ultimate martial art. Thanks to Rickson, I had discovered that there were better street-fighting moves out there and I had to learn them.

It had been five years since my last Olympics, and I had been depressed the entire time. My life needed a change in direction, and jujitsu was the avenue. The takedowns and conditioning of wrestling were superior to any martial art, and combining wrestling with the submissions of jujitsu would create an even better martial art than either of them alone.

Pedro Sauer was one of Rickson's students and had the Brazilian jujitsu club in Provo that had brought Rickson to town. Pedro was smart and fluid, his technique flawless. He was the perfect coach for me.

CHAPTER 16

Trouble at Foxcatcher

While I was experiencing life-altering moments in Utah, Dave's wrestling career was filled with disappointment, injury, and determination.

Following his setback to Kenny Monday in the 1988 wrestle-off for the Olympic team, Dave took a year off from competition to coach the US national team. Dave came back during the '89 season, when Kenny was in the prime of his outstanding freestyle career.

Dave and Kenny had a great rivalry going on the mat, and the two also had immense respect for each other. When Kenny won gold in Seoul, Dave was there to hoist him on his shoulders and take him on a victory lap around the mat.

Dave's international popularity was probably never more evident than at the 1991 tournament in Tbilisi. He had won there in '87, and no American had won the tournament twice.

Russian wrestling fans adored Dave. Zeke Jones, the current US freestyle national team coach, was coaching the Tbilisi team in '91, and he told me that Dave's finals match with a Russian ended in a tie, but the refs awarded the victory to the Russian because of Dave's passivity, which had been caused by a shoulder injury.

The fans went nuts, throwing things onto the arena floor and jeering. It took several minutes for officials to get the crowd under control. The refs reconvened, and both wrestlers' hands were raised in victory. The fans wildly cheered the decision even though their own countryman had appeared to have won the championship. Zeke said he felt as if he were in a scene right out of *The Twilight Zone*. I've been told that was the only time two gold medals have been awarded in the same weight class at the tournament.

Kenny beat Dave again in the '91 trials for the World Team. After that loss, Dave, tired of cutting weight, decided to move up to 180.5 pounds in his bid to return to the Olympics. Dave struggled with nagging injuries after the switch, and his new weight class was one of the strongest on the US team, with defending world champ Kevin Jackson, Royce Alger, and Melvin Douglas, who was a year away from beginning his run of four consecutive US national championships. All four of those guys probably could have medaled at the upcoming Olympics.

Dave lost his best-of-three to Douglas after winning the first match. Jackson wound up claiming the spot on the US team and won gold in Barcelona.

Dave turned thirty-three in the summer of '92. He wasn't the type of wrestler who got counted out of too many things during his career, but at that age, the widespread opinion was that Dave had missed out on his last opportunity to compete in the Olympics.

My brother, however, only grew more determined. He set his sights on the 1996 Games in Atlanta, Georgia. He dropped back down to 163, Kenny Monday retired, and Dave became our country's top-ranked wrestler. He won the national championship and placed second at Worlds. In '94, he won the national and World Cup titles and placed second at the Goodwill Games. In '95, he won his third consecutive national championship and seventh overall. He also won his fifth World Cup title that year.

Dave's inspiring comeback had become a good story. At age thirty-six, his performances were giving every indication that he was on his way to winning an Olympic medal twelve years after our double golds at the Los Angeles Games.

To the same degree that Dave's career had trekked upward, the atmosphere at Foxcatcher Farm seemed equally headed downward. The stories I heard from Dave, my good friend Dan Chaid, and other wrestlers there became increasingly perplexing. In the aftermath of Dave's murder, when the media began investigating du Pont's past, I heard even more bizarre stories detailing how erratic John's behavior had become.

Convinced there were spirits and spies inside the mansion, John had brought in a psychic to describe the spirits residing in the home. He also had workers check every inch of the walls and floors to locate the spies John knew were watching him. The spies weren't found. But still adamant they were there, John had all the mansion's columns and walls X-rayed.

He also assigned a group of wrestlers the task of searching for Nazi spies that du Pont had observed hiding in treetops, and he believed enemies were coming through the mansion's tunnels intent on killing him.

John ordered treadmills removed from the training center because he believed their clocks were transporting him back in time. He told a wrestler to take off his baseball cap because he believed the cap was transmitting some kind of signals. The balls on du Pont's billiards table were sent off for inspection because he suspected they had transmitting devices inside them.

A relative said John had called himself "the Dalai Lama of the United States" and would not acknowledge anyone who did not address him by that title. At other times, he also claimed to be the president of Bulgaria and of the Soviet Union.

He believed that rocks communicated with him, and he talked about a device he was convinced was inside the mansion that sprayed a unique oil on people that made them disappear. He shot geese that he insisted were trying to place him under a spell.

Older stories were made public, too.

In the mid '80s, John had blown up a family of newborn foxes with dynamite for no known reason. In 1990, he had blood running down his legs. When asked what was wrong, he explained that he could see bugs digging into his skin and was plucking them out, tearing pieces of flesh off with them.

John owned a tank, which had been stripped of its weapons, that he liked to drive around the estate and in parades. One night around Christmastime in 1984, he drove the tank to a home on his estate occupied by a policeman and his wife. John had driven through several trees and had scratches on his head from hitting the branches. Bloodied and drunk, he asked the wife if her husband could "come out to play."

Yet those who stepped forward to tell of their odd experiences with du Pont said they hadn't thought that he would hurt, much less kill, anyone. His behavior was usually dismissed with "That's just John," or attributed to his alcohol and cocaine use. Family members later said they had been concerned about John's mental health and tried to persuade him to get help. But he refused and, under Pennsylvania law, they were helpless to do more without his consent.

Although the stories went back more than a decade, it was clear that they had become increasingly outlandishness over recent years.

And just in the past year or so, I learned of a story that had been reported years earlier and I had not heard of even though I was working at Villanova at the time. In December 1987, John hit a flag man directing traffic. Du Pont wasn't driving fast, but he struck the man hard enough that the man rolled up onto the hood of John's Lincoln Town Car and then fell onto the ground when du Pont stopped. Du Pont told the man he was the Vanderbilt wrestling coach and dragged him to the sidewalk, although I still have a difficult time believing John was strong enough to drag another man. A witness said du Pont stayed with the man for a few minutes and before police or medical help could arrive, told the man in a slurred voice, "You'll be all right" and drove away.

When du Pont arrived at his estate, he immediately got into the helicopter with Chaid, Calabrese, and another man to go to the Philadelphia airport and fly to Wisconsin, where they would meet up with Dave to attend a wrestling match. Du Pont ordered everyone not to talk on the way to the airport. On board the Learjet, he told the group what had happened and that he might have killed the flagman. While they were en route to Wisconsin, du Pont's lawyer made several calls to Nancy to have John call him as soon as he arrived. In front of Dave and Nancy, and still with his travel partners, John again admitted he had hit a man with his car.

Du Pont, Dan, Rob, and the other man flew back home that night. When questioned by police the next day, John said that he hadn't thought the man was seriously hurt and that he left the scene because he had to make the trip to Wisconsin. The man, who was treated for minor injuries at a hospital and released, did not file a complaint and received an insurance settlement. John was given a minor traffic violation and fined a whopping total of $42.50.

Looking back, it seems like du Pont spent all of those years just one step from being exposed for what he truly was. The wrong person made angry could have ruined everything for him. But John had the connections, the power, and the money to keep from being made public the selfish, manipulative man that he was.

The problems at Foxcatcher seemed to become more frequent when Jordanov moved onto the farm. Valentin was from Bulgaria, and he had been one of the marquee wrestlers in that dual that du Pont had set up.

After Valentin arrived at Foxcatcher, he arranged matches for du Pont in Bulgaria against wrestlers in the Veterans division, for ages fifty and over. John would fly over to southeastern Europe and pay Bulgarians to lose to him. Some of those wrestlers made more money losing to John than they could make in a year competing in legitimate matches.

During one tournament, a special exhibition match was held between John and a Bulgarian wrestler. A du Pont win had been arranged, but the Bulgarian got out to a big lead in the first minutes. Du Pont couldn't do anything to the guy to score points. The Bulgarian realized he was in danger of winning and threw himself onto his own back, pinning himself. The ref called the fall and, for some reason, the Tunisian wrestlers there started celebrating with John, hoisting him on their shoulders and parading him around the arena. Who knows? He might have paid the Tunisians to help him celebrate, too.

I hadn't heard of such Veterans tournaments taking place in the United States. I had seen a Veterans match once and felt sorry for the two competitors because they were slow and uncoordinated. I think John exerted his influence to have Veterans tournaments set up in our country. I wouldn't be surprised to learn he had started donating money specifically to the Veterans program. Those tournaments started becoming popular and all kinds of retired wrestlers started competing again. My coach at UCLA, Dave Auble, became a Veterans World Champion.

According to what I was told, du Pont really became fixated on winning a World Championship in the Veterans division. He wrestled in a few tournaments but was unable to win. It wasn't uncommon for Veterans tournaments to have weight classes with no competitors, so to win a world title, John started showing up and signing up for an empty weight class, regardless of whether he qualified weightwise. No officials would say anything to stop him. They couldn't afford to bite the hand that fed their sport.

José Betancourt, who had thrown a match to John on the Villanova team's trip to Puerto Rico, became friends with du Pont. José took part in a fake match with John, which I don't think John knew had been rigged. Du Pont beat José by a score of 14–13 or something similar. Dave told me he considered José his hero for making John happy. When John was happy, life on the farm was better for everyone there.

Chaid told me a story, which has since become well documented, from when Mario Saletnik came to live in the "old schoolhouse," a renovated building at the farm. Mario was FILA's

highest-ranking official and head of its association of officials. He
had been influential in getting John to donate to FILA. He was
also head official at Olympics and World Championships. He had
been the "extra official" assigned to watch Dave and me at the '84
Olympics after Dave had hurt the Yugoslav and I had broken the
Turk's elbow.

Mario's moving to Foxcatcher surprised me. I still do not
know what caused him to move there. Mario was the most powerful official in wrestling, yet he had chosen to expose himself to
becoming corrupted. John got a kick out of manipulating people
to see if they would go against their principles in exchange for
money. It was a game for him. He really did believe that everyone
had a price. Now it was Mario's turn to be tested.

After a while, du Pont determined that Mario was trying to
get more money from him not only for FILA but also for himself.
John decided he no longer wanted Mario around.

During the winter, du Pont had somehow driven his new Lincoln Continental into a pond on the estate. A few days later, John
met Mario at the front gate in another Lincoln Continental. Mario
said he had heard from the wrestlers about John's driving his car
into a pond and asked how it had happened.

"I'll show you," du Pont told him. "Get in the back."

John handed Mario a plane ticket back to his home country
of Canada and proceeded to drive toward the same pond, through
the same set of trees, and right back into the pond. John jumped
out of his car on the way into the pond and returned to his mansion, leaving Mario there in the backseat. Mario managed to get
out and walked back to the wrestling facility, where, noticeably
freaked out, he described what had just happened. Mario was all

wet, and when he took his suit pants off, his legs were red from the near-freezing water.

It became a joke among the wrestlers, who would tease Mario by asking if he wanted to go for a swim. But that incident later would be looked back on as the first sign that du Pont intended to start getting rid of some of those around him and would do so by whatever means necessary, including causing physical harm.

John's history was to become enamored of a sport or activity—such as collecting, law enforcement, triathlon, or wrestling—and make it his "toy" until he became bored with it. Then he would discard it and set off to find a new toy.

In my opinion, John reached that point with wrestling. He had gained power within wrestling's governing bodies and over some of the sport's key players. He had climbed the sport's political ladder. He had bought himself more international influence and prestige than he could through any of his other collections. But still, wrestling was his toy, and it was time to discard it.

John and Chaid, who had come to Villanova in 1987, started having problems with each other that led to a story Dan told me. In October 1995, Dan was lifting weights in the Foxcatcher weight room when John came in carrying an automatic assault rifle with a perforated barrel. John crouched in an aggressive stance, pointed the rifle at Dan, and said, "Don't fuck with me. I want you off the farm now."

"John, I've only tried to be your friend," Dan responded. "But I'll leave."

Du Pont left the gym, and Dan started telling the other wrestlers what had happened and that du Pont was losing his mind and out of control. Their reaction was to tell Dan that du Pont was only mad at him.

Du Pont just never seemed dangerous, because no one thought he would ever actually follow through on his threats. John would do something crazy, then it would be dismissed with "John wouldn't hurt anybody."

The assault rifle incident came up in the media after du Pont murdered Dave, and Dan claimed that he had reported what had happened to the police, but that they hadn't taken him seriously, saying du Pont was "a little eccentric." The police department countered by stating that Chaid had never followed through on the paperwork and that with nothing more than an unsubstantiated allegation available to them, there was nothing more they could do.

Dan packed most of his belongings in a van that he left at Dave's house and returned home to California. He flew back to Philadelphia a few weeks later to finish packing and leave for good. John wasn't happy to hear that Dan was back on the property. Late that night, he went to Dave's house, drunk and looking for Dan. He searched through Dave and Nancy's house trying to find Dan, but he wasn't there.

John was so drunk that he was stumbling around, and he slipped and hit his head on a windowsill, opening a big cut.

Dave and his wife helped John to his car so Dave could drive him to the emergency room, and Nancy noticed a rifle in the car and took it into their house. John kept saying he wanted his gun back before they left, and finally Dave returned it to him, but not before removing the bullets.

Dave ran red lights driving John to Crozer-Chester Medical Center, where the trauma center had been named for him. On the way, John told Dave that he was going to file a police report claiming Chaid had hit him in the head with a bat and that he wanted Dave to back up his story.

At the emergency room, John refused to fill out any forms, yelling, "I'm John du Pont! I don't need to wait in line! Get me a doctor right now!" The nurses were rushing around, trying to calm him and get the necessary paperwork filled out. But John kept barking orders and asking, "Don't you know who I am?" He wound up needing stitches to close the cut.

John stuck with his story about Dan and a bat. Dave and his wife told police what had really happened. When John learned later that Dave and Nancy had not gone along with his story, he requested a copy of the police report.

I haven't confirmed this officially, but I have been told that the police report was on du Pont's desk when they searched his mansion after arresting him for killing Dave. Only after the murder, as the media began investigating and later through information that came out as part of the judicial process, did the pieces of a complex puzzle begin to come together.

Apparently, du Pont developed a growing animosity toward Dave, who had been John's favorite when he moved onto the farm. Over time, Valentin Jordanov—who, like Dave, was married with children—took Dave's place in that role.

I think Valentin was the only wrestler on the farm who could tolerate John, and that was only because Valentin didn't know a lot of English at that time. When I had first met Valentin, while he was living on the estate, I told him, "If you want to stay at Fox-catcher, don't learn English. He'll talk your head off and you'll hate it here."

The odd thing was that Dave and Valentin were very close friends. Their friendship had begun during that Foxcatcher-Bulgaria match of John's.

John fired Dave after a party on New Year's Eve 1994 because Dave came dressed in a Russian soldier's uniform to get a laugh out of his Bulgarian friend. John had a fascination with Bulgaria and had made up bizarre stories about his mother having had sex with a Bulgarian soldier, meaning he and Valentin were both Bulgarian. John must have viewed Dave as a threat to his friendship with Valentin.

The next day, John called Dave to the mansion and fired him. Jordanov and Calabrese both told du Pont that they would leave the team if Dave was forced out. John backed down and apolo-gized to Dave.

In 1995, Foxcatcher head coach Greg Strobel's contract ex-pired and he took the head coach's job at Lehigh University. Greg recommended that du Pont appoint Dave as his replacement. Du Pont, however, chose Jordanov over Dave even though Dave was clearly more qualified. When Valentin expressed his disappoint-ment over his new salary, it was Dave who went to du Pont on Valentin's behalf and talked John into paying Valentin more.

Dave was the person at Foxcatcher whom the others went to when they had problems with du Pont. Dave was the only one among the wrestlers who would stand up to John yet also could calm him down and convince him to, in most cases, act rationally. Dave was not a yes-man, and he wasn't afraid to speak up and tell du Pont when he was screwing something up. He thought he could help John.

John listened to Dave more than anyone else at Foxcatcher, but Valentin had become the one John most wanted to impress.

That November, the athletes advisory council of USA Wrestling gathered via conference call to consider requesting that the organization officially discontinue its association with du Pont. The discussion centered on two complaints.

First, one wrestler had reported du Pont pointing guns at some of the wrestlers at Foxcatcher.

Second, earlier in the year, du Pont had kicked three black wrestlers off the farm because of their skin color, saying the Ku Klux Klan ran Foxcatcher. It wasn't just the black wrestlers du Pont had removed from the farm. He had developed a fear of the color black and ordered anything black on the estate either removed or painted a different color.

Dave defended John more than anyone else on the call, and the council decided not to call for action by USA Wrestling. The council members were not convinced that du Pont was racist or a threat to anyone's safety. Plus, du Pont's interest in wrestling appeared to have begun to wane. He had already sent word to USA Wrestling that his financial contributions would cease after 1996. He had been talking about how he might get out of the sport altogether.

Once du Pont had made it known that he would stop making his annual donation to USA Wrestling, a separation began to develop between him and the governing body. John had become a problem within wrestling, but he was also in the process of removing himself from the sport without USA Wrestling's having to force it.

Dave planned to stay at Foxcatcher through the 1996 Olympics, which would end in early August—he wanted to cap his comeback on wrestling's biggest stage—and then return home to Palo Alto, where I only recently learned he had been offered the chance to coach at Stanford again. When other wrestlers heard of Dave's intent, some packed up and moved and others made plans to leave with Dave. Valentin was one of those.

During the Christmas holidays of 1995, Dave and his family came to visit me in Utah. I forgot to give him the security code to my house and while I was at the school he went into the house, set off the alarm, and the police came. We had a good laugh over that.

I took Dave's family to Salt Lake City to visit Temple Square, which is the most-visited tourist spot in Utah. I talked to them about my faith, the positive impact it had made in my life, and what I had learned about the validity of the Book of Mormon.

Dave and I did some jujitsu in the BYU wrestling room. I explained to Dave how I had quit wrestling for good and had become exclusively a jujitsu guy. He wanted to see what jujitsu felt like. I got on my back, which a wrestler never does. I lay there and waited for Dave to get on top of me. Then I got him in an armlock and, a little more than seven months from the Olympics, I cracked his elbow. On the way to the hospital, I kept firmly saying to him, "Why didn't you tap? I told you to tap!"

Doctors discovered bone fragments that had already been in

his elbow, and he had to later have them surgically removed. I felt bad even though I hadn't caused the injury.

On our last day together, I took Dave skiing at Snowbird. The forecast called for a severe snowstorm, but as this was his last day in Utah, we went anyway. The storm lifted and the conditions were almost perfect for skiing. There was all this pure powder to ski on, and we were the only ones on the mountain. We skied all day and had the greatest time together.

After Dave's family got back to Foxcatcher, he mailed me a card. In his note he reflected back to when, after winning my second World Championship, I had started signing my name "Mark Schultz, Olympic and two-time World Champion." Chris Horpel had given me a hard time for not being a World Champion, which was why I made that a part of my signature. Dave told me he thought that was funny.

Then he added the reason he had sent me the card: He wanted me to know how much he loved me and how happy he was to be my brother.

CHAPTER 17

Why?

We'll never know why John du Pont killed my brother. But the date has always loomed as important when I try to come up with a reason: January 26, 1996. Valentin Jordanov's thirty-sixth birthday.

There had been a party at the gym late that morning to celebrate Valentin's birthday and to send off a group of Bulgarian wrestlers who had been training there and were leaving that afternoon. Du Pont was there with the wrestlers.

As far as motive goes, I believe that du Pont had a birthday present he wanted to give Jordanov that would demonstrate how much du Pont loved him, how true he was to Valentin.

A few hours after the party, du Pont asked Pat Goodale, his security expert, to take a ride with him around the estate. It had been a rugged winter in southeastern Pennsylvania. The great blizzard of '96 had dumped about two feet of snow on Delaware County less than three weeks earlier, and after a more recent snowfall, du Pont wanted to survey the damage on his eight hundred acres.

John typically carried a .38 caliber handgun with him around the property. But on this day, Goodale noticed du Pont grabbing a longer-barreled, .44 Magnum revolver—one of the most powerful handguns in the world—before heading to the car.

Du Pont's car was being repaired, and he slid behind the wheel of the silver Lincoln Town Car loaner. After driving around the snow-covered estate, du Pont made his way toward the white two-story house Dave and his family lived in on the edge of the estate, a mile from the main house.

It was about two forty-five on a cold, gray Friday afternoon. Dave's kids were at school, a couple of blocks away. Dave was crazy about Alexander and Danielle, and I just know he had been checking the time as he repaired his car radio, counting down the minutes until it was time to pick up Alexander and Danielle and start the weekend.

Dave was part in, part out of his car when du Pont turned into the driveway and pulled near him. Dave had no idea of du Pont's intention and no way of protecting himself as he said, "Hi, Coach," and started toward du Pont's car.

The first shot and Dave's scream drew Nancy's attention toward the front door. She grabbed the phone to call 911 on her way. Du Pont's second shot was fired before she stepped outside. When she opened the front door, she told John to stop. He pointed the gun at her and she turned back into the house. Then, quickly, came the third and final shot.

Goodale testified at du Pont's trial that he was on his way out of the car through the passenger-side door. He had two guns on him, and he had drawn one and pointed it at du Pont. Goodale said du Pont turned to face him, with the barrels of their guns pointing at each other.

Needing to get du Pont out of there so she could check on Dave, Nancy returned outside and informed John the police were on their way. Goodale scurried for cover behind a metal barrel. He said du Pont tossed his gun onto the seat and hurried out of the driveway.

Nancy and Goodale tried to stop Dave's bleeding until the paramedics could arrive. But hollow-point bullets expand, or mushroom, on impact. They are designed to inflict more damage to the target than a conventional bullet. John had loaded his gun to kill.

Dave died in his wife's arms.

I have never quite grasped Goodale's actions during the shooting. I've wondered if he actually had jumped out of the car and hidden behind the barrel in self-defense and *then* pointed his gun at du Pont. He could have put a bullet in du Pont and ended it at any point, but he didn't. He took criticism because he was the only person who could have saved Dave's life, but I tried to have sympathy toward him. Only he and du Pont knew what truly happened.

I don't blame Goodale for anything. How could he have expected anything like that to happen? The three shots occurred so much more quickly than it seems when you read about them, and Goodale had to make a split-second decision. Even as I still wonder what else could have happened in Dave's driveway, it's difficult to fault Pat.

My dad called me probably within half an hour of the shooting. I was in the midst of just another middle-of-the-season afternoon at the office, answering phone calls and opening mail. Practice was a little more than an hour away.

I don't think anyone in the history of BYU cursed as much as I did after throwing the phone.

I sat in the corner, sobbing, wishing I had told Dave to leave Foxcatcher earlier. Or further back, not to move there at all. Before he moved to Foxcatcher, I had recommended to Dave that he get things in writing with du Pont and warned him that John was a manipulator. Then when Chaid had told me about John bringing the assault rifle into the weight room, I thought I needed to tell Dave to leave right then.

I didn't tell him. I should have listened to my gut.

And I hated myself for thinking this, but I realized that Dave would never break my record for World Championships won. We were always competitors. Both of us. But I have carried so much guilt all these years for having that thought. I've had to rely on my faith, which assures me that God wants me to be happy and that I need to forgive myself instead of punishing myself for thinking about having more championships than Dave.

Larry Nugent, my assistant coach, was the first person to come into the office. He slumped in his chair. I think he started crying, but I'm not too sure because I wasn't paying much attention to him. I don't even know how long we stayed in the office, but before Larry drove me home, I noticed I had never hung up the phone. My dad had been listening to me scream and curse and cry the entire time.

Alan Albright and Ben Ohai, a BYU Hall of Fame wrestler and one of my closest friends along with Alan, were waiting for Larry and me at my house. Dave's murder was already becoming big news, especially with the early reports saying one of the du Pont heirs was suspected as the killer. The TV was tuned to CNN. I would watch for a while, then have to leave the room to go cry. I remember one of those times when I had to go off to be alone, Ben followed me into the room to be with me, and he was crying, too.

Someone in my house took a phone call from the police in Newtown Square who said they were aware I might want to do something to du Pont and told me not to go to Pennsylvania. I had already thought about driving out there. I wanted to blow du Pont's brains out, but I knew that with the cops already at the estate, there was no way I could get to him.

John had driven back to the mansion, without Goodale, after shooting Dave and walked directly into the windowless, steel-lined vault on the first floor that his mother had installed as a bomb shelter. John used the vault—complete with combination lock and lever, just like a bank vault—as his library and, often, snorting room. It was in his library that John was known to go with the cocaine supplier he kept on his payroll and later emerge acting different and with white stuff visible around his nose.

Du Pont removed the three empty cartridges from his .44, replaced them with three fresh bullets so the revolver would be fully loaded, and slid the gun out of sight onto a high shelf. He stepped out of the library and shouted instructions to his employees upstairs that under no circumstances were they to allow the police in. They acknowledged, assuming he was referring to a subpoena he expected to be served regarding a continuing legal matter.

The police, uncertain of du Pont's location, started gathering at the entrance to the estate. Eventually, the standoff would include seventy-five police officers from ten departments and thirty SWAT team members. The local police knew firsthand that du Pont possessed an arsenal of weapons, some high-powered. They were also aware of du Pont's marksman skills because he had trained many of them to shoot until the day in 1992 when, abruptly and for no known reason, he decided to cut off access of the police to the range on his farm.

The media began to assemble at the estate, too. Reporters worked their sources for any details they could uncover about the man whose philanthropy had covered over his eccentricities but who now was holed up in his home as an alleged murderer.

Why did he shoot Dave? How could John du Pont kill anyone?

The reporters would have plenty of time to ask those questions before the standoff came to an end.

Police drove around the farm escorting employees and residents of the outlying homes safely off the property. After more than an hour, a policeman monitoring the mansion through binoculars spotted du Pont inside. John wasn't alone. Two of his employees, Georgia Dusckas and Barbara Linton, plus a painter, working unassumingly upstairs, remained inside. There were early concerns that John was holding Dusckas and Linton as hostages, but those were dismissed when police spotted both walking freely around the mansion. They were unaware that Dave had been killed, and nothing in du Pont's mannerisms indicated that anything out of the ordinary had happened.

Du Pont asked Dusckas, his executive assistant, to call Pat Goodale on the cell phone. A fire a few months earlier had taken out phone service to the mansion and du Pont hadn't thought it necessary to have the line repaired. The cell phone was the only way to make or receive calls.

Dusckas could not reach Goodale.

Then John asked Dusckas to call his lawyer, Taras Wochok. He wanted Wochok to come to his home. But Wochok had left work early and his office would have to try to make contact with him.

By the time Wochok received the message, reports of the standoff were all over the Philadelphia-area media outlets. Wochok headed immediately for the farm.

The painter was the first of the remaining three to leave the mansion. Dusckas and Linton later noticed officers with rifles near the mansion but assumed they were there to serve the subpoena. Wochok, by phone, informed Dusckas about what was really taking place.

Dusckas made several more attempts to reach Goodale by phone. When she finally connected with him, she told Goodale that du Pont wanted Pat to come see him. Goodale said he couldn't and advised Dusckas that she and Linton needed to leave. Goodale hung up. Dusckas called Goodale back, and John Ryan, the policeman leading the negotiations team, answered instead.

Linton exited the mansion at 5:45 P.M. and was whisked away to safety.

A little later, du Pont reminded Dusckas that Jordanov would be stopping by for his nightly visit. Du Pont asked Dusckas to invite the other wrestlers at the farm to come, too.

"In fact," du Pont added with an eerie chuckle, "invite Schultz up."

Dusckas placed a call to Ryan. She realized she needed to get out, but would have to wait for an opportunity to leave without John's noticing. She wanted the police to be prepared for her to escape the first chance she could. That chance came when John asked her to take his coffee cup to the kitchen.

At 6:45 P.M., Dusckas slipped out of the mansion. John remained inside, alone.

With only du Pont in the mansion, police could be patient and wait him out. Having reliable phone contact with du Pont would be essential to their operations, though, so Friday night, workers from the telephone company were escorted into a tunnel to repair the phone line. To reduce noise for the workers, and to ensure that du Pont couldn't sneak up on the workers and police in the tunnel, the heater was turned off.

The usual time for Jordanov to visit du Pont passed, and du Pont began making repeated cell phone calls to Jordanov's family home on the farm, leaving messages for Valentin to come to the mansion. John would not talk to the police, however, until an overnight call from Goodale rang the phone inside.

Goodale, calling from the police line, tried to convince du Pont to give up and come out of the house, but du Pont was not interested. Instead, he asked that Valentin, Wochok, and Mario Saletnik come visit him. Before du Pont hung up, he wanted to make sure that Goodale understood with whom he was talking. Du Pont was, he reminded Goodale, the president of the United States.

Intermittent conversations continued into a chilly and stormy Saturday, with police continuing to ask du Pont to come out of the house and du Pont insisting he wanted to see Valentin, Wochok, and Saletnik instead.

In one conversation, du Pont remarked, "His Holiness is under siege here." In another, he called the estate "holy property" and "a forbidden city." In another, he referred to himself as "president of the Soviet Union."

Du Pont engaged in longer conversations with police as Saturday progressed, with some calls lasting up to twelve minutes, but he still could not be talked out of the house. Nor would he acknowledge that a shooting had taken place on his property. That night, the police decided that a rested du Pont would be better to deal with and halted their phone calls so John could sleep.

Early Sunday morning, before seven o'clock, du Pont used the cell phone to call Wochok at home. John identified himself as Jesus Christ and warned that the death of Jesus would bring an end to the world. Then he asked for cigars and pipe tobacco. Du Pont told Wochok he could be called again at 10:00 A.M. and clicked off the call. The police began calling shortly before then. Du Pont declined to answer calls until it was 10:00 A.M.

The police allowed Wochok to talk to du Pont that morning, and the conversation followed much the same pattern as those the day before: John would not leave the house and he wanted to see Valentin.

Du Pont complained about being cold. Temperatures had dipped into the twenties overnight, and the fireplace wasn't generating enough warmth as John burned copies of the second book he had written and paid to have published. The book's title: *Never Give Up*.

John told his lawyer that he wanted to go into the tunnel to see why the boilers were not working. The heater had been turned off only to help with the repair of the phone lines, but cutting the heat to inside the mansion proved to be the most significant step in ending the standoff.

In what would be the final phone conversation, with police negotiator Sergeant Anthony Paparo, du Pont demanded during the afternoon that the heater be repaired. Paparo said that was not possible. But du Pont had tired of being cold. Could he be allowed, du Pont asked, to go outside to the greenhouse so he could enter the tunnel and see what was wrong with the boilers?

Paparo, not wanting du Pont to end the call, dragged out the conversation until supervisors were consulted and police officers stationed around the mansion were placed on alert. Paparo began negotiating a trip outside for du Pont. Paparo made John promise— repeatedly—that he would not carry a gun outside with him.

Wearing a dark Bulgarian team sweat suit with a light blue Team Foxcatcher shirt underneath, du Pont exited the house and took his first steps down the path toward the greenhouse. A SWAT team member, concealed behind a tree, waited for du Pont to walk far enough that he wouldn't be able to turn and run back into the house. The officer then pointed his gun at du Pont and ordered him to stop and raise his hands.

John did as instructed, then dropped his hands and made a run for the house. The officer stepped out from behind the tree and again ordered du Pont to stop. Du Pont stopped for only a second before dashing for the door again.

The officer chased him down and grabbed him. Other officers converged on du Pont and handcuffed him.

From du Pont's neck hung a laminated pass from the previous year's World Championships. The pockets of his sweatpants contained keys and a passport. As du Pont had promised, he had left the house unarmed.

Du Pont was placed in a police van and, forty-eight hours after the standoff began, was on his way to jail.

CHAPTER 18

My Ultimate Victory

I took leave from my job at BYU and remained in Utah. Dave's body was cremated, so I did not go back to Philadelphia until the memorial service on Sunday, February 11.

The memorial was held at the University of Pennsylvania's sports arena called the Palestra, which comes from the word for the place in ancient Greece used for training in wrestling and athletics. Among those in attendance were wrestlers and officials who had canceled trips for competitions in Bulgaria and Turkey.

I wore a striped, long-sleeved shirt and jeans. Others dressed up more than I had, with most in suits, but I intentionally wore clothes I would never wear again. I didn't want any clothing to serve as a reminder of the service.

Hal Miles drove from Petersburg, Virginia, to be with me. We went into a room away from the crowd. We kneeled, and Hal prayed for Dave and me. Years later, Hal honored me by allowing me to baptize him into the LDS Church. He is still one of my best friends.

For ninety minutes, wrestlers, friends, and family members shared their memories of Dave.

Roger Reina, the wrestling coach at Penn, called Dave "a hero of the people." Roger described how Dave had admirably managed to be both tough and sensitive, both childish and wise.

Larry Sciacchetano, the president of USA Wrestling, called

Dave "the Muhammad Ali, the Magic Johnson, the Michael Jordan of our sport."

Larry pointed out that most people were lucky to have one or two true best friends, but Dave had ten thousand. "He made everyone feel important," Larry said. "When you were with him, he was genuinely interested in you, in what you were doing in your life, and how he could help."

Valentin also spoke. "My best friend is gone forever," he said. He called training with Dave the best six years of his life.

Tears were visible on Valentin's face as he left the stage and walked into the stands to take a seat. Alexander and Danielle noticed how upset Valentin was, followed him into the seats, and hugged him. Those kids—I can't imagine what they were going through. Alexander was nine, Danielle six. Dave was so proud of them. They demonstrated at that service how they had learned the importance of caring for others from their dad.

I cried the entire service. Some of the speakers laughed as they told stories about Dave. I couldn't laugh. Once when I was sobbing, Alexander and Danielle came over to console me. It should have been the other way around. I should have been consoling them, but that memorial service was so, so hard.

When my dad spoke, he referred to Dave as "Jesus in a woolen cap" and "the Michelangelo of wrestling." It had been two weeks since we lost Dave, and Dad told the audience he still could not comprehend what had happened. "Such sweetness so swiftly taken from our lives," he lamented.

Dad played the piano and sang a song called "The Boy by the Sea." He had written the song about Dave playing at Half Moon Bay near San Francisco as a young kid.

Dad also told a story that jarred me.

When we were living in Oregon, when I was in the fifth or sixth grade, I asked Dave what his earliest memory was.

"Tell me yours first," he said.

"Rolling down the stairs at Grandma's," I told him. "What's yours?"

"Actually, I have a memory from before I was born," he said.

Incredulous at such a notion, I interrupted in a disrespectful tone.

"Oh, really?"

Dave never brought up the memory around me again. Not until the memorial service did I hear the story.

Dad recalled when Dave was four and the two of them were walking in the woods, holding hands. Dave asked if Dad wanted to hear "a really big secret."

"Sure," Dad told him. "What is it?"

"You won't laugh at me, will you?" Dave asked.

"No, I won't laugh," Dad assured him.

"Before I was born," Dave began, "I was standing in the clouds and surrounded by twelve men. The oldest one looked down on earth and said, 'You're going down there to be tested.'"

Story complete, Dave walked away.

Dad stood there stunned for a few seconds, and then started running to catch up with Dave.

"Did you pass the test?" Dad asked.

"Oh, yeah, I'm going to pass the test," Dave told him. "But I'm not going to be here very long."

Dave then left Dad to go off and play.

When it was my turn to speak, I could not prevent my voice

from cracking. I don't remember ever crying in public before then. But there I stood, with television cameras focused on me, bawling.

I told the audience that I considered Dave my best friend, my teacher, and my coach, and how he was the most honest person I had ever known. I shared how strong he had become by diligently working to compensate for the weaknesses he dealt with as a child. He was wise beyond his years, I said, and tougher than anyone I had ever met.

I asked that everyone please pray for our family "until this murder trial is over and justice in this life will be served."

When I changed clothes after the service, I threw my shirt and jeans in the trash.

Less than four months after the conclusion of the O. J. Simpson murder trial, nine charges were filed against du Pont, including first- and third-degree murder.

Simpson might have been the highest-profile murder defendant the US court systems had seen, but John was the richest. Two things became apparent right away: Du Pont might have no defense other than insanity, and no expense would be spared in defending against the charges.

The process would become frustratingly slow as his team of lawyers—dubbed "Dream Team East" by the media, after Simpson's dream team of lawyers—used stall tactics to drag out the process and, presumably, buy time before having to declare whether an insanity defense would be employed.

At du Pont's preliminary hearing two weeks after the murder, one of his attorneys said John did not understand his legal rights as explained by the judge.

The defense team had du Pont undergo neurological tests, hoping to find a physical cause for du Pont's peculiar behavior. The tests were made public, the results were not. It was easy to draw a conclusion as to what the tests revealed. Or didn't reveal.

During courtroom proceedings, du Pont sat emotionless, often with a blank stare. He continued to tell his lawyers he did not understand the charges or the procedures laid out by the judge.

I knew how to stall on the mat. However, my stalling was nothing compared to the defense team's tactics in the courtroom. But they didn't get penalized as I had been. Twice du Pont's lawyers went to the Pennsylvania Supreme Court, appealing the judge's denial of their request to have du Pont leave prison for a psychiatric exam in a doctor's office.

They also tried to have overturned the judge's refusal to allow du Pont to go back to the farm to look for materials that could be used in his defense. The judge rightly ruled that du Pont, with his resources, was a flight risk. The defense did, however, manage to have John's arraignment postponed while the two sides wrangled over whether he was competent to stand trial.

I was no legal expert, but even I knew du Pont's lawyers were trying to avoid or delay prosecution and build support for an insanity plea. But still, it was annoying to recognize that John's wealth was gaining him every advantage possible in his defense. To keep up, the district attorney's office had to hire two people to deal with the media and handle all of the defense's appeals.

The district attorney's office also determined it would not seek

the death penalty, citing the belief that a better chance for conviction would come if the death penalty was not placed on the table.
I was fine with that decision. I just wanted du Pont to spend the
rest of his life in prison.

I didn't want him in a state hospital, though, because that
would have been easy time compared to prison. John had lived a
life of luxury and it had not been enough for him. He had wanted
more. I wanted the rest of his life to be as uncomfortable as possible. Yet, his being in prison with all of his possessions taken from
him could not come remotely close to what he taken away from
our family.

You never get over losing a brother. For me, Dave's dying was
like cutting loose the anchor on a boat and setting the boat
adrift on the sea to float aimlessly. Dave had always been my
anchor.

Because we had bounced back and forth between our parents
growing up, Dave had been the one constant in my life. He had
always been there to advise me, to help me stop worrying about
things. We were like a two-man sect; he was my leader, and I was
his follower.

When John killed Dave, he took my brother and my happiness from me.

For eight years, the ending to my wrestling career had nagged
me. In Wayne Baughman's book, *Wrestling On and Off the Mat*, he
discussed the importance of going out a winner. More than anything, I had wanted to win the '88 Olympics and walk away a
champion. But du Pont ruined that possibility for me. Every day

since moving away from Foxcatcher, I had thought about my dream, about du Pont, and about what he had done to me.

Now, every day, I added to those thoughts what he had done to my brother.

One day, I received a call from my jujitsu coach, Pedro Sauer. He was training "Dangerous" Dave Beneteau to fight in the upcoming UFC IX: Motor City Madness, Ultimate Fighting Championship's pay-per-view event of mixed martial arts bouts. Beneteau had been the heavyweight runner-up at the Canadian wrestling team's Olympic trials, and Pedro wanted me to work out with him.

Mixed martial arts—a combination of wrestling, submission holds, and kickboxing—was introduced to the United States in 1993, when UFC was created. MMA became extremely popular in a short period of time. Wrestlers performed well in MMA, because the conditioning and takedowns of wrestling proved to be advantageous in the sport. If you look at any fight, with only rare exceptions, the fighters wind up on the ground. Fighters who were not good at grappling were at a disadvantage. It was easy for a wrestler to transition to MMA. You can't teach a kickboxer how to wrestle, but you can teach a wrestler how to kickbox.

Beneteau came to Provo, and we trained together for a few weeks. During one session, I took Beneteau down and he landed wrong on his right hand, breaking it. I took Dave to a doctor, who gave him two options: undergo surgery to have a plate screwed into the bones so he could compete, or have a cast put on his hand that would take him out of action until after UFC IX.

At age thirty-five, I had been training full-contact with my heavyweight at BYU, Mike Bolster. Although I did not believe that

Dave would opt to miss his bout, I told him that if he did have to default because of injury, I would take his place.

Dave, as I expected, chose surgery and went on to Detroit as scheduled for his bout with Gary "Big Daddy" Goodridge. The day before UFC IX, I flew to Detroit to be with Beneteau in his corner.

The standard UFC news conference was the night before the bouts, with all the fighters, promoters, referees, doctors, and trainers there. After answering the media's questions, Beneteau asked a doctor to look at his broken hand, and the doctor told him he couldn't fight. I sought out the promoter and asked if I could fight in Dave's place. He liked the idea, and we started talking money.

I was offered $25,000. I asked for double that. The promoter countered with $25,000 if I lost and $50,000 if I won. I told him I would decide the next morning.

I had trouble sleeping that night. At six-foot-three and 245 pounds, Big Daddy had five inches and forty pounds on me. He had finished as runner-up at UFC VIII: David vs. Goliath, when the format consisted of a tournament bracket. He had victories in the quarterfinals by knockout and in the semifinals by technical knockout.

The call from the promoters asking for my answer came at 6:30 A.M. From not sleeping well, I felt like crap. I said I needed more time. I fell asleep, only to be awakened by another call from the promoters. I gave the same answer and went back to sleep. They called back again. No decision yet. At ten thirty that morning, they called and said they needed my answer right away or they would sign someone else.

I called Pedro and asked him to go down to the hotel lobby

with me. The promoters were waiting for me, with a contract sitting on the desk in front of them. I asked for one more minute, walked over to a corner, knelt, and asked God to tell me what I should do.

I stayed in that position for probably three minutes until I was overcome with the undeniable feeling that if Dave were alive, he would tell me I had to fight. I stood and turned from the corner. Pedro and a group of people were looking at me.

"I'll do it," I announced.

That was eight hours before the fight, and the only clothes I had brought with me were a suit and tie and a pair of shorts for working out.

I took the required AIDS test and then bought a mouth guard. Beneteau gave me his protective cup to wear. One of Pedro's students loaned me his wrestling shoes—good thing our feet were the same size—and I wore the shorts I had been given at the LA Olympics.

The list of rules for UFC fights was short. Fights were bare knuckles and inside an octagon-shaped cage, with no biting, no eye gouging, and no punching with closed fists. If a fighter opted to wear shoes over going barefoot, he was prohibited from kicking. Everything else was legal. You could head-butt, fishhook your opponent's mouth (insert your fingers or hands into the sides of his mouth and pull hard in opposite directions), attack the groin, pull ears, choke, dislocate or break joints, break bones, scratch, twist or snap the neck, and whatever else you could imagine. Bouts lasted twelve minutes, with a three-minute overtime period if needed.

Politicians led by Senator John McCain had targeted ultimate fighting for regulation, or perhaps even banning, because of its violence. To avert a possible cancellation of the event, UFC announced during the day that closed-fist strikes would be banned that night. Pedro told me the news and I was like, "All right! Goodridge can't strike me with his fists!"

The referee, "Big" John McCarthy, came into my dressing room about thirty minutes before the fight to inform me of the new ban on closed-fist punches. He asked me to show him a closed fist. I made one. Then he asked me to show him an open fist. I opened my hand as I would to deliver a karate chop.

"No, an open fist is like this," Big John corrected me, making a fist and pulling his thumb away from the fist. If either of us violated the ban, he warned, we would be fined fifty dollars per offense and the fine would be collected, well, whenever. In other words, we could punch all we wanted.

Goodridge was one hell of a striker, but he wasn't a wrestler, and I knew I would be able to take him down. I didn't think he would be able to get on top of me, from where he could punch and elbow me, and even when he did manage to get on top, I believed my wrestling skills would prevent him from being in that position for long.

When the match started, we both came out cautious. I made the first move, taking him down about thirty seconds in by running him into the cage with a double leg takedown. Goodridge was wearing a gi, the loose-fitting suit associated with martial arts like karate and judo. Grabbing his gi made it easier to pull his legs out from under him as soon as he had stopped against the cage. It was the easiest takedown ever for me, and that's why MMA fighters stopped wearing gis.

Goodridge wrapped his arm around my head and grabbed his own gi. He held my head so tightly that I wondered if I would pass out. I responded by pointing my chin into his ribs so that the tighter he squeezed me, the deeper my chin would sink into his ribs.

I started feeling a little light-headed. With not much time to get out of his hold before passing out, I made him break his grip by reaching up with my left hand and pinching his trachea by jamming my thumb into his throat. I could have hurt him badly, maybe even killed him, if I had used all my strength and broken his trachea. After Goodridge let go of me, I hit him in the head a few times.

Ultimate fighting refs could stop a fight if there was a lack of action and restart the bout with both fighters on their feet. After I had been released and we settled into holding on to each other for a bit, Big John stepped in and had us stand.

I took Gary down again and pounded him with my fists some more, opening a cut beside his right eye. The ref stopped us to check Goodridge's cut and restarted us from our feet. Once again, I took Goodridge down and got the mount position on him and hit him in the face several times, targeting the cut beside his eye.

I was in the mount position with about ten seconds to go in the fight and looked into Gary's eyes. I think we both knew it was over. I could have elbowed him a few more times or gone for an armlock, but I knew he had kids.

Is it really necessary? I asked myself.

Regulation time ran out.

I don't know if the doctor stopped the fight because of Goodridge's cut or if Gary stopped the bout himself, but he didn't come out for overtime.

I was glad the fight was over. I had been training, but not for competition, and my conditioning was not very good.

That night was a spiritual moment for me. There was a reason Dave Beneteau had suffered his injury. There was a reason I had gone to Detroit. There was a reason the doctor had told Beneteau he couldn't fight.

I didn't fight again after that night. My back herniated soon after the match. Within a week I couldn't walk and had to be hospitalized. My athletic career was over at that point, and I retired from UFC with a 1-0 record.

That one win erased eight years of pain and prevented who knows how many more years of hurting. I had felt like a loser ever since the '88 Olympics, but that changed that night in Detroit. I went out a winner. It felt as though I was telling John du Pont in capital letters that he had lost his battle to make me miserable like him. I had won, and he was still a loser.

In some respects, I became a winner again the instant I stepped into the octagon. I proved that I could get into that cage and fight with, basically, no rules. I fought against a tough man who was bigger than I was—significantly—and a highly respected fighter.

I had spent my entire life trying to become the ultimate martial artist. I had thought all those years that wrestling was the ultimate martial art. Then jujitsu opened my eyes and showed me that I had been confining myself within the rules of the NCAA and FILA. Their rules had forced me to focus on conditioning and learning how to stay on top of opponents. Jujitsu had taught me a new array of techniques. And then in MMA, where the rules had been removed, I was free to show who I had become.

It had been eight years since Seoul, but I believed I had received a stamp of endorsement from the most brutal combat sport that existed: I could make people submit to me.

On May 16, 1996, my happiness returned.

All that remained was for justice to be served.

D u Pont's first public words since the murder came two weeks
after UFC IX, at his delayed arraignment.

Wearing a full, graying, unkempt beard—I thought he was
trying to *look* insane—du Pont again claimed he did not understand the charges against him.

His attorney then asked John who he was.

"The Dalai Lama," he told the court.

It had been slightly more than four months since Dave's
death, but finally a not guilty plea had been entered on du Pont's
behalf. At last, the case seemed to take a full step forward. The
clock was now running for the defense team to declare if it would
employ an insanity defense.

The Olympic wrestling medals were awarded on August 31 in
Atlanta. The United States did not medal in Dave's weight class. I
couldn't help but think that day about Dave's dream of capping his
comeback on that medal stand. He would have made it up there,
too. No doubt.

Three weeks after the Olympics, the momentum of the com-
monwealth's case against du Pont took a wrong turn. The judge,
weighing the testimony of doctors from both sides and two lawyers
whom du Pont had fired since the case began, ruled him incompe-
tent for trial and ordered him sent to a state hospital for treatment.
Within sixty days, doctors at the state hospital were to report if he
could stand trial.

The prosecutors had argued that du Pont was faking his incompetence in order to delay proceedings. I agreed. Du Pont had too long a history of manipulation to ignore.

The incompetency ruling dealt only with John's perceived ability to help his lawyers prepare his defense, not his overall mental state. John had never stopped running his estate while in prison, including approving the purchase of a truck for the farm.

He had a fence topped with barbed wire put up around the estate, and a sign reading FOXCATCHER PRISON FARM was erected. In my opinion, that was a desperate attempt on John's part to turn his estate into a prison so he could return home to live out his life in the comfort of his estate.

Most interesting, though, was that relatives filed a civil lawsuit asking that du Pont be declared mentally incapacitated so that the family could gain guardianship of du Pont and control of his estate. In one court, John's lawyers were claiming that he was not mentally able to help them with his case. Yet if the family's lawsuit was not delayed, in another court, his lawyers would have to argue he was still capable of managing his property and money. That delay did occur.

Finally, in December, the judge ruled du Pont competent to stand trial in January. Lead defense lawyer Thomas Bergstrom told the judge he planned to pursue a defense of not guilty by reason of insanity.

That was a crucial statement because, according to research that multiple media outlets cited at the time, an insanity defense was used in less than 1 percent of felony cases. Of those, the strategy was successful only a fourth of the time.

But with two witnesses to the murder, the defense, in effect, had no other option.

The jury that would decide the case was selected in the next-to-last week of January. From a pool of seventy-five prospective jurors, six men and six women—predominantly middle-aged—were chosen. With the trial expected to last four weeks, six alternates were also chosen.

The insanity plea would boil down to one question for jurors to answer: At the time when John shot Dave, did he know that his actions were wrong?

CHAPTER 19

Justice

Opening arguments began on Monday, January 27, 1997, in the courtroom of Delaware County Court Judge Patricia Jenkins. I did not attend the trial, receiving constant updates from my parents, friends such as Dan Chaid, and media coverage on the Internet.

During the preliminary hearings phase, the prosecution had asked me to testify about witnessing John use cocaine. At first, I didn't want to. There were other wrestlers who had observed John do cocaine. I had been in Utah and hadn't seen him on coke since 1989. I was also concerned that admitting I had done coke could cost me my job at BYU. Plus, I didn't like the idea of possibly helping du Pont's lawyers use some kind of diminished capacity reason for his actions.

I hired a lawyer who talked to the prosecutors and told them I did not want to testify.

The likelihood of the insanity defense changed things. Testimony about du Pont's cocaine use would be needed to rebut the insanity defense.

I flew to Philadelphia and told prosecutors what I knew about du Pont's drug use and about doing coke with John a few times in '89. I was asked if I would testify and I said yes, knowing it could kill my career. But for some reason, the judge did not allow me to testify, and I was in Utah during the entire trial.

John wore a blue-and-yellow Foxcatcher sweatshirt and blue sweatpants the first day. He would wear the same outfit throughout the trail. Knowing his lack of hygiene all too well, I would guess that John probably wore the exact same outfit each day.

Dave's wife was the first to testify, detailing what she witnessed of the murder. In cross-examination, the defense focused on one statement during her 911 call. Nancy had identified John as the shooter and when the 911 operator asked why du Pont would have shot Dave, she responded, "He's insane."

It had to be easy for the prosecution to counter that Nancy's statement was far from a medical analysis, but it seemed early on that the defense would have to grasp at any little thing it could.

Of the prosecution's witnesses, Pat Goodale was probably most scrutinized by the defense. He was the only person who heard John ask Dave, "You got a problem with me?" before the first shot—an important statement toward intent that admittedly warranted every attempt by the defense to attack Goodale's credibility.

Joseph McGettigan, coprosecutor with Dennis McAndrews, used Goodale's recounting of his time with du Pont in the thirty-five minutes or so before the shooting to establish that du Pont had been carrying on business as usual right up until he pointed his gun out of the car window.

Goodale had previously worked for a security firm du Pont had hired and returned to work for du Pont a few weeks before the murder because John had wanted a .50 caliber machine gun mounted on his tank. Bergstrom attempted to create the picture that Goodale, and his previous company, had taken advantage of du Pont's wealth with needless expenses and excessive charges. Hey, everyone tried to take advantage of du Pont's wealth. Even wrestlers. I think one of the things that attracted John to wrestlers was that even though we were trying to survive financially, unlike most of the people around him, our greatest interest was in things of intrinsic value, not material.

Of course, with the insanity defense in play, the list of witnesses included a parade of psychiatrists, with four testifying for the defense and two for the prosecution. Defense psychiatrists testified that du Pont suffered from paranoid schizophrenia.

Testimony ended on Thursday, February 13, after thirteen days in the courtroom. Following a long weekend, closing arguments were delivered on Tuesday, and the jury was handed the responsibility of deciding du Pont's fate.

From what I had gathered, the prosecution laid out its case quite clearly. The defense had seemed to score its best points regarding du Pont's cocaine use. Hair analysis tests—given as the reason for du Pont's allowing his hair to grow out—indicated the likelihood that John had not used cocaine in the past fifteen months.

The prosecution needed du Pont's cocaine use to help create an explanation other than insanity for his behavior. There were enough witnesses to prove du Pont had a cocaine habit, but the defense team was able to prevent prosecutors from connecting John to cocaine near enough to late January 1996 for drugs to be a determining factor in the murder.

The jury, which had not been sequestered to that point, was sequestered for the duration of deliberations.

As with any high-profile trial, every set of questions the jurors sent out for the judge to answer touched off a wave of speculation in the media about which way the jury seemed to be leaning. Deliberations lasted for seven days. For my parents, they were seven long, stressful days of waiting, wondering what was going on in the jurors' discussions, praying that justice would be served, and hoping that du Pont's wealth had not gotten him off the hook one more time and that Dave's murderer would suffer the consequences he deserved.

My parents had been there for the entire trial, but that final week was especially tough on both of them. It was tough on me in Utah, and I had the benefit of the "distraction," so to speak, of working through my daily routine and coaching my team while wondering if at any moment someone would call to say a verdict was on its way. I at least had plenty to keep me busy. I can't imagine what my parents went through being there, having to sit and wait.

The jury sent word to the judge that it had reached its verdict late in the afternoon on Tuesday, February 25. The courtroom was filled yet hushed when the verdict was read: The jury had determined that John du Pont was guilty of third-degree murder but mentally ill. He was also found guilty but mentally ill of the lesser charge of simple assault for pointing a gun at Pat Goodale. The jury decided du Pont was not guilty of the same charge for pointing his gun at Dave's wife.

The "third-degree" part meant the jury found that du Pont had not intended to kill Dave. The "but mentally ill" part meant that the jurors believed the testimony of defense psychiatrists who called du Pont a paranoid schizophrenic. The verdict opened the possibility that du Pont would be treated for his mental illness in a state hospital before serving the rest of his sentence in prison.

That sentence could be as short as five years and as long as forty.

When I learned of the verdict, I experienced mixed emotions. The insanity defense had failed, so du Pont was legally responsible for the murder. He knew what he was doing each time he pulled the trigger and killed Dave. But at the same time, the "mentally ill" finding provided du Pont some leniency. I wanted du Pont in prison, not in a state hospital. More than that, I didn't want him to enjoy one moment of freedom.

I wondered if the jury had decided to split the difference between first-degree murder and the insanity plea or involuntary manslaughter. The key ramification of their finding was that the penalty phase moved out of their hands and into the judge's.

The day for sentencing came two and a half months later, on May 13. I was there that day to make my victim-impact statement.

I hadn't seen John in person in years. His long, greasy hair and shaggy beard from the trial were gone; his hair was its customary short length and his beard was neatly trimmed. His teeth had been fixed, too. I heard that his lawyer claimed it cost nine thousand dollars for all the dental work John needed. But his apparent "I'm insane" act was still around.

John made eye contact with me one time, his head cocked back, just staring down his huge beak of a nose at me. His mouth was open like a fish gulping water and stayed open in that manner most of the time during the sentencing phase.

When it came to my turn to speak to the court, I shared how I had watched du Pont use cocaine and that I didn't believe him to be insane. But I talked mostly about my brother and how great he was.

It wasn't easy to sit up there and talk about Dave in that setting. I'm not typically a crier. The two times I have cried in public are at the memorial service and that day in the courtroom. I didn't try to prevent myself from crying, though. I knew that the more emotion I showed, the harsher du Pont's penalty might be. I didn't have to fake or exaggerate any emotions; they were real and plentiful. I just wanted to reveal on the outside what I was feeling on the inside.

Du Pont spoke before he was sentenced. He said he had been ill when he killed Dave. He said he was sorry for any inconvenience he caused to Dave's wife and children. *Inconvenience?* He didn't apologize to me or our parents. It was just as well, because I didn't believe a word he said.

He knew that he was facing spending the rest of his life in prison. His money had bought him an outstanding defense team—Thomas Bergstrom probably won his client a lesser verdict that most attorneys would not have—but his money wasn't going to benefit him now. His lack of ability had been the reason he had come up short of achieving his athletic dreams. Now how he would spend the rest of life came down to his ability to act as if he was sorry and place the blame on something other than who he truly was: a greedy manipulator who would do whatever it took to get whatever he wanted.

Judge Jenkins sentenced du Pont to thirteen to thirty years in prison for the murder of Dave and three to six months for the simple assault. John was fifty-eight at the time.

Following the sentencing, I returned to BYU. Provo had been a good place for me. My personal life had never been as stable as it was after I moved to Provo and became a member of the Church of Jesus Christ of Latter-day Saints.

The city and university were pleasantly clean, and becoming a part of the LDS Church caused me to clean up my act. I also earned a master's degree in exercise science at BYU, with a 3.7 GPA.

We had a good wrestling program building at BYU. When I became head coach in 1994, it was known that the program was in danger of being dropped by the school. In 1995, Rondo Fehlberg was hired as athletic director. Rondo had wrestled at BYU in the late '60s and early '70s. A three-time conference champion and once an All-American, Rondo was a member of BYU's athletic Hall of Fame. Rondo was supportive of our program.

Our team improved each season. We also took care of business in the classroom: Three times, we had the highest grade-point average of any wrestling team in the nation; three other times, we had the second-highest. It was just pure luck I was there at the time. We had good kids in the program.

But a change in the university presidency during Rondo's tenure eventually meant the end of our program. In 1999, the school announced it would phase out wrestling, along with gymnastics, over the next school year. The demands of meeting the standards of Title IX were cited as the reason, but the root existed in revenue shortages, because wrestling was a nonrevenue sport.

During that time, I also went through a difficult divorce. It was a long process in and out of courts that kept me from moving out of Utah until the divorce was settled. That prevented me from taking a wrestling job elsewhere in the country, although the number of available jobs continued to decrease.

As a result of the divorce, I lost my kids, my money, and the house I had built with my two hands. By that point, I couldn't land a job interview with any university.

Losing my job and the divorce rocked my world, but I bounced back because I had proved to myself I had what it took to overcome adversity. I was a fighter.

Team Foxcatcher had been in decline even before Dave's death and du Pont's conviction. I don't know the exact number, but at its peak in wrestling, there had been a few dozen wrestlers across the country representing du Pont's team. At the time of the murder, I believe there were about fifteen wrestlers on the team, and I knew of only four still living and training at the farm.

Most of the remaining team members held a bonfire to burn their Team Foxcatcher uniforms after du Pont was arrested.

At the US Olympic trials in June 1996, less than five months after Dave's death, a few wrestlers were still being funded by du Pont and wore their Team Foxcatcher gear, outraging members of the team who had left because of the murder.

"Throw that Foxcatcher guy out of there!" Dan Chaid yelled during one of the wrestler's matches.

Coach Dan Gable told the media he had advised the wrestlers not to wear the gear. One Foxcatcher wrestler claimed he wore his singlet to honor Dave and put it away after the first round.

Brian Dolph, who had been at Foxcatcher with Dave, had Dave's initials tattooed on the underside of one of his arms. Whenever that arm was raised in victory, Dave's initials would be displayed. Other former team members wrestled with black patches on their singlets.

USA Wrestling created grants to temporarily aid wrestlers who had been funded by du Pont. Dave's widow formed the Dave Schultz Wrestling Club largely to help former Foxcatcher wrestlers continue competing, including '96 Olympic gold medalist Kurt

Angle. In 1999, she won a wrongful death lawsuit settlement against du Pont. The amount was not disclosed, but media reports called it the largest ever paid by one person in the United States. The wrestling club remained in existence until 2005.

All throughout wrestling, steps were taken to honor Dave's memory and recognize his contributions to the sport.

The Dave Schultz National High School Excellence Award was established by the National Wrestling Hall of Fame to annually honor the country's outstanding high school senior wrestler. Dave's name was added to the Most Outstanding Wrestler Award presented each year at the California high school state championships. The recipient received a trophy with Dave's image etched in glass.

USA Wrestling created the annual Dave Schultz Memorial International tournament at the US Olympic Training Center in Colorado Springs. The tournament still attracts the top international freestyle and Greco-Roman wrestlers in the world.

In 1997, Dave was inducted into the National Wrestling Hall of Fame in Stillwater, Oklahoma, an honor I had received two years earlier. In 2010, I had the thrill of standing alongside Alexander and Danielle as Dave and I were inducted together into the San Jose Sports Hall of Fame. We were introduced as the best wrestling brothers the United States has ever produced.

Du Pont first came up for parole in December 2009. After sentencing, he had spent three months receiving treatment at a state hospital before being transferred to a state prison for the duration of his sentence.

I called his prison once to ask what kind of living conditions he had there. I was told he was in an eight-foot by ten-foot cell with another prisoner. He was in a special wing, with older prisoners on one side of the block and child molesters on the other. Those were the two groups of prisoners most likely to be abused by the general population, so they were kept in a more secure area. What an idiot du Pont must have been to trade tens of millions of dollars for that kind of existence.

During the trial, I didn't agree with testimony that du Pont was paranoid schizophrenic. I didn't like that the prosecutors accepted the diagnosis, either. My analysis of du Pont was that he was an evil, selfish drug addict. But now I agree that John was mentally ill. He was not insane as his lawyers claimed, but I recognize that he did have a sickness.

When John became eligible for parole, I wrote a letter to the parole board requesting that his bid be denied. I didn't think they would let him out, but with what he could do with his money, you just could never be too sure about anything regarding John.

He earlier had hired a private investigator to come to my house in Utah and ask if I would be willing to help John get out of prison. I opened the door with a video camera rolling and asked the private investigator what he wanted. When he told me, I shut the door and sent the video to the Delaware County prosecutor's office.

Du Pont was denied parole.

On Thursday, December 9, 2010, I received word that John had passed away. He was found early that morning in his cell, unresponsive. John had been receiving treatment for severe emphysema and chronic obstructive pulmonary disease. He was seventy-two when he died.

In accordance with instructions in his will, du Pont was buried in a red Foxcatcher wrestling singlet. Eighty percent of his estate was bequeathed to Valentin Jordanov and members of Valentin's family.

Du Pont's death was a nonevent for me. I think my dad said it best when he told a reporter that as far as he was concerned, John had died the day he killed Dave.

There was a bit of a feeling for me that John's dying meant there was one thing fewer to think about. I had considered that if he ever did get out of prison, he might put out a hit on someone in our family.

But other than that, I didn't care about John.

He had taken my brother and my career from me, but I had found my ultimate victory over John in 1996 when I won in UFC.

Du Pont underestimated me as a fighter. He never gave me enough credit for who I was, for how tough I was. John is dead now, though. He is a part of my past that I have died to.

But still, sometimes when I'm thinking about my brother, remembering the good times we experienced together, the adversity we battled to overcome, both together and on our own, when I'm regretting that Dave can't be here to be proud of what I have become, I catch myself thinking about his murderer, too.

And I wish John du Pont had never lived.

I miss you, Dave.

Afterword

Wʜᴀᴛ started as simply wanting my children to know about their old man's life has turned into a bestselling book and Oscar-nominated movie.

I started writing my story after my UFC bout, when the BYU president barred me from cage-fighting if I wanted to keep my job and because my back went out on me. I knew my athletic career was over, so I started typing.

That sixty-page, single-spaced document wound up in the hands of movie director Bennett Miller sometime around 2006. He began reading and decided my story was one he needed to make into a movie.

Bennett had directed *Capote*, which was released in 2005 and earned five Academy Award nominations. After he had worked on *Foxcatcher* for several years, the economy crashed and money dried up. Then Brad Pitt offered him another sports drama, *Moneyball*, which wound up being nominated for six Oscars. Right after *Moneyball* was released in 2011, with the accolades Bennett was picking up, was when I realized *Foxcatcher* could really make it into theaters.

When I learned that Channing Tatum would play me in *Foxcatcher*, I looked up to heaven and shouted, "Yes!" His credentials were impressive, but let's be completely honest: Who wouldn't want to be played by someone good-looking enough to be named *People* magazine's "Sexiest Man Alive" in 2012?

I wish I could say that we look exactly alike. Instead I'll have to settle for boasting that there are some similarities between Channing and me when I was younger. For the movie, they gave Channing implants in his mouth so his jaw was more pronounced, like mine. Implants also were used in his nose to make it wider and not as straight, because I'd had my nose broken in wrestling. Channing was given cauliflower ears, too. That made him look like a real wrestler.

Channing is one of the most unique, talented, and special people I've ever met. He worked hard to play me and picked up wrestling really quickly. He and Mark Ruffalo (who played Dave) trained for five or six months before shooting, and I was involved in training them.

Filming began in the fall of 2012 in and around Pittsburgh. I was able to visit the set, and Bennett gave me a cameo appearance in the movie as Weigh-in Official #1.

I met Steve Carell, who turned in an *outstanding* performance as du Pont, on the set. It was weird because it had been seventeen years since Dave was murdered, and all the emotions I had gone through had settled down. But I first saw Steve out of the corner of my eye while he was dressed as du Pont. He looked and walked exactly like John. I realized almost immediately that it was Steve, but for that split second, it was eerily strange because it felt as if du Pont had been raised from the dead.

Steve was a good guy, and he really got du Pont's mannerisms down, from delivery of speech to facial movements to looking down that long beak of a nose at you. Steve used a prosthetic piece to make his nose larger, but I think du Pont's was even bigger.

As much as I pity du Pont, I have to admit that his being loony and eccentric made for a good movie character. Playing du Pont gave Steve an opportunity to show his dramatic side with a really good role.

I enjoyed spending time with the actors in their trailers. It was obvious that they were doing what they love and were treated well. They were some of the happiest people I've met.

All the actors and actresses wanted to be sensitive to the real-life personalities whose stories they were portraying. A few of us were talking about Dave, and Mark said, "Your brother really loved you."

"I know," I said. "And I really loved him."

My first look at the finished product came in May 2014 at the Cannes International Film Festival in France, where *Foxcatcher* was nominated for the prestigious Palme d'Or (Golden Palm) award for best picture.

I had watched a rough cut the year before and had focused on the acting of Channing (playing me) and Steve (playing du Pont). They were amazing. But at Cannes, I watched Mark's portrayal of Dave more than before, and he was just as good as Channing and Steve. All three of them nailed their roles.

It was all I could do to not stand up and cheer during the movie. It was awesome!

The most difficult part was watching the scene in which Dave is murdered. The first time I saw the scene on screen, tears flowed. The second time, at Cannes, I was prepared to keep my emotions in control, but it still wasn't easy to relive.

When the movie ended, the audience broke out in a standing ovation that lasted more than six minutes. Just as the cheering was beginning to wane, Bennett walked over to my seat, grabbed me by the hand, and led me to the middle section to join the actors and producers.

Everybody had to be wondering who I was. Channing grabbed my wrist and lifted it as if I had won a match. I took Bennett by the wrist and raised his, too, as the applause picked back up. Then I hugged him, Steve, Channing, and Mark. Bennett raised both arms of Megan Ellison, the producer from Annapurna Pictures who cofinanced *Foxcatcher*. Channing and Mark then hoisted Bennett by his legs and raised him in the air. The ovation had to have lasted a full ten minutes.

I read a lot of reviews and watched a lot of videos about Cannes, and I was relieved to see that a very large majority of the critics liked *Foxcatcher*. I read numerous reviews that began hyping the movie for the Oscars, and especially for the performances of Channing, Steve, and Mark.

Foxcatcher received five nominations for Academy Awards: Steve for Best Actor in a Leading Role, Mark for Best Actor in a Supporting Role, Bennett for Directing, Bill Corso and Dennis Liddiard for Makeup and Hairstyling, and E. Max Frye and Dan Futterman for Best Writing, Original Screenplay.

When you watch the Oscars on television, you can tell it would be a big deal to be there in person, but man, I had no idea how cool attending the Oscars could be. It's Hollywood's Super Bowl.

I drove to the Dolby Theatre in Los Angeles with executive producers Michael Coleman and Tom Heller. Security was incredible. There was no attempt to try to hide how many security personnel were there. It was almost like a show of force.

We walked through hallways with metal detectors to a red curtain at the end, which opened up to the famed red carpet. I wore my Olympic gold medal, the ultimate prize in my sport, because the *Foxcatcher* nominees were going for the ultimate prize in their business.

Our first stop on the carpet was in front of a wall of photographers next to a giant Oscar statue. Reporters from all over the world lined the red carpet, asking celebrities for interviews. Mario Lopez of *Extra* interviewed me. He was fun to talk with because he had finished third in his state as a high school wrestler. A Brazilian news crew asked me questions about Brazilian jujitsu. I took a bunch selfies, including with Steve, Ethan Hawke of *Boyhood*, and Zendaya, who is just a beautiful, gracious eighteen-year-old.

I met up with Bennett and laughed about all the ups and downs during the eight years of getting *Foxcatcher* into theaters. Bennett then asked me to follow him into the theater. I sat in the second tier, behind the nominees, and enjoyed the show.

We didn't win any Oscars. I was disappointed because I really thought the movie and the people who made it happen were deserving of the awards. But still, to me, five nominations was a huge win regardless.

Back when I was a kid and I wondered what my life would look like as a movie, I never imagined anything like what has played out through *Foxcatcher*. This obviously has grown well beyond sharing my story with my kids.

I've worked hard and suffered so much with little financial compensation for so long. I'm not going to get rich, but I do want people to understand what I've gone through. There is a lot of sorrow and pain in the world. Suffering is a universal theme. What I hope my life demonstrates is that with great suffering and sacrifice also come great blessings. As many bad things as I have had to live through, I have been blessed an equal amount. I wouldn't trade my life with anyone's.

I believe in God and that all things happen for a reason. I think that sometimes we have to meet the wrong people before we can be introduced to the right ones, and I've come to know some good people who have helped me tell my story in the movie and this book.

Ultimately, I have faith that all the pain and suffering I have endured will pay off, because this much I have learned through my journey: When you work hard, miracles happen.

Acknowledgments

I'd like to thank Domenic Romano and Rose Massary of Romano Law for all of their help, as well as Chip MacGregor at MacGregor Literary Agency. David Thomas helped me write a great book.

At Dutton, Jill Schwartzman and Stephanie Hitchcock have been invaluable in seeing this project through to completion.

I also want to acknowledge Bennett Miller, Megan Ellison, Annapurna Productions, Channing Tatum, Steve Carell, and Mark Ruffalo, for getting my story on-screen. I appreciate the care you all took in honoring Dave's legacy.

Finally, the biggest thanks go to my parents, Jeannie St. Germain and Philip Gary Schultz. And to my brother, Dave. Things may not have been easy for us at times but we always had each other.

Dramatis Personae

STAN ABEL
a member of the National Wrestling Hall of Fame, was head coach of the University of Oklahoma wrestling team for which Mark Schultz and Dave Schultz wrestled.

ALAN ALBRIGHT
was head wrestling coach at Brigham Young University and hired Mark to work there as an assistant.

DAVE AUBLE
is a member of the National Wrestling Hall of Fame who coached Mark and Dave at UCLA.

ED BANACH
wrestled at Iowa along with his older brother, Steve, and twin brother, Lou. Mark defeated Ed in the finals of the 1982 NCAA Wrestling Championships.

BRUCE BAUMGARTNER
was Mark's US teammate at the 1984 and 1988 Olympics, at which he won two of his four Olympic wrestling medals.

DAVE BENETEAU
known as "Dangerous Dave," was an ultimate fighter whom Mark helped train.

TIM BROWN
was Mark's high school wrestling coach in Ashland, Oregon.

ROB CALABRESE
was the first wrestler to join John du Pont's Team Foxcatcher and coached with Mark at Villanova University.

DAN CHAID

was a teammate of Mark and Dave's at Oklahoma. Chaid coached at Villanova with Mark and worked out frequently with him at Villanova and on Team Foxcatcher.

JOHN DU PONT

was an heir to the du Pont family fortune who hired Mark as an assistant wrestling coach at Villanova and to wrestle and coach for his Team Foxcatcher. He murdered Dave in January 1996 and then died in prison in December 2010.

DAN GABLE

one of the most decorated wrestlers and coaches in US wrestling history, coached the University of Iowa to sixteen NCAA championships. He was head coach of the US freestyle team when Mark won the gold medal at the 1984 Olympics.

PAT GOODALE

was security expert for John du Pont and one of two witnesses to the murder of Dave.

GARY GOODRIDGE

known as "Big Daddy," was the opponent in Mark's only bout in Ultimate Fighting Championship.

SADAO HAMADA

gymnastics coach at Stanford University, coached Mark in the sport before Mark switched to wrestling.

ED HART

coached Mark and Dave at Palo Alto High School in California.

CHRIS HORPEL

was an All-American wrestler at Stanford who coached Mark early in his wrestling career. He also coached Mark and Dave while he was an assistant coach at UCLA, and he later hired Mark and Dave to work as his assistants at Stanford.

JIM HUMPHREY
was assistant coach at the University of Oklahoma when Mark and Dave wrestled there. He was also head coach of the US freestyle team for which Mark competed in the 1988 Olympics and later coached Team Foxcatcher.

VALENTIN JORDANOV
was a seven-time World Champion wrestler from Bulgaria who trained at Foxcatcher while Mark's brother lived and coached there.

REŞIT KARABACAK
was a Turkish wrestler who was ranked number one in his weight class entering the 1984 Olympics. Mark's victory against Karabacak was overturned after Mark broke Karabacak's elbow during the match.

LEE KEMP
was a three-time World Champion who shared with Mark the record for most wrestling world titles won by an American.

ANDRE METZGER
was a teammate of Mark and Dave's at Oklahoma, where he earned All-American honors four times. He later coached at Villanova.

VLADIMIR MODOSYAN
was a World Champion wrestler from the Soviet Union.

CHRIS RINKE
was a Canadian wrestler whom Mark defeated en route to winning the gold medal at the 1984 Olympics.

MARIO SALETNIK
was the highest-ranking official in FILA, wrestling's international governing body, and lived for a time on the Foxcatcher estate.

DAVE SCHULTZ
was Mark's older brother, whose wrestling accomplishments included an NCAA championship, an Olympic gold medal, and one World Championship.

NANCY SCHULTZ
was Dave's wife.

PHILIP SCHULTZ
was father to Mark and Dave.

MIKE SHEETS
wrestled at Oklahoma State University, where he competed against both Mark and Dave. After college, he was an opponent of Mark's in key matches on the national level.

ISREAL SHEPPARD
was a two-time All-American wrestler and teammate of Mark and Dave's at Oklahoma.

JEANNIE ST. GERMAIN
was mother to Mark and Dave.

RICKY STEWART
was a wrestler with Oklahoma State who was a redshirt freshman the one season Dave competed there.

GREG STROBEL
was head wrestling coach for Team Foxcatcher.

TARAS WOCHOK
was John du Pont's longtime lawyer.

CHUCK YARNALL
was Villanova's head wrestling coach when Mark moved there.

Bibliography

"An Eccentric Heir's Wrestle with Death." *Newsweek*, February 5, 1996. http://www.newsweek.com/eccentric-heirs-wrestle-death-179902 (accessed June 29, 2014).

Buckley, J. Taylor, and Gary Fields. "John du Pont's Life a Clash of Contradictions." *USA Today*, February 5, 1996.

Gensler, Howard. "Yarnall Resigns as Villanova Wrestling Coach." *The Philadelphia Inquirer*, February 15, 1987. http://articles.philly.com/1987 -02-15/news/26180898_1_du-pont-high-school-wrestler-team-foxcatcher (accessed June 29, 2014).

"Heir Trigger." *Daily News* (New York), January 29, 1996.

Koury, Renee. "Du Pont Case: Accused Killer of Wrestler Lived in Atherton." *San Jose Mercury News*, February 1, 1996.

Longman, Jere, Pam Belluck, and Jon Nordheimer. "A Life in Pieces: For du Pont Heir, Question Was Control." *The New York Times*, February 4, 1996.

Neff, Craig. "Fatal Obsession." *Sports Illustrated*, February 5, 1996.

Ordine, Bill, and Ralph Vigoda. *Fatal Match: Inside the Mind of Killer Millionaire John du Pont*. New York: Avon Books, 1988.

Ordine, Bill, and Ralph Vigoda. "Loved Ones Mourn Slain Wrestler." *The Philadelphia Inquirer*, February 12, 1996.

Ordine, Bill, and Ralph Vigoda. "Prosecutors: Du Pont Still Runs Things." *The Philadelphia Inquirer*, July 21, 1996.

Plaschke, Bill. "Unwelcome Mat." *Los Angeles Times*, June 9, 1996. http:// articles.latimes.com/1996-06-09/sports/sp-13287_1_dave-schultz -wrestling-club (accessed June 29, 2014).

Pucin, Diane. "Schultz Is Gone, but Still Dominating Olympic Trials." *The Philadelphia Inquirer*, June 9, 1996.

Schaefer, Mari A. "John du Pont Was Buried in His Wrestling Singlet." *The Philadelphia Inquirer*, February 16, 2011.